THE
LIMITATIONS
OF
THEOLOGICAL
TRUTH

THE
LIMITATIONS
OF
THEOLOGICAL
TRUTH

*Why
Christians Have
the Same Bible
but Different
Theologies*

NIGEL BRUSH

Kregel
Publications

The Limitations of Theological Truth: Why Christians Have the Same Bible but Different Theologies
© 2019 by Nigel Brush

Published by Kregel Publications, a division of Kregel Inc., 2450 Oak Industrial Dr. NE, Grand Rapids, MI 49505–6020.

ISBN 978-0-8254-4470-8

Printed in the United States of America

19 20 21 22 23 / 5 4 3 2 1

To my wife Anne, whose love, good sense, and artistic talents have created a peaceful and beautiful home where one can escape from the cares of the world and have time to think, read, write, and enjoy the simple things of life.

CONTENTS

Acknowledgments

I would like to thank Cathy Hancock and Judy Sabo, two retired schoolteachers, whose encouragement, as well as their cheerful and tireless proofreading of this book (as well as many other manuscripts), have greatly enhanced the quality and readability of this present work.

INTRODUCTION

IT HAS NOW BEEN MORE than a decade since I wrote *The Limitations of Scientific Truth: Why Science Can't Answer Life's Ultimate Questions* (Brush 2005). That book was the result of many years of effort trying to harmonize biblical truth with scientific truth. I found that such linkages were not only possible but indeed plentiful, since the God who reveals himself through the Scriptures is the same God who reveals himself through the natural world which he has created, as both David (Ps. 19:1) and Paul (Rom. 1:20) have noted. Since Christians and non-Christians alike often find science to be a stumbling block to developing a deep faith in God, it was my desire to bring these two sources of revelation into agreement with each other. Many of the bridges I built between science and Scripture, however, would eventually collapse because science kept altering the shoreline on its side of the bridge. In other words, scientists' understanding of the natural world was constantly changing as more and more empirical evidence was acquired and new discoveries were made. This realization forced me to abandon my youthful dream of harmonizing Scripture and science, but it gave me a new question to ponder: Why does scientific truth continue to change? Moreover, if scientific truth was not fixed but instead, was in constant flux, how was it superior to philosophical truth or religious truth—as some scientists asserted? The end result of this line of research was a book on the various limitations that keep science from arriving at absolute truth.

Although I failed in my initial quest to harmonize science and Scripture, it was my hope that by writing a book that delineated some of the limitations of scientific truth, I could free many of my fellow Christians from their fear of science and its pronouncements, since all scientific truths are provisional and permanently so. Why fear theories that are here today, but may be gone tomorrow? Instead of fearing and avoiding science, perhaps Christians, once they understood the limitations of scientific truth, would be more willing to examine current scientific theories and even participate in science research. Many Christians might thereby obtain a deeper understanding of the natural world that God has made, as well as the character of the God who has made it. Why should science, one of the most powerful methodologies for seeking truth ever devised by human beings, become the exclusive property of nonbelievers?

Many Christians who read my previous book were happy or relieved to learn about the limitations of scientific truth. Because of their faith in God, many Christians (including myself) had always believed that the Bible, being God's Word, was both superior and much more trustworthy than the ideas or theories of men. My book provided Christians with evidence, drawn from the writings of scientists and philosophers of science, that scientific truth had a number of significant limitations. Therefore, I concluded that scientific truth was not superior to biblical truth. After publishing *The Limitations of Scientific Truth*, however, I came to realize that theologians also shared the same limitations as scientists. Although the Bible was the Word of God, theology was not. Theology is the study of God and his relationship to humanity. It is a human discipline that attempts to understand and interpret God's Word. As a result, it has many of the same limitations that other human disciplines, such as science and philosophy, have. Moreover, it was obvious that some theological truths were not static, but were also changing over time—just like scientific truths. Indeed, many of the ideals being advocated or the practices being condoned in churches today were rare or nonexistent in those same churches only fifty years ago. Although God does not change, nor does his Word, our theology—our understanding and interpretation of God's Word—has changed in the past, is changing in the present, and will no doubt continue to change in the future. Many of the bridges I had previously attempted to build between Scripture and science had collapsed, not only because science kept shifting the shoreline on its side of the divide, but because theology was also shifting its shoreline as well. Theological truth is not superior to scientific truth; both are built on the shifting sands of human knowledge and understanding.

Instead of continuing to celebrate the limitations of scientific truth, therefore, perhaps it is time for Christians to carefully examine the limitations of theological truth. Why have our theological truths changed over time? What are the limitations we face as we try to understand the Bible? How is it possible that the church sometimes ends up with theological positions that actually run counter to the teachings of Christ? In this present book, *The Limitations of Theological Truth: Why Christians Have the Same Bible but Different Theologies*, I am going to argue that many of the limitations that scientists face in trying to understand God's world are the very same limitations that theologians face in trying to understand God's Word. The problem is not with the Bible: "All Scripture is inspired by God and profitable for teaching, for reproof, for correction, for training in righteousness; so that the man of God may be adequate, equipped for every good work" (2 Tim. 3:16–17). The problem is with us, as fallen men and women: "All of us like sheep have gone astray, Each of us has turned to his own way; But the LORD has caused the iniquity of us all To fall on Him" (Isa. 53:6). Our theology is often flawed because we are flawed. When we fail to take this fundamental fact into consideration, we are vulnerable to a host of errors that may actually separate us from the God whom we are seeking to know better through our theological studies.

PART 1

THE HUMAN FACTOR QUEST

Chapter 1

HUMAN DISCIPLINES AND THEIR HUMAN WEAKNESSES

ADAM AND EVE'S WILLFUL disobedience in the garden of Eden has impacted every aspect of our human experience. How can things ever be completely right in our lives or in the world around us when we are out of harmony with our Creator? The fallen nature of mankind pervades every aspect of our lives including our imaginations and intellectual pursuits. In this context, all human disciplines are flawed because the humans who work within these disciplines are themselves flawed.

I. THE QUEST FOR TRUTH

In my introductory classes at college, I point out to my students that we, as human beings, are on a quest for truth that began as soon as we became conscious of the world around us and will continue throughout our lives until the day we die. We seek truth in all aspects of our lives, including the places we live, the jobs at which we work, the hobbies we choose, our relationships with other people, or our own self-knowledge. For example: Is this city a safe place to live and raise a family? Does this job provide opportunities for advancement? Which team has the best players and is most likely to win a championship? Will this man or woman be a good husband or wife? What career should I choose based on my talents and interests? For some, the most intensive period of this quest for truth will be during their college years when they have the opportunity to rapidly sharpen their intellectual skills and deepen their knowledge of the world around them. I also point out to my students that there are three basic approaches that humans have devised in their search for truth: religion, philosophy, and science. Of the three, religion is the oldest and science is the youngest. Unfortunately, the truths derived from each of these approaches often seem to contradict each other. Two of the primary reasons that the truths of one discipline are often out of harmony with the truths of another discipline are that each discipline confines its search for truth to a limited area and each discipline uses a different methodology in its search for truth within that area.

Scientists search for truth in the natural realm—the physical universe. The methodology they use is based on empirical evidence derived through the five senses: what we can see, hear, touch, taste, or smell. Scientists have also devised various instruments that enhance these senses, such as microscopes, telescopes, stethoscopes, sonar, etc. From the scientific perspective, what you apprehend with the five senses is all there is; or at least, all there is that is amenable to scientific research. Philosophy, on the other hand, seeks truth within the confines of the human mind. One can practice philosophy by simply sitting in a dark room and thinking about the meaning of life. The methodology of philosophy is based on rules for rational thought and various techniques for achieving this end, such as induction and deduction. Religion, however, seeks truth in the realm of the supernatural. A fundamental belief of most peoples and cultures down through the ages is that there is a deeper reality behind or beyond the physical realm in which we live. What you see or think is not all there is. There are hidden laws and deeper realities that govern the visible realm. Many believe that it is in this *supernatural* realm that ultimate truth resides. The problem is that we are confined to the natural realm and do not have direct physical access to the supernatural realm. The only way to acquire truth from this realm is through revelation: these truths must be revealed to us by beings living in that other, hidden realm. Therefore, the methodology of religion is revelation, and all the great world religions are based on such disclosures of otherwise hidden and unknowable truths. Of course, all these revelations cannot be true since they often contradict each other. All religions, however, are founded on the *claim* that revelation has been received from the supernatural realm, just as all sciences are based on the claim that their theories are supported by empirical evidence.

In Hinduism, the most important scriptures are the *Vedas,* which were composed from the utterances of seers and sages who had received revelation from divine beings. In Islam, Mohammad heard a ringing in his ears that he came to realize was the voice of Allah speaking to him. He wrote down what Allah was saying to him and this became the *Koran.* In Judaism, the Ten Commandments were written on tablets of stone by the very finger of God before they were given to Moses. Knowledge of the law, and probably the early history of mankind and the Israelites, was also given to Moses by God on Mount Sinai and subsequently written down by Moses in the first five books of the Old Testament: Genesis through Deuteronomy (Exod. 24:4; Num. 33:2; Deut. 31:9; John 7:19; Acts 7:38). In Christianity, God's ultimate revelation to humanity was in the person of Christ, his only begotten Son. As Jesus said: "For I did not speak on My own initiative, but the Father Himself who sent Me has given Me a commandment as to what to say and what to speak" (John 12:49). Through Christ, God entered the natural realm and dwelt among us. As Jesus said, "He who has seen Me has seen the Father" (John 14:9).

Christianity is unique among all the world's religions because the Word (Christ) "became flesh, and dwelt among us" (John 1:14). In other words, a door between the natural and supernatural realm was opened and God entered the natural realm of space and time in material form through his beloved Son. The existence of God could now be confirmed, not only through supernatural revelation, but also by empirical evidence: "What was from the beginning, what we have heard, what we have seen with our eyes, what we have looked at and touched with our hands, concerning the Word of Life" (1 John 1:1). Since Christ subsequently ascended back into heaven, we no longer have access to empirical evidence for God's existence, although we do have the testimony of the apostles who were eyewitnesses: "For we did not follow cleverly devised tales when we made known to you the power and coming of our Lord Jesus Christ, but we were eyewitnesses of His majesty" (2 Peter 1:16).

II. THEOLOGY: A HUMAN DISCIPLINE WITH A HEAD OF GOLD BUT FEET OF CLAY

Humans have devised various academic disciplines to aid them in their quest for truth, whether through science, philosophy, or religion. There are a number of academic disciplines within science that seek to study the natural realm, including astronomy, geology, and biology. In philosophy, some of these academic disciplines include metaphysics, logic, and ethics. The primary academic discipline within religion is theology. *Webster's New Collegiate Dictionary* defines theology as: "the study of God and his relation to the world" (Woolf 1981:1200).

After completing my book *The Limitations of Scientific Truth* in 2005, I subsequently came to understand that philosophy and religion shared many of the same limitations in their search for truth that I had previously identified for science, including temporal, logical, cultural, spatial, and empirical limitations. The common denominator behind these limitations in all three disciplines was the human factor. Science is an academic discipline devised by humans and practiced by humans; philosophy is an academic discipline devised by humans and practiced by humans; theology is an academic discipline devised by humans and practiced by humans—and all humans are flawed because of their sinful nature. Therefore, the ultimate reason that the truths of science are often difficult to harmonize with the truths of philosophy or religion is that all academic disciplines devised and practiced by humans are also flawed: they are composed of mixtures of truths, half-truths, and falsehoods. If science, philosophy, or theology ever arrived at absolute truth, they would cease to change with time and would be in agreement with each other. Despite periodic bursts of optimism, this has not happened in the past, it is not happening today, nor will it happen in the future. Like the base of a rainbow, absolute truth always recedes beyond our reach every time we try to approach it through a human discipline.

The flaws in humans that practice these academic disciplines can be summarized in terms of three basic problems: (1) human ignorance—we don't have all the facts, (2) human error—we sometimes misinterpret the facts, and (3) human bias—we sometimes distort the facts. In my earlier book, I quoted from Stephen Jay Gould concerning the very human nature of the scientific discipline: "I criticize the myth that science itself is an objective enterprise, done properly only when scientists can shuck the constraints of their culture and view the world as it really is. . . . Rather, I believe that science must be understood as a social phenomenon, a gutsy, human enterprise, not the work of robots programmed to collect pure information" (1981:21). This same critique can also be applied to philosophy and religion. The idea that Christian theology, because of its subject matter (God) or its reliance upon divine revelation (the Bible), is somehow purer or less prone to error than other human disciplines is also a myth. Theologians, like scientists and philosophers, are also sinners, fallen humans who have limited knowledge about that which they study, who often make mistakes, and who all have their own unique set of biases. Although the focus of Christian theology is on the divine, it is nevertheless a very human discipline that is devised by humans and conducted by humans. As Witherington has noted, "It is time, indeed it is well past time, to recognize that 'theology' is what we do to and with the text" (2005:245). From this perspective, the academic discipline of theology is very similar to the troubling image that King Nebuchadnezzar saw in a dream:

> The head of that statue was made of fine gold, its breast and its
> arms of silver, its belly and its thighs of bronze, its legs of iron, its

feet partly of iron and partly of clay. You continued looking until a stone was cut out without hands, and it struck the statue on its feet of iron and clay and crushed them. Then the iron, the clay, the bronze, the silver and the gold were crushed all at the same time and became like chaff from the summer threshing floors; and the wind carried them away so that not a trace of them was found. But the stone that struck the statue became a great mountain and filled the whole earth. (Dan. 2:32–35)

Like the statue in Nebuchadnezzar's dream in the book of Daniel, the discipline of theology may have a head of gold, the study of God and his Word, but it has feet of iron and clay. We are the feet of iron and clay that can easily be crushed, causing the entire structure to come crashing down into a pile of dust. Thus, Christian theology is subject to the same human limitations that afflict all human disciplines. These limitations are not in God's Word, but in ourselves. I believe that the Bible is God's Word, perfect, complete, and able to accomplish all things for which God made it. On the other hand, I do not believe that our understanding of the Bible is perfect or complete. Theology is a human discipline and the weak link in all human disciplines is the humans who practice those disciplines.

III. THEOLOGY'S IMPERFECTIONS MANIFESTED: A HOUSE DIVIDED

One of the most glaring examples of the limitations of theological truth is highlighted by the difference between *what* Jesus prayed that his church should be, and *what* the church has actually become. After the Last Supper, just before he left with his disciples for the Mount of Olives where Judas would betray him, Jesus concluded his prayer for the disciples with this request to his Father: "I do not ask on behalf of these alone, but for those also who believe in Me through their word; that they may all be one; even as You, Father, are in Me and I in You, that they also may be in Us, so that the world may believe that You sent Me" (John 17:20–21). Far from being of one mind and one heart, a pure mirror with no imperfections that clearly reflects the love of the Father and the Son, the church has shattered into dozens of different glass shards. As we see in the writings of Luke and the apostle Paul, dissension within the church arose shortly after its founding on the Day of Pentecost (Acts 6:1, 15:1–2; Rom. 16:17–18; 1 Cor. 1:10–11, 11:18–19). Although these early arguments were settled by the authority of the apostles, similar theological disagreements and doctrinal squabbling within the church would punctuate church history for the next 2,000 years.

During the early part of the first millennium, a number of theological arguments arose within the church that ultimately had to be settled by the calling of major church councils, such as the Council of Nicaea over the Trinitarian Controversy. In this controversy, Arius contended that Christ, being the only begotten Son of God, had a beginning and was therefore not like God who had no beginning, whereas his bishop, Alexander, argued that Christ was coeternal with God and therefore of equal stature (Latourette 1953:152–153; Walton 1986: Chart 14). The Council of Nicaea decided in favor of Alexander and out of this council was forged the Nicene Creed:

> We believe in one God, the Father Almighty, maker of all things visible and invisible, and in one Lord, Jesus Christ, the Son of God, the only-begotten of the Father, that is, of the substance [*ousias*] of the Father, God from God, light from light, true God from true God, begotten, not made, of one substance [*homoousion*] with the Father, through whom all things came to be, those things that are in heaven and those things that are on earth, who for us men and for our salvation came down and was made flesh, and was made man, suffered, rose the third day, ascended into the heavens, and will come to judge the living and the dead. (Latourette 1953:155)

Arius was wrong, however, not only because of the decision of the Council of Nicaea, but because of what Christ had testified concerning himself: "'Your father Abraham rejoiced to see My day, and he saw it and was glad.' So the Jews said to Him, 'You are not yet fifty years old, and have You seen Abraham?' Jesus said to them, 'Truly, truly, I say to you, before Abraham was born, I am.' Therefore they picked up stones to throw at Him, but Jesus hid Himself and went out of the temple" (John 8:56–59). The reason the Jews were ready to stone Jesus was that he used the very same words, *I am*, to describe himself as God had used to describe himself to Moses: "Then Moses said to God, 'Behold, I am going to the sons of Israel, and I will say to them, "The God of your fathers has sent me to you." Now they may say to me, "What is His name?" What shall I say to them?' God said to Moses, 'I AM WHO I AM'; and He said, 'Thus you shall say to the sons of Israel, "I AM has sent me to you""" (Exod. 3:13–14).

Another division that arose within the early church was concerning the dual nature of Christ, being both the Son of God and the Son of Man, with some elements within the church stressing the divine character of Christ, while others giving more weight to his human attributes. Several church councils were held over this controversy, concluding with the Council of Chalcedon in 451, which resulted in another statement of faith, the Creed of Chalcedon: "Following the holy fathers we all, with one voice, define that there is to be confessed one and the same Son, our Lord Jesus Christ, perfect in Godhead and perfect in manhood, truly God and truly man, of rational soul and body, of the same substance [*homoousion*] with the Father according to the Godhead, and of the same substance [*homoousion*] with us according to the manhood, like to us in all respects, without sin, begotten of the Father before all time according to the Godhead...." (Latourette 1953:171). Other controversies arose in the early church over issues such as whether sins that were committed after baptism could be forgiven, whether those who had denied their faith during periods of Roman persecution should be allowed back into the church (the Donatist Controversy), or whether we are all born without sin, or into sin because of Adam's transgression (the Pelagian Controversy). Although these and many other theological controversies led to the shedding off of many small groups of dissenters from the main body of believers, the church was able to preserve its overall integrity through councils where these theological disputes were settled and doctrinal unity maintained.

The first great schism in the church did not occur until A.D. 1054 when the Eastern Church in Constantinople and the Western Church in Rome went their separate ways after Pope Leo IX of Rome and Patriarch Michael Cerularius of Constantinople excommunicated each other from the church. This split between the Orthodox Church and Catholic Church was due to a variety of factors including cultural differences between the Greeks and the Romans and political differences between the Byzantine Empire and the Holy Roman Empire, but it also involved several theological controversies, such as: (1) the Filioque Controversy over whether the Holy Spirit proceeds from the Father (Eastern Church) or from both the Father and the Son (Western Church); (2) the Iconoclastic Controversy over whether statues should be prohibited in worship (Eastern Church), or permitted (Western Church); (3) celibacy of the clergy; (4) the use of leavened or unleavened bread in the Eucharist; and (5) different emphasis on the divinity and humanity of Christ (Latourette 1953:571–572; Walton 1986: Chart 22). After this division, the Patriarch of Constantinople's control over the Orthodox Church would be weakened by the capture of Constantinople in 1453 by a Muslim army and the city's subsequent incorporation into the Ottoman Empire, as well as later, in 1472, when Ivan the Great of Russia attempted to assume the role of protector of the church. The Orthodox Church subsequently fragmented along national lines into fourteen different autocephalous (self-governing) branches, each with their own leader or leaders, including the Eastern Orthodox Churches of: Albania, Bulgaria, Czech and Slovak Republics, Georgia, Poland, Romania, Russia, and Serbia; the Oriental Orthodox Churches of: Alexandria, Antioch, Constantinople, Cyprus, Greece, and Jerusalem; and the Orthodox Church in America.

The Catholic Church would also be subject to further fragmentation, such as during the Great Schism of the papacy between 1378 and 1417. From 1309 to 1378, because of political unrest in Italy, the popes had chosen to live at Avignon (which is now located in southern France). Italians sometimes refer to this period as the Babylonian captivity of the papacy. Then, after some sixty-nine years, Pope Gregory XI (1370–1378) moved his residence back to Rome in 1378, but died shortly thereafter. In an attempt to break the power of the French over the papacy, the Italians elected a pope from among their members, Urban VI (1378–1389), but the French Cardinals rejected this choice and elected their own pope, Clement VII (1378–1394). After failing to overthrow Urban VI and recapture Rome after three years of warfare, Clement VII moved his residence back to Avignon while Urban VII remained in Rome. Thus, for the next thirty-one years the Catholic Church had two popes. Then in 1409, the Council of Pisa appointed their own pope, Alexander V (1409–1410). The three popes and their successors in Avignon, Rome, and Pisa vied for power over the next eight years. The papacy was finally restored to Rome in 1417 when the Council of Constance in 1414 and 1417 deposed all three contenders and named Martin V (1417–1431) as the new pope at Rome (Chadwick 1995:175–176; Walton 1986: Chart 29). Many other divisions, both theological and political, threatened the Catholic Church during the latter half of the first millennium and the first half of the second millennium, but the church was able to maintain its integrity, perhaps in part by allowing limited forms of dissent through the growth of various monastic orders such as the Knights Templar, Teutonic Knights, Benedictines, Augustinians, Carthusians, Carmelites, Dominicans, Franciscans, and Jesuits. These orders, while emphasizing certain ideas or behaviors, nevertheless remained within the broader fold of the Catholic Church. The more radical theological excursions of other groups, however, such as the Cathari, Waldensians, Lollards, and Hussites, were not tolerated by the Catholic Church, and these groups were subject to persecution and even death (Walton 1986: Chart 28).

The second great schism within the Catholic Church would occur in 1517 when Martin Luther nailed his Ninety-five Theses on the door of All Saints' Church in Wittenberg, Germany, thereby ushering in the Protestant Reformation. In this document Luther attacked the clergy's abuse in the selling of indulgences for the remission of sins. For this action, the pope requested that Luther come to Rome to answer to the charge of heresy, but Luther's friends managed to keep him safe in Germany. In 1520 Luther published five tracts that set forward his theological positions: (1) Sermon on Good Works, (2) The Papacy at Rome, (3) The Address to the German Nobility, (4) The Babylonian Captivity of the Church, and (5) The Freedom of the Christian Man:

> In these tracts were set forth the convictions which became distinctive features of Protestantism—justification by faith alone, the priesthood of all believers, the authority of the word of God as contained in the Scriptures, and the right and duty of each Christian to interpret the Scriptures. Some of these convictions had been foreshadowed in groups which had been cast out of the Catholic Church in the centuries before Luther. Yet, as compared with them the emphasis was new, especially the basic affirmation, justification by faith. Luther and his fellow-Protestants maintained that they were simply reasserting historic Christianity as it had been before its corruption by Rome. (Latourette 1953:715)

For these theological positions, Luther was excommunicated from the Catholic Church by Pope Leo X in 1521.

With the growing use of the printing press, following its introduction into Europe by Johannes Gutenberg around 1440, the writings of Luther were soon being printed and disseminated throughout the Holy Roman Empire. The impact of Luther's theology was first felt in northern Germany, but it soon spread to the Netherlands, Scandinavia, Scotland, and England (Chadwick 1995:202–203). Moreover, beginning with the printing of the Gutenberg Bible (in Latin) in the 1450s, Bibles were also becoming more readily available to the general populace across Europe, and translations of the Bible into the languages of the various countries made the Scriptures even more accessible to the common people. In the fourteenth century alone, translations of the Bible, or the New Testament, into Russian, German, English, French, Icelandic, Finnish, and Spanish were completed. Unfortunately, the growing availability of the Bible, along with Luther's advocacy for the priesthood of all believers, also led to a proliferation of individual interpretations of the Scriptures. Without the authority of apostles, a pope or patriarch, a Christian emperor, or large church councils, the Protestant Reformation rapidly splintered into a multitude of denominations—each with its own distinctive structure and theological emphasis. In fact, over the past two centuries this fissuring trend seems to have accelerated, and this is not factoring in all the various types of Lutherans, Presbyterians, Methodists, Baptists, etc. (see Table 1).

Table 1: The Proliferation of Protestant Churches	
1500s	Lutheran, Reformed, Anabaptist, Anglican, Mennonite, Presbyterian, Congregationalist
1600s	Baptist, Dutch Reformed, Quakers, Amish
1700s	Church of the Brethren, Moravians, Methodist, Episcopalian, Shakers
1800s	Mormon, Disciples of Christ, Holiness Churches, Seventh-day Adventist, Salvation Army, Jehovah's Witnesses, Christian Science, Church of God, Evangelical Free Church, Church of God in Christ
1900s	Church of the Nazarene, Assemblies of God, United Church of Christ, Foursquare Church, Vineyard Fellowship, Calvary Chapel, International Church of Christ, Potter's House, Willow Creek

Looking on the bright side of 2,000 years of church history, one might argue that the church has shown great resiliency and vitality down through the ages. Just when the Christian faith seems to be stagnating, bound in the fetters of human traditions and institutions, it breaks out anew in fresh manifestations of religious fervor and devotion, returning once more to its first love, the Lord Jesus. (Latourette 1961:542) From this perspective, the plethora of denominations and branches within Christianity provides strong evidence that the message of the gospel is still very much alive in the hearts and minds of men and women. On the other hand, one has to wonder how much stronger our witness to the world would be if the church had remained one body as the Lord had prayed it would, instead of letting our various theological disputes, often over quite trivial matters, get in the way. Indeed, not only are we divided by our theologies, we often use these theological differences to judge one another, even to the point of stating who is and who isn't saved—a direct violation of what Jesus commanded during his Sermon on the Mount: "Do not judge so that you will not be judged. For in the way you judge, you will be judged; and by your standard of measure, it will be measured to you" (Matt. 7:1–2). If the church had remained one body, rather than many, if we had not allowed our theological interpretations to split us apart, then our witness to the world would be far stronger and much more effective than it is today. As the Lord prayed: "that they may all be one; even as You, Father, are in Me and I in You, that they also may be in Us, so that the world may believe that You sent Me" (John 17:21).

In conclusion, theology is very much a human discipline with all the flaws and limitations inherent in any enterprise undertaken by fallen humanity. Although we are dealing with the infallible Word of God, our knowledge, understanding, and interpretation of that revelation is far from perfect. Church history is strewn with the wreckage of theological positions that were once thought to be true and unalterable but which were later abandoned or discredited. Therefore, we must prayerfully and continuously reexamine our theological positions to make sure we are indeed building on the solid rock of God's Word and not the shifting sands of human knowledge, human traditions, and human biases. In the next five chapters we will examine some of the limitations that may impact the accuracy and validity of our theology.

PART 2

THEOLOGICAL LIMITATIONS

Chapter 2

THE TEMPORAL LIMITATIONS OF THEOLOGICAL TRUTH

IN *THE LIMITATIONS OF SCIENTIFIC TRUTH*, I stated that: "The first and perhaps greatest limitation of scientific knowledge is that it is constantly changing. Few things are more certain than this: that which is current scientific knowledge today will be outdated scientific knowledge tomorrow" (Brush 2005:27). This limitation is also true of theological knowledge. Although Christian theology is founded upon the Word of God, our understanding of that revelation has continued to change over time. While it may be argued that our understanding of most of Christianity's core truths has not changed over the past 2,000 years, our understanding of many of the more peripheral truths certainly has changed, and continues to change. Moreover, some of these peripheral truths are occasionally elevated to core truths among some churches or denominations.

I. A STUDENT'S CHANGING THEOLOGY

I was first introduced to the temporal limitations of theological truth as a young ministerial student at Bible college. As a part of our training for the ministry, we were encouraged to find positions of service in local churches as ministers, youth ministers, choir directors, Sunday school teachers, etc. Since we were still acquiring the knowledge and skills necessary for Christian Service, however, I would occasionally find that some of the things I had been teaching or preaching the previous Sunday in church were partially negated by what I was learning in class the following week. Thus, I had inadvertently been teaching or preaching falsehoods because of deficiencies in my understanding of the Scriptures. Although the Word of God was not changing, my understanding of that Word, my theology, was changing and (hopefully) maturing for the better. At the time, I wondered if I should stop preaching until my knowledge of the Bible was more complete, maybe after I had finished my degree work. Fortunately, I did not pursue this course of action since I came to realize that while my knowledge of the Scriptures was still developing, it was nevertheless more advanced than many of the people in my congregation. Moreover, I was constantly learning deeper truths from my professors at Bible college that I could share with the people in my church. Therefore, although I occasionally made theological mistakes that I subsequently had to correct, my preaching and teaching could still make a meaningful contribution to the spiritual growth of the people in the churches where I ministered. The church was indeed like a family with each of God's children learning from those who were more spiritually mature, and passing that knowledge on to those who were less mature or knowledgeable in the faith. Even more importantly, I later came to realize that God constantly takes the imperfect and perfects it to accomplish his will. All ministers, like all humans, are imperfect vessels of clay that God can nevertheless use to accomplish his purposes.

The temporal character of my theological knowledge was not resolved when I received my four-year degree from Bible college or by several degrees thereafter. If we are honest about it, our learning in any subject (especially theology) is a lifelong process and we never arrive at the point where there is nothing left to learn, no new insights left to be gained, or no new discoveries yet to be made. We can never stand on a pedestal and declare that we have now arrived at absolute truth and our utterances from henceforth should no longer be questioned. Taking such a position would surely be blasphemy, since God alone is omniscient. Instead, it is a hallmark of both intellectual and spiritual maturity that the more we learn about a subject, the more we realize how little we actually know. Great knowledge does not breed arrogance, but humility. Starting at small springs of truth, we travel down narrow brooks, then larger streams, and finally broad rivers until, after many years, we arrive at the edge of the great ocean of truth and realize how truly vast it actually is. There, at this seashore, we find many other seekers of truth, gazing out into the hazy distance of eternity. There we find individuals like Isaac Newton, "diverting myself in now and then finding a smoother pebble or a prettier shell than ordinary, whilst the great ocean of truth lay all undiscovered before me" (Evans 1968:484).

II. THE DISCIPLES' CHANGING THEOLOGY

A. Concerning the Identity of John the Baptist

We can also see the transitory nature of theology in the lives of the disciples as we read through the Gospels. The disciples' knowledge and understanding of who Jesus was only gradually developed during the course of Christ's ministry. The disciples were Jews: God's chosen people, to whom his law and revelations had been entrusted. The disciples were also in face-to-face contact with the Son of God on a daily basis. Nevertheless, the disciples' theology (i.e. their understanding of who Christ was and the nature of his mission on earth) was patchy at best throughout the time of Christ's earthly ministry. Only after Christ's resurrection and the coming of the Holy Spirit did their understanding of the events surrounding Christ's birth, ministry, death, and resurrection come fully into focus. Moreover, even their understanding of the identity of John the Baptist and his mission on earth was rather hazy and incomplete, despite the fact that at least two of Jesus's disciples had formerly been John's disciples.

John's role in preparing the Jewish nation for the appearance of the Messiah had first been foretold by the prophet Isaiah some 700 years before John's birth:

> "Comfort, O comfort My people," says your God. "Speak kindly to Jerusalem; And call out to her, that her warfare has ended, That her iniquity has been removed, That she has received of the LORD'S hand Double for all her sins." A voice is calling, "Clear the way for the LORD in the wilderness; Make smooth in the desert a highway for our God. Let every valley be lifted up, And every mountain and hill be made low; And let the rough ground become a plain, And the rugged terrain a broad valley; Then the glory of the LORD will be revealed, And all flesh will see it together; For the mouth of the LORD has spoken." (Isa. 40:1–5)

Some 300 years later, this prophecy concerning John would be reiterated by Malachi in the last book of the Old Testament: "'Behold, I am going to send My messenger, and he will clear the way before Me. And the Lord, whom you seek, will suddenly come to His temple; and the messenger of the covenant, in whom you delight, behold, He is coming,' says the LORD of hosts" (Mal. 3:1) and "Behold, I am going to send you Elijah the prophet before the coming of the great and terrible day of the LORD. He will restore the hearts of the fathers to their children and the hearts of the children to their fathers, so that I will not come and smite the land with a curse" (Mal. 4:5–6).

So important was John's role in preparing the way for the Messiah, that his conception, like that of Christ, was announced by the angel Gabriel:

> And an angel of the Lord appeared to him, standing to the right of the altar of incense. Zacharias was troubled when he saw the angel, and fear gripped him. But the angel said to him, "Do not be afraid, Zacharias, for your petition has been heard, and your wife Elizabeth will bear you a son, and you will give him the name John. You will have joy and gladness, and many will rejoice at his birth. For he will be great in the sight of the Lord; and he will drink no wine

> or liquor, and he will be filled with the Holy Spirit while yet in his mother's womb. And he will turn many of the sons of Israel back to the Lord their God. It is he who will go as a forerunner before Him in the spirit and power of Elijah, TO TURN THE HEARTS OF THE FATHERS BACK TO THE CHILDREN, and the disobedient to the attitude of the righteous, so as to make ready a people prepared for the Lord." (Luke 1:11–17)

Although the angel Gabriel struck Zacharias dumb because of his failure to believe Gabriel's declaration, Zacharias's speech was returned to him upon the birth of his son and he made the following prophecy:

> "And you, child, will be called the prophet of the Most High; For you will go on BEFORE THE LORD TO PREPARE HIS WAYS; To give to His people the knowledge of salvation By the forgiveness of their sins, Because of the tender mercy of our God, With which the Sunrise from on high will visit us, TO SHINE UPON THOSE WHO SIT IN DARKNESS AND THE SHADOW OF DEATH, To guide our feet into the way of peace." And the child continued to grow and to become strong in spirit, and he lived in the deserts until the day of his public appearance to Israel. (vv. 76–80)

Luke (3:1–3) later records that, "in the fifteenth year of the reign of Tiberius Caesar…the Word of God came to John, the son of Zacharias, in the wilderness. And he came into all the district around the Jordan, preaching a baptism of repentance for the forgiveness of sins." Many that heard John's preaching wondered if John might himself be the Christ, but John, fulfilling his mission, assured the people that "One is coming who is mightier than I, and I am not fit to untie the thong of His sandals; He will baptize you with the Holy Spirit and fire" (v. 16). Indeed, at the beginning of his ministry, Jesus came to John to be baptized "to fulfill all righteousness" (Matt. 3:15): "John testified saying, 'I have seen the Spirit descending as a dove out of heaven, and He remained upon Him. I did not recognize Him, but He who sent me to baptize in water said to me,' 'He upon whom you see the Spirit descending and remaining upon Him, this is the One who baptizes in the Holy Spirit.' 'I myself have seen, and have testified that this is the Son of God'" (John 1:32–34).

On the day following Jesus's baptism, John saw Jesus walking by and said to his disciples "Behold the Lamb of God!" (v. 36). Two of John's disciples immediately left John and began to follow Jesus. Andrew, the brother of Simon Peter, was one of these disciples, the other was probably John, one of the sons of Zebedee (in his gospel, John usually refers to himself as the *disciple*). After this initial introduction, Andrew and his brother Simon Peter, as well as John and his brother James, would later be called by Jesus from their boat along the shore of the Sea of Galilee to become fishers of men. Nevertheless, despite Andrew and John's early discipleship with John the Baptist, and later with Jesus, they, as well as the other disciples, would subsequently struggle to understand exactly who these two individuals were, John the Baptist and Christ, both of whose coming had been prophesied of old.

John the Baptist, himself, seems to have wavered slightly in his faith concerning Jesus after being imprisoned by Herod. Both Matthew (11:2–3) and Luke (7:18–19) record that John, after hearing of the works of Jesus, sent two of his disciples to Jesus and asked: "Are You the Expected One, or shall we look for someone else?" (Matt. 11:3). Jesus told John's disciples to report to John what they were seeing and hearing: "the BLIND RECEIVE SIGHT and the lame walk, the lepers are cleansed and the deaf hear, the dead are raised up, and the POOR HAVE THE GOSPEL PREACHED TO THEM. And blessed is he who does not take offense at Me" (vv. 5–6). All these miracles that Jesus was performing were the fulfillment of prophecies in the book of Isaiah concerning the ministry of the Messiah, the same book that prophesied concerning John's own ministry: "I am the LORD, I have called You in righteousness, I will also hold You by the hand and watch over You, And I will appoint You as a covenant to the people, As a light to the nations, To open blind eyes, To bring out prisoners from the dungeon And those who dwell in darkness from the prison" (Isa. 42:6–7). Isaiah also prophesied:

> The Spirit of the Lord GOD is upon me, Because the LORD has anointed me To bring good news to the afflicted; He has sent me to bind up the brokenhearted, To proclaim liberty to captives And freedom to prisoners; To proclaim the favorable year of the LORD And the day of vengeance of our God; To comfort all who mourn, To grant those who mourn in Zion, Giving them a garland instead of ashes, The oil of gladness instead of mourning, The mantle of praise instead of a spirit of fainting. So they will be called oaks of righteousness, The planting of the LORD, that He may be glorified. (Isa. 61:1–3)

After John's disciples left with this report to give to their master in prison, Jesus began to instruct the multitudes concerning John and his ministry:

> This is the one about whom it is written, "BEHOLD, I SEND MY MESSENGER AHEAD OF YOU, WHO WILL PREPARE YOUR WAY BEFORE YOU." Truly I say to you, among those born of women there has not arisen anyone greater than John the Baptist! Yet the one who is least in the kingdom of heaven is greater than he. From the days of John the Baptist until now the kingdom of heaven suffers violence, and violent men take it by force. For all the prophets and the Law prophesied until John. And if you are willing to accept it, John himself is Elijah who was to come. He who has ears to hear, let him hear. (Matt. 11:10–15)

Despite this very clear affirmation by Jesus as to the identity of John the Baptist and his coming in the spirit and power of Elias (Mal. 3:1, 4:5–6), many of the people continued to speculate that Christ, himself, was Elijah, Jeremiah, one of the other prophets, or, after John's death, even John the Baptist—as the disciples told Jesus along the coasts of Caesarea Philippi before Peter made his good confession: "You are the Christ, the Son of the living God" (Matt. 16:13–16). But even after this, some of the disciples still seemed confused about the identity of John the Baptist and Elias. Some six to eight days after Peter's good confession, Peter, James, and John accompanied Jesus to the mount where he was transfigured and appeared in glory with Moses and Elias (Matt. 17:1–3). Yet, as Jesus and these three disciples came down from the mount of transfiguration, the disciples, having now seen Elijah, were still confused over when he would come. Jesus had to explain it to them once more: "And His disciples asked Him, 'Why then do the scribes say that Elijah must come first?' And He answered and said, 'Elijah is coming and will restore all things; but I say to you that Elijah already came, and they did not recognize him, but did to him whatever they wished. So also the Son of Man is going to suffer at their hands.' Then the disciples understood that He had spoken to them about John the Baptist" (vv. 10–13).

Therefore, despite the Old Testament prophecies in Isaiah and Malachi, the announcement of John's birth by the angel Gabriel, the prophetic utterance of Zacharias, the discipleship of Andrew and John under John the Baptist, and the teaching of Jesus about John the Baptist after the visit of John's two disciples, it was not until after the transfiguration that these three disciples finally understood that John the Baptist and Elijah were one—at least in terms of spirit and power. Like a seminary student's theology, the disciple's theology was also imperfect and constantly changing as their understanding of God and his purposes gradually developed over time. Under the guidance of Jesus, and later the Holy Spirit, the disciples finally came to understand John's role in preparing the way of the Messiah, as both Matthew and Luke would later record in their gospels:

> Now in those days John the Baptist came, preaching in the wilderness of Judea, saying, "Repent, for the kingdom of heaven is at hand. For this is the one referred to by Isaiah the prophet when he said, 'THE VOICE OF ONE CRYING IN THE WILDERNESS, MAKE READY THE WAY OF THE LORD, MAKE HIS PATHS STRAIGHT!'" (Matt. 3:1–3)

> Now in the fifteenth year of the reign of Tiberius Caesar, when Pontius Pilate was governor of Judea, and Herod was tetrarch of Galilee, and his brother Philip was tetrarch of the region of Ituraea

and Trachonitis, and Lysanias was tetrarch of Abilene, in the high priesthood of Annas and Caiaphas, the word of God came to John, the son of Zacharias, in the wilderness. And he came into all the district around the Jordan, preaching a baptism of repentance for the forgiveness of sins; as it is written in the book of the words of Isaiah the prophet, "THE VOICE OF ONE CRYING IN THE WILDERNESS, 'MAKE READY THE WAY OF THE LORD, MAKE HIS PATHS STRAIGHT. EVERY RAVINE WILL BE FILLED, AND EVERY MOUNTAIN AND HILL WILL BE BROUGHT LOW; THE CROOKED WILL BECOME STRAIGHT, AND THE ROUGH ROADS SMOOTH; AND ALL FLESH WILL SEE THE SALVATION OF GOD.'" (Luke 3:1–6)

B. *Concerning the Divinity of the Messiah*

Another area where we see the temporal limitations of the disciples' theology is with regard to the divine nature of the Messiah. Andrew and John began to follow Jesus because of God's revelation to John the Baptist during his baptism of Jesus that this was indeed the Son of God (John 1:32–34), and John's declaration of that fact on the following day: "Behold the Lamb of God!" (v. 36). Nevertheless, the disciples apparently did not fully understand all that this implied. For instance, while crossing the Sea of Galilee, a storm came up that threatened to sink their ship, but Jesus was asleep in the back of the boat. When they awoke Jesus with the cry "Teacher, do You not care that we are perishing?" (Mark 4:38), he upbraided them for their lack of faith before rebuking the wind and the waves and causing a great calm on the sea. But this result was obviously not what the disciples had expected: "The men were amazed, and said, 'What kind of a man is this, that even the winds and the sea obey Him?'" (Matt. 8:27); "They became very much afraid and said to one another, 'Who then is this, that even the wind and the sea obey Him?'" (Mark 4:41).

What did the disciples expect? If Jesus were awake, perhaps he could tell them what to do in order to save themselves? If Jesus were awake, perhaps that would protect them all from perishing since God would not allow his son to die? If Jesus were awake, perhaps he would pray to his Father to save them and the storm would abate? Instead, Jesus himself commanded the wind and waves to cease—as if he were God. Here was a deep theological issue indeed: Who exactly was the Son of God and what was his relationship to God?

Another example of the disciples' limited theological understanding of who the Son of God actually was occurred during the feeding of a crowd that had gathered to hear Jesus. Before the feeding of these 5,000, Jesus asked Philip, "'Where are we to buy bread, so that these may eat?' This He was saying to test him, for He Himself knew what He was intending to do" (John 6:5–6). Philip, however, not understanding the power and divinity of the one who posed this question, answered: "Two hundred denarii worth of bread is not sufficient for them, for everyone to receive a little" (John 6:7). For the one who created the plants and animals that feed the whole earth, however, feeding a few thousand people was a very small matter indeed—he had no need of money. Jesus later showed his contempt for the value of money when the money collectors in Capernaum asked Peter if his master paid tribute, and Peter answered in the affirmative. Jesus then explained to Peter that the children of kings do not pay tribute, only those outside the royal family. Nevertheless, to avoid offense, Jesus told Peter to cast a hook into the sea and the first fish he would catch would have a coin in its mouth with which the tribute could be paid (Matt. 17:24–27). To the One who owns every beast of the forest, the cattle upon a thousand hills, all the fowls of the mountains, and all the wild beasts of the field (Ps. 50:10–11), human tokens of wealth are irrelevant and unnecessary.

One further example of the Son of God's dominion over nature occurred following the feeding of the 5,000. After sending the crowds away, Jesus went up on a mountain to pray but told his disciples to go in their ship, back to Bethsaida. By evening the ship was still in the middle of the sea, hindered by the waves because the winds were contrary. Then, in the fourth watch of the night, Jesus came to them walking upon the water and the disciples cried out because they thought he was a spirit. Then Jesus spoke to them and said: "Take courage, it is I; do not be afraid" (Matt. 14:27).

Once again, we see the surprise and consternation of the disciples with regard to the power Christ had over nature: "When they got into the boat, the wind stopped. And those who were in the boat worshiped Him, saying, 'You are certainly God's Son!'" (vv. 32–33); "Then He got into the boat with them, and the wind stopped; and they were utterly astonished, for they had not gained any insight from the incident of the loaves, but their heart was hardened" (Mark 6:51–52). Although Matthew tells us that those in the ship came and worshiped Jesus after this miracle, Mark tells us that they, nevertheless, were so amazed because they had not considered the miracle of the feeding of the 5,000 because their hearts were hardened. They had also apparently forgotten their previous experience on this same lake when Jesus had calmed the wind and the waves during a great storm (Matt. 8:23–27).

It is evident that, even after Jesus calmed the wind and the waves during the great storm, even after the feeding of the 5,000, and even after they witnessed him walking upon the water, the disciples still failed to understand the true divine nature of the Son of God. When subsequently faced with another crowd who were hungry, the 4,000, the disciple's response was the same: "And Jesus called His disciples to Him, and said, 'I feel compassion for the people, because they have remained with Me now three days and have nothing to eat; and I do not want to send them away hungry, for they might faint on the way.' The disciples said to Him, 'Where would we get so many loaves in this desolate place to satisfy such a large crowd?'" (Matt. 15:32–33). Apparently, the disciples response was not a rhetorical question with an obvious answer, such as: Lord, will you provide food as you did at the feeding of the 5,000? Rather, their understanding of the divinity of the Son of God was still woefully insufficient. After the feeding of the 4,000, Jesus and the disciples left on a ship and came to the coast of Magdala, where the Pharisees and Sadducees confronted Jesus, desiring a sign from heaven. The miracles that Jesus had already performed in public, including the feeding of the 5,000 and the 4,000, had no more impact on the Pharisees and Sadducees than it had on the disciples. After telling the Pharisees and Sadducees that the only sign they would be given was the sign of the prophet Jonas, Jesus and his disciples got back aboard their ship and left for Bethsaida. During this voyage, Jesus warned his disciples to beware of the leaven of the Pharisees and of the Sadducees, but they thought this was because they had forgotten to buy bread before leaving port and now had only one loaf of bread on board (Matt. 15:39–16:7; Mark 8:10–16). Jesus once more had to remind them of what they had already witnessed concerning his power:

> But Jesus, aware of this, said, "You men of little faith, why do you discuss among yourselves that you have no bread? Do you not yet understand or remember the five loaves of the five thousand, and how many baskets full you picked up? Or the seven loaves of the four thousand, and how many large baskets full you picked up? How is it that you do not understand that I did not speak to you concerning bread? But beware of the leaven of the Pharisees and Sadducees." Then they understood that He did not say to beware of the leaven of bread, but of the teaching of the Pharisees and Sadducees. (Matt. 16:8–12)

> And Jesus, aware of this, said to them, "Why do you discuss the fact that you have no bread? Do you not yet see or understand? Do you have a hardened heart? HAVING EYES, DO YOU NOT SEE? AND HAVING EARS, DO YOU NOT HEAR? And do you not remember, when I broke the five loaves for the five thousand, how many baskets full of broken pieces you picked up?" They said to Him, "Twelve." "When I broke the seven for the four thousand, how many large baskets full of broken pieces did you pick up?" And they said to Him, "Seven." And He was saying to them, "Do you not yet understand?" (Mark 8:17–21)

The disciples' theology concerning the Son of God was still firmly grounded within the realm of human possibilities, not divine possibilities. If Christ had fed thousands with a few loaves and fishes, could he not provide sustenance for a few disciples on a boat?

The flaws in the disciples' theology were not due to human ignorance—they had been eyewitnesses of these miracles. Human error could have played a role; they could have, somehow, misinterpreted what these events meant. Mark, however, argues that the primary problem was human bias (they distorted the facts) because their hearts were hardened. In other words, they only saw what they wanted to see. They simply could not face the shattering reality that they were in the presence of God through the person of his Son. Near the end of Jesus's earthly ministry, the disciples were still struggling with this idea:

> Philip said to Him, "Lord, show us the Father, and it is enough for us." Jesus said to him, "Have I been so long with you, and yet you have not come to know Me, Philip? He who has seen Me has seen the Father; how can you say, 'Show us the Father'? Do you not believe that I am in the Father, and the Father is in Me? The words that I say to you I do not speak on My own initiative, but the Father abiding in Me does His works. Believe Me that I am in the Father and the Father is in Me; otherwise believe because of the works themselves." (John 14:8–11)

John would finally come to fully understand the divinity of the Son of God and would later open his gospel with this beautiful and powerful proclamation: "In the beginning was the Word, and the Word was with God, and the Word was God. He was in the beginning with God. All things came into being through Him, and apart from Him nothing came into being that has come into being. In Him was life, and the life was the Light of men. The Light shines in the darkness, and the darkness did not comprehend it" (John 1:1–5). Christ was able to command the wind and the waves and walk on the waters because he had made the air and the seas. He was able to feed the 5,000 and the 4,000 with a few loaves and fishes because he had made the plants and animals. He was able to heal the lame, bring hearing to the deaf, sight to the blind, and even life to the dead because he had made those whom he now healed. As the disciples daily walked and talked with Christ and witnessed these miracles, their understanding (their theology) of who the Son of God was, gradually deepened and was enriched until finally, they understood that they were in the presence of their Creator.

C. Concerning the Messiah's Mission to the Gentiles

The disciples' theology was not only limited in terms of who the Son of God was, it was also limited in terms of what his mission was on earth. We see hints of this misunderstanding in John's record of Jesus's conversation with the Samaritan woman at the well in Sychar: "The woman said to Him, 'I know that Messiah is coming (He who is called Christ); when that One comes, He will declare all things to us.' Jesus said to her, 'I who speak to you am He.' At this point His disciples came, and they were amazed that He had been speaking with a woman, yet no one said, 'What do You seek?' or, 'Why do You speak with her?'" (John 4:25–27). Although the disciples were surprised that Jesus was even talking with this Samaritan woman, they held their peace at this time. Later, however, as Jesus was on his final journey to Jerusalem before his crucifixion, a Samaritan village refused to provide lodging for Jesus and his disciples, whereupon James and John, the sons of thunder, asked Jesus if they should call fire down from heaven and destroy this village, but Jesus answered, "'You do not know what kind of spirit you are of; for the Son of Man did not come to destroy men's lives, but to save them' And they went on to another village" (Luke 9:55–56).

Now of all the Gentiles, the Jews probably hated the Samaritans the most because these ten tribes of Israel had split away from Judah and Benjamin in the days of Solomon's son Rehoboam. The leader of these ten tribes, Jeroboam, became their king and set up his royal seat at Shechem (which was later moved to Samaria in the time of Omri). Jeroboam also set up idols in Dan and Bethel so that the people would not go up to Jerusalem to worship and offer sacrifices to God. Samaria was later captured and destroyed and the peoples of these ten tribes were taken into captivity by the Assyrians. During their captivity, some of the Israelites intermarried with Assyrians or other peoples. When the Assyrian Empire later collapsed, some of these captives and their descendants came back to live in northern Israel, but the Jews viewed them as traitors, idolaters, and half-breeds. Therefore, as the chosen people, the Jews generally held the Gentiles in disdain since they were not the children of Abraham. Of all the Gentiles, however, they particularly disliked the Samaritans. Despite this Jewish bias, prophecies concerning the Messiah in the Old Testament clearly indicated that the Messiah would be the Savior, not only of the Jews, but also of the Gentiles (see Table 2).

Table 2: Prophecies That the Messiah Would Be Savior to All Peoples
Then in that day The nations will resort to the root of Jesse, Who will stand as a signal for the peoples; And His resting place will be glorious. (Isa. 11:10)
Behold, My Servant, whom I uphold; My chosen one in whom My soul delights. I have put My Spirit upon Him; He will bring forth justice to the nations. (Isa. 42:1)
I am the LORD, I have called You in righteousness, I will also hold You by the hand and watch over You, And I will appoint You as a covenant to the people, As a light to the nations, To open blind eyes, To bring out prisoners from the dungeon And those who dwell in darkness from the prison. (Isa. 42:6–7)
Arise, shine; for your light has come, And the glory of the LORD has risen upon you. For behold, darkness will cover the earth And deep darkness the peoples; But the LORD will rise upon you And His glory will appear upon you. Nations will come to your light, And kings to the brightness of your rising. (Isa. 60:1–3)

Therefore, the disciples' surprise that Jesus would talk to a Samaritan woman and their willingness to bring down fire on a Samaritan village, was probably not due to their ignorance of these Scriptures, or even due to their misinterpretation of these Scriptures, but instead because of the bias that they shared with their fellow Jews toward the Samaritans. This bias blinded them to the fact that all nations of the world would be blessed through the Messiah, as God had promised Abraham: "In your seed all the nations of the earth shall be blessed, because you have obeyed My voice" (Gen. 22:18). Jesus was to be the Savior to the entire world: both Jews and Samaritans; both Jews and Gentiles; Jews and Romans; as well as Greeks, Persians, Babylonians, Assyrians, etc. This broader flaw in the disciples' theology concerning the mission of Christ to the Gentiles would surface again after Christ's death and resurrection. The Holy Spirit instructed the apostle Peter in a vision to go to the house of Cornelius, a centurion of the Italian band, and preach the gospel to him and his household. Cornelius and his whole household accepted the Lord Jesus and received the same baptism of the Holy Spirit that the disciples had received on the Day of Pentecost. Many of the Jewish Christians were upset when they learned that Peter had entered the house of a Gentile and eaten with them: "And when Peter came up to Jerusalem, those who were circumcised took issue with him, 'You went to uncircumcised men and ate with them'" (Acts 11:2–3). When Peter explained his vision, however, and rehearsed all that had happened in the house of Cornelius, including God's outpouring of the Holy Spirit upon these Gentiles, even before they were baptized with water, his accusers realized that their theology concerning this issue was flawed and were willing to accept the Lord's guidance in this matter: "When they heard this, they quieted down and glorified God, saying, 'Well then, God has granted to the Gentiles also the repentance that leads to life'" (v. 18). In conclusion, the disciples' understanding of the Son of God's mission to the Gentiles changed through time as God led them into an ever-deeper understanding of the Scriptures and how the prophecies concerning the Messiah would be fulfilled.

D. Prophecies concerning the Messiah's Suffering and Death

A much more severe limitation in the disciples' theology was with regard to exactly how the Messiah would save the Jews and Gentiles from their sins. Their focus was on the glorious promises of *what* the Messiah would do for his people, rather than on *how* he would accomplish this redemptive work. Sacrifice as a means of atoning for sin was an integral part of God's dealings with the human race throughout the Old Testament. Some biblical scholars have suggested that sacrifice may have even been foreshadowed in the garden of Eden by God killing animals and using their skins to clothe Adam and Eve after they had sinned (Gen. 3:21); many biblical scholars see God's curse on the Serpent in the garden of Eden as being the first messianic prophecy in the Old Testament: Christ bruising the Serpent's head (ultimate victory over Satan), while Satan is bruising Christ's heel (the crucifixion): "The LORD God said to the serpent, 'Because you have done this, Cursed are you more than all cattle, And more than every beast of the field; On your belly you will go, And dust you will eat All the days of your life; And I will put enmity Between you and the woman, And between your seed and her seed; He shall bruise you on the head, And you shall bruise him on the heel'" (vv. 14–15).

After the flood, Noah built an altar and made a burnt offering unto the Lord of every clean beast and every clean bird (Gen. 8:20). God tested Abraham by asking him to offer his son Isaac as a burnt offering on Mount Moriah, a prefigurement of what God himself would actually do one day with his own beloved Son (Gen. 22:1–14). In Egypt, the Lord instructed each household of the Israelites to take a lamb without blemish at the beginning of the first month, and on the fourteenth day kill it and take its blood and strike it on the door posts of their houses so that the Lord would pass over their homes and not slay their firstborn, as he was going to do to the Egyptians (Exod. 12:1–13). The law that was given to Moses on Mount Sinai by the Lord, made very implicit the various sacrifices that were to be made by the Israelites for the atonement of their sins. Indeed, as the writer of Hebrews has noted:

> For when every commandment had been spoken by Moses to all the people according to the Law, he took the blood of the calves and the goats, with water and scarlet wool and hyssop, and sprinkled both the book itself and all the people, saying, "THIS IS THE BLOOD OF THE COVENANT WHICH GOD COMMANDED YOU." And in the same way he sprinkled both the tabernacle and all the vessels of the ministry with the blood. And according to the

> Law, one may almost say, all things are cleansed with blood, and
> without shedding of blood there is no forgiveness. (Heb. 9:19–22)

Since, as the apostle Paul noted, "the Law has become our tutor to lead us to Christ, so that we may be justified by faith" (Gal. 3:24), the law's emphasis on the shedding of blood for the forgiveness of sins should have prepared the disciples for what Christ would have to do in order to redeem his people—but it didn't. Instead, the disciples desperately wanted to believe otherwise. After waiting a thousand years for the promised Messiah, and then finding and loving him, how could they even consider losing him? It is an innate part of human optimism that when we remember the past or look forward to the future, we usually focus on the positive things and forget or ignore the negative things.

Although the disciples' own wishes and desires blinded them to Jesus's ultimate mission upon the earth, the Old Testament Scripture not only foretold the glory and ultimate victory of the coming Messiah, but also of his suffering and death (see Table 3):

Table 3: Prophecies concerning the Persecution and Death of the Messiah
Behold, My servant will prosper, He will be high and lifted up and greatly exalted. Just as many were astonished at you, My people, So His appearance was marred more than any man And His form more than the sons of men. Thus He will sprinkle many nations, Kings will shut their mouths on account of Him; For what had not been told them they will see, And what they had not heard they will understand. (Isa. 52:13–15)
Who has believed our message? And to whom has the arm of the LORD been revealed? For He grew up before Him like a tender shoot, And like a root out of parched ground; He has no stately form or majesty That we should look upon Him, Nor appearance that we should be attracted to Him. He was despised and forsaken of men, A man of sorrows and acquainted with grief; And like one from whom men hide their face He was despised, and we did not esteem Him. Surely our griefs He Himself bore, And our sorrows He carried; Yet we ourselves esteemed Him stricken, Smitten of God, and afflicted. But He was pierced through for our transgressions, He was crushed for our iniquities; The chastening for our well-being fell upon Him, And by His scourging we are healed. (Isa. 53:1–5)

Table 3: Prophecies concerning the Persecution and Death of the Messiah
His grave was assigned with wicked men, Yet He was with a rich man in His death, Because He had done no violence, Nor was there any deceit in His mouth. But the LORD was pleased To crush Him, putting Him to grief; If He would render Himself as a guilt offering, He will see His offspring, He will prolong His days, And the good pleasure of the LORD will prosper in His hand. As a result of the anguish of His soul, He will see it and be satisfied; By His knowledge the Righteous One, My Servant, will justify the many, As He will bear their iniquities. Therefore, I will allot Him a portion with the great, And He will divide the booty with the strong; Because He poured out Himself to death, And was numbered with the transgressors; Yet He Himself bore the sin of many, And interceded for the transgressors. (Isa. 53:9–12)

These passages from Isaiah make it very clear that the Messiah would redeem his people, but at a great price to himself. He would bear their sins and be wounded for their transgressions, even unto death and the grave. Other prophecies in the Old Testament are even more specific with regard to the manner in which the Messiah would suffer and die—by crucifixion.

The prophet Zechariah tells us that the Messiah will be pierced and his hands would be wounded: "I will pour out on the house of David and on the inhabitants of Jerusalem, the Spirit of grace and of supplication, so that they will look on Me whom they have pierced; and they will mourn for Him, as one mourns for an only son, and they will weep bitterly over Him like the bitter weeping over a firstborn" (Zech. 12:10); "And one will say to him, 'What are these wounds between your arms?' Then he will say, 'Those with which I was wounded in the house of my friends.' 'Awake, O sword, against My Shepherd, And against the man, My Associate,' Declares the LORD of hosts. 'Strike the Shepherd that the sheep may be scattered; And I will turn My hand against the little ones'" (Zech. 13:6–7). These prophecies in Zechariah were fulfilled when the hands and feet of Jesus were nailed to the cross (as was the Roman custom for cruci-fixion) and his side was pierced with a spear by a Roman soldier to ensure that he was indeed dead: "So the soldiers came, and broke the legs of the first man and of the other who was crucified with Him; but coming to Jesus, when they saw that He was already dead, they did not break His legs. But one of the soldiers pierced His side with a spear, and immediately blood and water came out" (John 19:32–34).

A thousand years before the coming of the Messiah, King David's prophetic utterances in the book of Psalms provided even more specific details about the Messiah's death on a cross, including: (1) both his hands and feet being pierced, (2) the crowd's actions and words of scorn as he hung on the cross, (3) the specific pain one would feel while hanging on a cross, (4) the soldiers casting lots for his clothing, (5) the fact that his legs were not broken to speed his death (as was done to two thieves who were also being crucified with Christ), (6) his being given vinegar to drink, and (7) his last words on the cross (see Table 4):

Table 4: Prophecies in Psalms concerning Christ's Crucifixion
They open wide their mouth at me, As a ravening and a roaring lion. I am poured out like water, And all my bones are out of joint; My heart is like wax; It is melted within me. My strength is dried up like a potsherd, And my tongue cleaves to my jaws; And You lay me in the dust of death. For dogs have surrounded me; A band of evildoers has encompassed me; They pierced my hands and my feet. I can count all my bones. They look, they stare at me; They divide my garments among them, And for my clothing they cast lots. (Ps. 22:13–18)
But I am a worm and not a man, A reproach of men and despised by the people. All who see me sneer at me; They separate with the lip, they wag the head, saying, "Commit yourself to the LORD; let Him deliver him; Let Him rescue him, because He delights in him." (Ps. 22:6–8)
He keeps all his bones, Not one of them is broken. (Ps. 34:20)
They also gave me gall for my food And for my thirst they gave me vinegar to drink.(Ps. 69:21)
My God, my God, why have You forsaken me? (Ps. 22:1)

Many of these prophecies in the Psalms, however, may have been obscured or hidden from the disciples' understanding until after the actual events had occurred, since human hindsight is often clearer than foresight. Moreover, in the highly detailed Psalm 22, there is no introduction as to whom this psalm is referring, whether to David himself, or someone else. It was only after Christ uttered the opening words of this Psalm (22:1), "MY GOD, MY GOD, WHY HAVE YOU FORSAKEN ME?" while he was dying on the cross that the content of this Psalm came into clear focus:

> At the ninth hour Jesus cried out with a loud voice, "ELOI, ELOI, LAMA SABACHTHANI?" which is translated, "MY GOD, MY GOD, WHY HAVE YOU FORSAKEN ME?" When some of the bystanders heard it, they began saying, "Behold, He is calling for Elijah." Someone ran and filled a sponge with sour wine, put it on a reed, and gave Him a drink, saying, "Let us see whether Elijah will come to take Him down." And Jesus uttered a loud cry, and breathed His last. And the veil of the temple was torn in two from top to bottom. When the centurion, who was standing right in front of Him, saw the way He breathed His last, he said, "Truly this man was the Son of God!" (Mark 15:34–39)

Other brief but specific prophecies concerning the crucifixion, such as Psalm 34:20 (none of his bones were broken) or Psalm 69:21 (he was given vinegar to drink), are scattered as jewels among the Psalms, and the context in which these verses occur seems to offer little help in understanding what they refer to— until after the prophecy had been fulfilled. For example the verses that come before and after Psalm 34:20 are about the righteous in general, when suddenly this specific prophecy about the righteous one (the Messiah) appears (none of his bones shall be broken).

In any event, whether or not the disciples fully understood the relatively clear prophecies in Isaiah and Zechariah, or the some-what more obscure passages in Psalms concerning the price that the Messiah would have to pay to redeem his people, Jesus was very clear in his instruction to the disciples about his ultimate mission here on earth, but the disciples could not, or would not accept this teaching. According to the Gospels, Jesus first began to teach the disciples about his coming death at the hands of the scribes and Pharisees right after Peter made the good confession near Caesarea Philippi (Matt. 16:13–20; Mark 8:27–30; Luke 9:18–21) (see Table 5):

Table 5: Jesus's Teaching concerning His Coming Death

From that time Jesus began to show His disciples that He must go to Jerusalem, and suffer many things from the elders and chief priests and scribes, and be killed, and be raised up on the third day. Peter took Him aside and began to rebuke Him, saying, "God forbid it, Lord! This shall never happen to You." But He turned and said to Peter, "Get behind Me, Satan! You are a stumbling block to Me; for you are not setting your mind on God's interests, but man's." (Matt. 16:21–23)

And He began to teach them that the Son of Man must suffer many things and be rejected by the elders and the chief priests and the scribes, and be killed, and after three days rise again. And He was stating the matter plainly. And Peter took Him aside and began to rebuke Him. But turning around and seeing His disciples, He rebuked Peter and said, "Get behind Me, Satan; for you are not setting your mind on God's interests, but man's." (Mark 8:31–33)

But He warned them and instructed them not to tell this to anyone, saying, "The Son of Man must suffer many things and be rejected by the elders and chief priests and scribes, and be killed and be raised up on the third day." (Luke 9:21–22)

It must have been very confusing to the disciples as they daily tried to align their human perception and understanding with those of the Son of God. In a few short minutes, Peter went from the heights to the depths, first being praised by Christ for his recognition that Jesus was indeed the Son of God: "Blessed are you, Simon Barjona, because flesh and blood did not reveal this to you, but My Father who is in heaven" (Matt. 16:17), but then being rebuked by Christ for not understanding his ultimate mission upon the earth: "Get behind Me, Satan! You are a stumbling block to Me; for you are not setting your mind on God's interests, but man's" (v. 23). Even though the Father had revealed to Peter who Jesus actually was, Peter still had little understanding of why the Father had sent his Son to earth. As would later be seen in the garden of Gethsemane, Jesus would struggle mightily with the task that God had set before him: for he that knew no sin, to take on the sins of mankind. This was the ultimate temptation that Satan offered Christ, first in the wilderness at the beginning of his ministry, and later on the Mount of Olives at the end of his ministry: the crown without the cross. Now, near Caesarea Philippi, just when it seemed that his disciples were beginning to truly understand who he was, Peter becomes the mouthpiece for Satan, saying: "God forbid it, Lord! This shall never happen to You" (v. 22).

Yet, despite Jesus's very strong rebuke of Peter, the disciples were still not able or ready to accept his warning that the Messiah must soon suffer and die at the hands of men. Only about a week later, on the Mount of Transfiguration, Luke records that Moses and Elias appeared with Jesus and they talked together "of His departure which He was about to accomplish at Jerusalem" (Luke 9:31). As Peter, James, and John were coming down from the Mount of Transfiguration with Jesus, he introduced them to the idea, not only that he would die, but also that he would be raised from the dead. They may have thought he was referring to the final judgment when all the dead would be raised, but that didn't seem to make much sense if they were to keep silence until that time: "As they were coming down from the mountain, He gave them orders not to relate to anyone what they had seen, until the Son of Man rose from the dead. They seized upon that statement, discussing with one another what rising from the dead meant" (Mark 9:9–10). Upon reaching the bottom of the mountain, they were met by a crowd who had gathered around a man whose son was possessed by an evil spirit that the other disciples had not been able to cast out. After Jesus healed the boy, Luke records: "And they were all amazed at the greatness of God. But while everyone was marveling at all that He was doing, He said to His disciples, 'Let these words sink into your ears; for the Son of Man is going to be delivered into the hands of men.' But they did not understand this statement, and it was concealed from them so that they would not perceive it; and they were afraid to ask Him about this statement" (9:43–45).

Later, after returning to Galilee, Jesus continued to teach his disciples about his coming death and resurrection. Although they finally began to accept the idea that Jesus was going to be put to death and were sorrowful, his resurrection was still a mystery to them and would remain so until after he had actually risen from the dead: "From there they went out and began to go through Galilee, and He did not want anyone to know about it. For He was teaching His disciples and telling them, 'The Son of Man is to be delivered into the hands of men, and they will kill Him; and when He has been killed, He will rise three days later.' But they did not understand this statement, and they were afraid to ask Him" (Mark 9:30–32); "And while they were gathering together in Galilee, Jesus said to them, 'The Son of Man is going to be delivered into the hands of men; and they will kill Him, and He will be raised on the third day.' And they were deeply grieved" (Matt. 17:22–23).

When the time finally came for Jesus to make his last trip to Jerusalem for the Feast of the Passover, he once again took his disciples aside and warned them of what was about to come to pass. Because of the disciples' lack of faith, their misunderstanding of the Scriptures and Christ's teachings, as well as their own personal hopes and fears (i.e. their bias), their minds were still clouded and troubled (see Table 6):

Table 6: Jesus's Final Teaching about His Coming Death on the Cross

As Jesus was about to go up to Jerusalem, He took the twelve disciples aside by themselves, and on the way He said to them, "Behold, we are going up to Jerusalem; and the Son of Man will be delivered to the chief priests and scribes, and they will condemn Him to death, and will hand Him over to the Gentiles to mock and scourge and crucify Him, and on the third day He will be raised up." (Matt. 20:17–19)

They were on the road going up to Jerusalem, and Jesus was walking on ahead of them; and they were amazed, and those who followed were fearful. And again He took the twelve aside and began to tell them what was going to happen to Him, saying, "Behold, we are going up to Jerusalem, and the Son of Man will be delivered to the chief priests and the scribes; and they will condemn Him to death and will hand Him over to the Gentiles. They will mock Him and spit on Him, and scourge Him and kill Him, and three days later He will rise again." (Mark 10:32–34)

Table 6: Jesus's Final Teaching about His Coming Death on the Cross

Then He took the twelve aside and said to them, "Behold, we are going up to Jerusalem, and all things which are written through the prophets about the Son of Man will be accomplished. For He will be handed over to the Gentiles, and will be mocked and mistreated and spit upon, and after they have scourged Him, they will kill Him; and the third day He will rise again." But the disciples understood none of these things, and the meaning of this statement was hidden from them, and they did not comprehend the things that were said. (Luke 18:31–34)

Then after this He said to the disciples, "Let us go to Judea again." The disciples said to Him, "Rabbi, the Jews were just now seeking to stone You, and are You going there again?".... Therefore Thomas, who is called Didymus, said to his fellow disciples, "Let us also go, so that we may die with Him." (John 11:7–8, 16)

After the Lord's triumphal entry into Jerusalem, he later retired with his disciples to the upper room of a house where they observed the Passover together (The Last Supper). After their meal, Jesus taught them one last time. During this discourse he once again told them of his impending death and subsequent resurrection, but once again, they did not understand: "'A little while, and you will no longer see Me; and again a little while, and you will see Me.' Some of His disciples then said to one another, 'What is this thing He is telling us, "A little while, and you will not see Me; and again a little while, and you will see Me"; and, "because I go to the Father"?' So they were saying, 'What is this that He says, "A little while"? We do not know what He talking about'" (John 16:16–18). Jesus, once more, responds to their failure to understand:

> Then Jesus, knowing their confusion, spoke plainly to them "I came forth from the Father and have come into the world; I am leaving the world again and going to the Father." His disciples said, "Lo, now You are speaking plainly and are not using a figure of speech. Now we know that You know all things, and have no need

for anyone to question You; by this we believe that You came from God." Jesus answered them, "Do you now believe? Behold, an hour is coming, and has already come, for you to be scattered, each to his own home, and to leave Me alone; and yet I am not alone, because the Father is with Me." (John 16:28–32)

Later that same evening on the Mount of Olives, Christ's prophecy would indeed come true following his arrest by the chief priests and Pharisees and the scattering of his disciples.

Following Christ's arrest, trial, and crucifixion, the disciples were no longer in doubt as to the meaning of the Lord's teaching concerning his death at the hands of the Gentiles. On the other hand, they still did not comprehend what he meant about rising from the dead. Even when they begin to hear accounts of those who had seen the risen Lord, they remain in doubt (see Table 7):

Table 7: The Disciples' Confusion after Christ's Resurrection

But on the first day of the week, at early dawn, they came to the tomb bringing the spices which they had prepared. And they found the stone rolled away from the tomb, but when they entered, they did not find the body of the Lord Jesus. While they were perplexed about this, behold, two men suddenly stood near them in dazzling clothing; and as the women were terrified and bowed their faces to the ground, the men said to them, "Why do you seek the living One among the dead? He is not here, but He has risen. Remember how He spoke to you while He was still in Galilee, saying that the Son of Man must be delivered into the hands of sinful men, and be crucified, and the third day rise again." And they remembered His words, and returned from the tomb and reported all these things to the eleven and to all the rest. Now they were Mary Magdalene and Joanna and Mary the mother of James; also the other women with them were telling these things to the apostles. But these words appeared to them as nonsense, and they would not believe them. But Peter got up and ran to the tomb; stooping and looking in, he saw the linen wrappings only; and he went away to his home, marveling at what had happened. (Luke 24:1–12)

Table 7: The Disciples' Confusion after Christ's Resurrection

And so Simon Peter also came, following him, and entered the tomb; and he saw the linen wrappings lying there, and the face-cloth which had been on His head, not lying with the linen wrappings, but rolled up in a place by itself. So the other disciple who had first come to the tomb then also entered, and he saw and believed. For as yet they did not understand the Scripture, that He must rise again from the dead. (John 20:6–9)

Now after He had risen early on the first day of the week, He first appeared to Mary Magdalene, from whom He had cast out seven demons. She went and reported to those who had been with Him, while they were mourning and weeping. When they heard that He was alive and had been seen by her, they refused to believe it. After that, He appeared in a different form to two of them while they were walking along on their way to the country. They went away and reported it to the others, but they did not believe them either. (Mark 16:9–14)

And behold, two of them were going that very day to a village named Emmaus, which was about seven miles from Jerusalem. And they were talking with each other about all these things which had taken place. While they were talking and discussing, Jesus Himself approached and began traveling with them. But their eyes were prevented from recognizing Him…. And He said to them, "O foolish men and slow of heart to believe in all that the prophets have spoken! Was it not necessary for the Christ to suffer these things and to enter into His glory?" Then beginning with Moses and with all the prophets, He explained to them the things concerning Himself in all the Scriptures…. When He had reclined at the table with them, He took the bread and blessed it, and breaking it, He began giving it to them. Then their eyes were opened and they recognized Him; and He vanished from their sight. They said to one another, "Were not our hearts burning within us while He was speaking to us on the road, while He was explaining the Scriptures to us?" And they got up that very hour and returned to Jerusalem, and found gathered together the eleven and those who were with them, saying, "The Lord has really risen and has appeared to Simon." They began to relate their experiences on the road and how He was recognized by them in the breaking of the bread. (Luke 24:13–16, 25–27, 30–35)

Table 7: The Disciples' Confusion after Christ's Resurrection

But Thomas, one of the twelve, called Didymus, was not with them when Jesus came. So the other disciples were saying to him, "We have seen the Lord!" But he said to them, "Unless I see in His hands the imprint of the nails, and put my finger into the place of the nails, and put my hand into His side, I will not believe." After eight days His disciples were again inside, and Thomas with them. Jesus came, the doors having been shut, and stood in their midst and said, "Peace be with you." Then He said to Thomas, "Reach here with your finger, and see My hands; and reach here your hand and put it into My side; and do not be unbelieving, but believing." Thomas answered and said to Him, "My Lord and my God!" Jesus said to him, "Because you have seen Me, have you believed? Blessed are they who did not see, and yet believed." (John 20:24–29)

In many ways, the disciples' experiences during their time with Jesus were similar to those of a ministerial student starting out in Bible college: Their knowledge of who Christ was, and what his mission was on earth, was severely limited by (1) their limited knowledge of the facts, (2) their misinterpretation of the facts, and (3) their distortion of the facts because of their biases. Especially in the presence of the Lord, these human weaknesses were all too apparent. As a result, the temporal limitations of the disciples' theology were constantly being exposed; their understanding of the Scriptures and the nature of the Messiah were repeatedly changing or being refined. But Jesus led them patiently and lovingly into an ever-deeper understanding of who he was and why the Father had sent him; he led the disciples out of their darkness and into his glorious light, thereby fulfilling yet another one of Isaiah's prophecies: "Behold, My Servant, whom I uphold; My chosen one in whom My soul delights. I have put My Spirit upon Him; He will bring forth justice to the nations. He will not cry out or raise His voice, Nor make His voice heard in the street. A bruised reed He will not break And a dimly burning wick He will not extinguish; He will faithfully bring forth justice" (42:1–3).

Now we believe that the correction and perfection of the disciples' theology only occurred with the coming of the Holy Spirit that Jesus promised his disciples in the upper room before they left for the Mount of Olives where Judas would betray him: "But the Helper, the Holy Spirit, whom the Father will send in My name, He will teach you all things, and bring to your remembrance all that I said to you" (John 14:26); "But when He, the Spirit of truth, comes, He will guide you into all the truth; for He will not speak on His own initiative, but whatever He hears, He will speak; and He will disclose to you what is to come. He will glorify Me, for He will take of Mine and will disclose it to you. All things that the Father has are Mine; therefore I said that He takes of Mine and will disclose it to you" (John 16:13–15). Therefore, because the Holy Spirit was directing the writers of the New Testament into all truth, we are confident that the account of Jesus's divinity and ministry as recorded in the Gospels and Epistles of the New Testament is now a finished work with no need of further additions or corrections. The theology of the writers of the New Testament was perfected and ceased to change under the ministration of the Holy Spirit. The human limitations of the disciples were replaced by the unlimited power and knowledge of the Holy Spirit who now dwelled within them. It is for this reason that the apostle Paul states: "All Scripture is inspired by God and profitable for teaching, for reproof, for correction, for training in righteousness; so that the man of God may be adequate, equipped for every good work" (2 Tim. 3:16–17); "But even if we, or an angel from heaven, should preach to you a gospel contrary to what we have preached to you, he is to be accursed! As we have said before, so I say again now, if any man is preaching to you a gospel contrary to what you received, he is to be accursed!" (Gal. 1:8–9).

III. THE CHURCH'S CHANGING THEOLOGY

The temporal limitations of theological truth can also be seen with regard to the church's changing theological positions over time. The church struggles with the same human limitations that the disciples did before the Holy Spirit led them into truth. As was pointed out in Chapter 1, theological debates within the church have caused it to fragment into multiple trunks, branches, and twigs. Unlike the theology of the disciples, however, the church's theology has not been perfected but continues to change through time. Although we believe that the Holy Spirit also dwells within us, it is painfully obvious that, collectively, we have not allowed the Spirit to lead us into all truth. Instead, Satan has used our theology to set us to arguing with each other, thereby destroying the unity that our Lord prayed would characterize his followers.

Now it can certainly be argued, as C. S. Lewis did in *Mere Christianity* (1952), that there is a central core of beliefs that the majority of Christians down through the ages have adhered to, whether they were Catholic, Orthodox, or Protestant. This central theological core has not significantly changed over the last two millennia. As Witherington has pointed out: "We must recognize the wisdom that has come from our predecessors in doing theology. What has been believed 'everywhere, by everyone, all the time' to use a phrase from ancient church history, is more likely to be true and biblically on the mark than the latest fad theology, or something that has only been believed lately and by one stream of Christian tradition alone" (2005:253). Occasionally, theological debates have arisen over one or more of these central tenets of the faith, but much more frequently Christians have spent their time arguing over theological points that are secondary, or even tertiary to this central core of beliefs. Nevertheless, many of these theological arguments over marginal issues have assumed great importance in many peoples' minds, even to the point of justifying the severing of fellowship and the establishment of new churches.

One of the primary areas in which such debates have arisen is with regard to what is or is not proper Christian behavior. Laying aside the two great commands: "YOU SHALL LOVE THE LORD YOUR GOD WITH ALL YOUR HEART, AND WITH ALL YOUR SOUL, AND WITH ALL YOUR STRENGTH,

AND WITH ALL YOUR MIND; AND YOUR NEIGHBOR AS YOURSELF" (Luke 10:27), churches have repeatedly attempted to build theologies that codify exactly which behaviors or practices are godly or ungodly. Unfortunately, such theological *truths* are prone to change with time. Even within a single lifetime, we find that many of the things that were considered wrong when we were growing up in the church are now ignored, considered as being neither good nor bad, or even incorporated into church services and activities. Since God does not change through time, nor does his holiness change, how can things that were once considered to be bad now be considered good? Obviously, either our earlier theological constructs concerning these behaviors were flawed, or our current theological perspective is wrong. Our theology concerning these issues has obviously changed over time.

Another area where the church's theology has been highly volatile is with regard to time, especially the beginning of time (creation) or the end of time (the last judgment). Both of these time periods are exceptionally interesting to humans as they hold the key to two of the ultimate questions we ask throughout our lives: Where did we come from and what will happen when we die? Yet, both the beginning and ending of time are the two areas about which we know the least; the two periods that lie at the greatest distance from the present in which we live. Within only the past couple of hundred years, our theological understanding of the Genesis account has gone through many incarnations and revisions, including a variety of theories: Gap Theory, Day-Age Theory, Framework Theory, Temple Inauguration Theory, Historical Creationism Theory, Twenty-Four Hour Theory, etc. (Keathley and Rooker 2014: 111–165). Multiple theological theories have also plagued our recent attempts to better understand the Bible's teaching concerning the end of time, including: postmillennialism, premillennialism, amillennialism, and dispensationalism (Grenz 1992). As I explain to my students in college, multiple scientific theories about the cause of some effect we see in the natural world is a sure sign that we don't really understand what is causing that effect. Instead we are creating a number of possible solutions to the problem and hoping that one of them will eventually prove to be right. Despite the obvious confusion within the church as to which of these theological constructs about the beginning or ending of time is correct (if any of them are correct), it is here that many Christians have chosen to fight some of their major theological battles. We have deliberately chosen the low ground, the wet, marshy areas where solid footing is difficult to find, for the defense of our faith—rather than the high ground where we have a solid scriptural foundation upon which to build our fortifications. Perhaps it is time for many churches to abandon their fascination with matters in the distant, hazy past or the equally mysterious and unknown future, and focus their attention on the only true pearl of great price—Christ. Like the apostle Paul, we need to say: "For I determined to know nothing among you except Jesus Christ, and Him crucified" (1 Cor. 2:2). If the past is any indication of the future, the church's theology concerning creation and the end-times will no doubt continue to change through time, so we would be much better served to refocus our attention on the One who will not change, who is the Alpha and Omega, the Beginning and End, the one who created all things, and whose return will bring all things to an end.

A third area where we can clearly see the temporal limitations in the church's theology is with regard to our understanding of the natural world. Over the past 2,000 years, passages in the Old and New Testaments concerning the natural world have frequently been interpreted from the standpoint of then-current scientific or philosophical knowledge about the physical universe. These interpretations subsequently become part of the theology of the church. Unfortunately, humanity's knowledge about the physical universe is constantly changing and growing—especially since the Renaissance. It is inevitable, therefore, that new scientific discoveries will challenge older scientific beliefs—including those that have been incorporated into the church's theological interpretations of Scripture. As I tried to point out in my previous book, *The Limitations of Scientific Truth*, this is one of the great dangers of too closely linking one's theological beliefs with current scientific beliefs—the current scientific beliefs will inevitably change as more data is collected and new discoveries are made. This often results in long periods of conflict between the church and science with charges of heresy being leveled against those scientists who have made new discoveries or advanced new theories. New scientific discoveries, such as Copernicus's (sun-centered) model of the solar system challenged the church's theological understanding of the solar system which was based on Ptolemy's older, outdated, geocentric (earth-centered) model of the solar system. Thus, science–religion debates are often less about conflicts between science and religion, and more about conflicts between older scientific models (that the church had previously incorporated into its theology) and more recent scientific models (that the church has yet to incorporate into its theology). Eventually, the church's theological interpretation of the natural world also changes, and points of conflict, such as Copernicus's heliocentric model, are enfolded into the church's understanding of God's heavens and earth. Such debates often have little to do with the truth of the Scriptures, but much to do with our interpretations of the Scriptures or science's interpretations of the natural world. Therefore, the church's theological understanding of the richness and complexity of God's creation continues to change through time, along with science's understanding and knowledge of God's world, but not without much foot dragging and protests. We too often forget that the same God, who reveals himself through the Scriptures, also reveals himself through his creation. Theologians are focused on God's Word but scientists are focused on God's world.

In conclusion, we have examined the temporal limitations of theological truth in the life of a ministerial student, in the lives of the disciples, and in the life and history of the church. The main problem with theological truth is that it changes over time, just like scientific truth. The main reasons that theological truth changes over time are the human limitations of its practitioners. Theologians, like scientists, do not have all the facts, they often unintentionally misinterpret the facts, and they sometimes intentionally distort the facts because of their biases. Thus, theology, like science, is ultimately a human discipline. Therefore, theological truth is not absolute truth—even though its focus of study is upon the eternal, unchanging God and his perfect, unchanging Word.

THE LOGICAL LIMITATIONS
OF THEOLOGICAL TRUTH

INTRODUCTION

Scientists face severe logical limitations as they attempt to understand the universe which God has made. Although the scientific method is founded on the principle of induction, universal truths derived from induction can only be proven by making an infinite number of observations, which is, of course, impossible for finite human beings. This dilemma is often referred to as *Hume's Problem* in honor of the eighteenth century philosopher, David Hume, who first identified this flaw in the scientific method. When scientists attempted to circumvent this logical cul-de-sac by quantifying their observations and only speaking in terms of mathematical probabilities, they found that all mathematical systems are themselves flawed and incomplete, as explained in Gödel's Incompleteness Theorem (Brush 2005:68–71). Therefore, as the astronomer Timothy Ferris has noted: "there is not and never will be a complete and comprehensive scientific account of the universe that can be proved valid" (1988:384). Scientists bear witness to the reality of this situation on a regular basis as they continue to make new discoveries and expand their knowledge and understanding of God's world, modifying or abandoning old scientific truths and replacing them with improved or new ones. Theologians face even more insurmountable barriers as they attempt to use human logic to understand the thoughts and deeds of a holy, all-knowing, all-powerful God. Nevertheless, God has invited us to use our minds and logic capabilities to dialogue with Him: "'Come now, and let us reason together,' Says the LORD, 'Though your sins are as scarlet, They will be as white as snow; Though they are red like crimson, They will be like wool'" (Isa. 1:18).

Since God has fashioned us in his own image, communication and communion between the Creator and his creation is not only possible, but highly desired by the One who made us. If even the rocks can cry out in his presence (Luke 19:40), cannot we, his children, cry out "Abba! Father!" (Rom. 8:15)? Did God not call out Adam's name and come searching for him in the garden of Eden, desiring to speak with him (Gen. 3:9)? Nevertheless, it is imperative that we also understand the asymmetry of these conversations between ourselves and God. As the Lord pointed out to Isaiah: "'For My thoughts are not your thoughts, Nor are your ways My ways,' declares the LORD" (Isa. 55:8–9). Therefore, although we have been created with the capacity to converse with our Creator, many of the things he desires to teach or tell us may not easily be understood or perceived by us to be logical or fair. Children experience similar difficulties when conversing with their parents. Based on the child's limited knowledge of the world, it is often hard for them to fully comprehend what their parents are trying to teach them. Based on the child's limited experiences of life, the rules and demands of parents often seem arbitrary and unfair. Due to the child's short time upon the earth, the perspective and actions of their parents often seems painfully slow and plodding. Yet the gulf that separates parents from their children is only a matter of a few years, not eternity.

In a similar manner we, like children, often fail to understand what our Heavenly Father is trying to tell us, or we misinterpret his message, or even distort it. This malady affects us all, from the newborn Christian to the oldest saint. None of us is without sin and the frailty it imposes upon both our bodies and our minds. Consequently, it should not be surprising to see even our most learned ministers and theologians making mistakes in their interpretation of God's Word or even, on occasion, distorting it. Like children we often chafe beneath God's commands and even question the fairness of his judgments or the strength of his love for us. Through the frightening gift of free will, we not only have the opportunity to become servants and children of God, but also false teachers and false prophets. To the latter, however, God gives this warning: "Woe to the one who quarrels with his Maker—An earthenware vessel among the vessels of earth! Will the clay say to the potter, 'What are you doing?' Or the thing you are making say, 'He has no hands'? Woe to him who says to a father, 'What are you begetting?' Or to a woman, 'To what are you giving birth?'" (Isa. 45:9–10). Scientists face severe logical limitations as they attempt to understand the universe which God has made, but theologians face even more severe logical limitations as they attempt to understand the God who made that universe.

I. FROM A HOLY PERSPECTIVE

Perhaps the greatest logical stumbling block that limits our understanding of God and his Word is our fallen, sinful nature. God is holy, while we are not. "'Thou Holy One of Israel,' is the form of address which the Spirit puts into the lips of the people of God" (Hodge 1995:413). Over and over again the Scriptures emphasize the holiness of God: from Exodus to Revelation (see Table 8):

Table 8: Scriptures concerning the Holiness of God
Who is like You among the gods, O LORD? Who is like You, majestic in holiness, Awesome in praises, working wonders? (Exod. 15:11)
Then Joshua said to the people, "You will not be able to serve the Lord, for He is a holy God." (Josh. 24:19)

Table 8: Scriptures concerning the Holiness of God

There is no one holy like the LORD, Indeed, there is no one besides You, Nor is there any rock like our God. (1 Sam. 2:2)

Therefore, listen to me, you men of understanding. Far be it from God to do wickedness, And from the Almighty to do wrong. (Job 34:10)

Exalt the LORD our God And worship at His holy hill, For holy is the LORD our God. (Ps. 99:9)

For thus says the high and exalted One Who lives forever, whose name is Holy. (Isa. 57:15)

Your eyes are too pure to approve evil, And You can not look on wickedness with favor. (Hab. 1:13)

For the Mighty One has done great things for me; And holy is His name. (Luke 1:49)

YOU SHALL BE HOLY, FOR I AM HOLY. (1 Peter 1:16)

Who will not fear, O Lord, and glorify Your name? For You alone are holy. (Rev. 15:4)

How do we even describe the holiness of God? Words fail us because we have no points of reference against which to compare the holiness of God. All human examples of holiness are but pale imitations. We are attempting to describe the indescribable. When we do come into contact with God's holiness, our only response is to fall on our faces in speechless awe. Holiness is the most desirable thing in the world, yet the most unobtainable by human means or effort. Like moths attracted to a flame, we cannot approach God too closely without being destroyed in the searing light of his holiness. In that moment of self-revelation, when we truly see our fallen nature in contrast to the holiness of God, we are undone, we are destroyed. Even Moses could not look upon the face of God without dying (Exod. 33:20). In his *Systematic Theology*, Charles Hodge attempts to explain the holiness of God in the following manner:

This is a general term for the moral excellence of God.... Holiness, on the one hand, implies entire freedom from moral evil; and, upon the other, absolute moral perfection. Freedom from impurity is the primary idea of the word. To sanctify is to cleanse; to be holy, is to be clean. Infinite purity, even more than infinite knowledge or infinite power, is the object of reverence. Hence the Hebrew Word...as used in Scripture, is often equivalent to *venerandus*. 'The Holy One of Israel,' is He who is to be feared and adored. Seraphim round about the throne who cry day and night, Holy, Holy, Holy is the Lord of hosts, give expression to the feeling of all unfallen rational creatures in view of the infinite purity of God. They are the representatives of the whole universe, in offering this perpetual homage to the divine holiness. It is because of His holiness, that God is a consuming fire. And it was a view of His holiness which led the prophet to exclaim, "Woe is me! For I am undone; because I am a man of unclean lips, and I dwell in the midst of a people of unclean lips: for mine eyes have seen the king, the Lord of hosts" (Isa. 6:5). (Hodge 1995:413–414)

The first and greatest barrier, then, to our carrying on a completely logical dialogue with our Creator, is the fact that he is holy while we are sinners. How can we who have been deceived by the father of lies ever again completely trust our judgment or our ability to think completely logically? Having been repeatedly deceived by the enemy tends to warp one's perspective. In order to participate in a completely logical conversation, we must both understand and respect the one with whom we are conversing, otherwise misunderstandings soon arise. Yet we come to this conversation with God, clothed, not in white linen, but in filthy rags, our minds a complex jumble of contradictions and competing beliefs. We often do not even know who we are, let alone who the Father is with whom we seek an audience. To know who we are, is to recognize our depravity, as Paul once said: "Wretched man that I am! Who will set me free from the body of this death?" (Rom. 7:24).

II. From an Omniscient Perspective

> The knowledge of God is not only perfect in kind, but also in its inclusiveness. It is called *omniscience*, because it is all-comprehensive. In order to promote a proper estimate of it, we may particularize as follows: God knows Himself and in Himself all things that come from Him (internal knowledge). He knows all things as they actually come to pass, past, present, and future, and knows them in their real relations. He knows the hidden essence of things, to which the knowledge of man cannot penetrate. He sees not as man sees, who observes only the outward manifestations of life, but penetrates to the depths of the human heart. Moreover, He knows what is possible as well as what is actual: all things that might occur under certain circumstances are present to His mind. (Berkhof 1941:67)

The second great logical limitation we encounter as we attempt to understand and communicate with our Creator is his omniscience. He is the great, all-knowing One (1 John 3:20). He is the Alpha and Omega of all things (Rev. 22:13). He is the One who knows the end of all things, from their beginning (Isa. 46:10). We, on the other hand, after a lifetime of learning, only begin to perceive how little we actually know. What we do know is limited to that which we have been able to acquire from our five senses over the very short period of our lifetime on a small portion of a small planet that is orbiting one of billions of stars in a galaxy, that is but one among an estimated 180 billion galaxies. The starry night sky inspired King David to write: "When I consider Your heavens, the work of Your fingers, The moon and the stars, which You have ordained; What is man that You take thought of him, And the son of man that You care for him?" (Ps. 8:3–4). As modern man has looked out into these same heavens with his telescopes and other scientific instruments, his wonder has continued to grow, as well as his inability to ever comprehend it all. There are more stars in our Milky Way Galaxy than we could even count in one or many lifetimes, let alone name or visit. Someone has estimated that it would take almost 146 years to count to 4.6 billion (the age of the earth), but there are at least 100 billion stars in the Milky Way Galaxy. Thus, if we even tried to count the stars in the Milky Way Galaxy, it would take us around 3,212 years. The giant elliptical galaxy IC 1101 is estimated to contain more than 100 trillion stars, so it would take at least 3,173,894 years to count the stars in that galaxy, and there are billions of other galaxies. Yet, God has not only created, but numbered and named them all: "He counts the number of the stars; He gives names to all of them" (Ps. 147:4).

So how does a human with extremely finite understanding match wits with the One whose understanding is infinite? How do we deeply probe the thoughts of God? How do we explore the reasons behind God's choices or commands? Yet, we often try. Job questioned why God had allowed catastrophes to overwhelm his family and possessions. The scribes and Pharisees tried to lay traps and snares for Jesus. Television evangelists try to identify a word, phrase, or Scripture passage that will force God to bring about some humanly desired end. To all such attempts, God responds, as he did to Job: "Who is this that darkens counsel By words without knowledge?" (Job 38:2).

Theology is a human discipline that is fraught with danger, especially in the area of interpretation. Interpretations are always based on assumptions, some of which may be true while others are likely false. We often unconsciously (through ignorance or error) or consciously (through bias) make the Scriptures say more or less than God meant them to say. Consequently, theologians should always keep in mind the warning at the very end of the New Testament: "I testify to everyone who hears the words of the prophecy of this book: if anyone adds to them, God will add to him the plagues which are written in this book; and if anyone takes away from the words of the book of this prophecy, God will take away his part from the Tree of Life and from the holy city, which are written in this book" (Rev. 22:18–19). While this warning was given explicitly concerning the prophecies in the book of Revelation, it nevertheless should give pause to those who handle the Word of God carelessly, who pretend to know more than they

really do, who mold the Scripture to fit their own private interpretations, who presume to speak for God in areas where he has
not spoken. Will not the false prophet, as well as the beast, be cast
"into the lake of fire which burns with brimstone"? (Rev. 19:20).
Scriptures have been misinterpreted to justify a number of griev-
ous sins from apartheid to genocide, from the Inquisition to wars
of conquest. Do we really think these perversions of truth will
escape the notice of an all-knowing God? The Bible is very clear
that God's awareness and knowledge is all pervasive (see Table 9):

Table 9: Scriptures concerning the Omniscience of God
He who planted the ear, does He not hear? He who formed the eye, does He not see? (Ps. 94:9)
O LORD, You have searched me and known me. You know when I sit down and when I rise up; You understand my thought from afar. You scrutinize my path and my lying down, And are intimately acquainted with all my ways. (Ps. 139:1–3)
The eyes of the LORD are in every place, Watching the evil and the good. (Prov. 15:3)
Then the Spirit of the LORD fell upon me, and He said to me, "Say, 'Thus says the LORD, So you think, house of Israel, for I know your thoughts.'" (Ezek. 11:5)
But the very hairs of your head are all numbered. (Matt. 10:30)
SAYS THE LORD, WHO MAKES THESE THINGS KNOWN FROM LONG AGO. (Acts 15:18)
And there is no creature hidden from His sight, but all things are open and laid bare to the eyes of Him with whom we have to do. (Heb. 4:13)

It was this all-knowing, ever-present aspect of God that most
unnerved C. S. Lewis when he finally accepted the existence of
such a being. As he noted in his autobiography, *Surprised by Joy*:
"The real terror was that if you seriously believed in even such
a 'God' or 'Spirit' as I admitted, a wholly new situation developed" (1955a:227). Lewis went on to explain that "I had always

wanted, above all things, not to be 'interfered with.' I had wanted (mad wish) 'to call my soul my own'" (ibid.: 228). To acknowledge the existence of a personal, transcendent God, however, is to lose forever your sense of personal privacy and freedom to think whatever you like without anyone else ever knowing or interfering. Sometimes when we sin, we pretend that God is not watching us at that moment, but this is a lie we tell ourselves that will only lead to our own hurt and humiliation. To believe in God is to know that we are always in his presence; to know that our every action is seen by Him; to know that our every word is heard by Him; to know that our every thought is perceived by Him.

How do we use our human logic to understand a God about whom we know so little, but who knows and understands us so completely? He is a God who knows our every thought, desire, and fear. He is a God who has heard everything we have said and seen, everything we have done every day of our lives, yet he still loves us. Once all our delusions, pretensions, conceit, and pride are swept away in the presence of he who is the embodiment of truth, what do we have to say for ourselves? If the difference in years and knowledge sometimes makes it difficult for children to talk with their parents, or students with their professors, how much more so does the omniscience of God hinder our ability to talk with our Creator? Yet, Paul enjoins us to "Rejoice always; pray without ceasing; in everything give thanks; for this is God's will for you in Christ Jesus" (1 Thess. 5:16–18). God, in his mercy, gives us both the opportunity and the ability to engage in a dialogue with him on a daily basis, despite this seemingly insurmountable barrier of knowledge between what he knows and what we know. Nevertheless, in our theological interpretations of Scripture, we should never lose sight of the vast gulf between our ignorance and God's omniscience.

III. FROM AN OMNIPOTENT PERSPECTIVE

The third divine attribute that poses a logical limitation to the accuracy of our theological interpretations is God's omnipotence. God is all-powerful; there is nothing that he cannot do. He has made the heavens and the earth. He has brought forth life upon the earth. He has made us in his image. Like our Heavenly Father, we can make things, but all the materials that we use to make things were first made by him. Humans can only modify the things that God has already made. Therefore, the ultimate reason for all things resides in he who has created all things. The Creator holds the final answers to all of our questions about the physical universe in which we live. He is the final and absolute truth of all things. As Charles Hodge has noted: "The Lord God omnipotent reigneth, and doeth his pleasure among the armies of heaven and the inhabitants of the earth, is the tribute of adoration which the Scriptures everywhere render unto God, and the truth which they everywhere present as the ground of confidence to his people. This is all we know, and all we need to know on this subject; and here we might rest satisfied, were it not for the vain attempts of theologians to reconcile these simple and sublime truths of the Bible with their philosophical speculations" (Hodge 1995:407–408). As with his holiness and omniscience, the Scriptures are also very clear about God's omnipotence (see Table 10):

Table 10: Scriptures concerning the Omnipotence of God
I am God Almighty. (Gen. 17:1)
Whatever the LORD pleases, He does, In heaven and in earth, in the seas and in all deeps. (Ps. 135:6)
Ah Lord GOD! Behold, You have made the heavens and the earth by Your great power and by Your outstretched arm! Nothing is too difficult for You. (Jer. 32:17)
Even from eternity I am He, And there is none who can deliver out of My hand; I act and who can reverse it? (Isa. 43:13)
All the inhabitants of the earth are accounted as nothing, But He does according to His will in the host of heaven And among the inhabitants of earth; And no one can ward off His hand Or say to Him, "What have You done?" (Dan. 4:35)

Table 10: Scriptures concerning the Omnipotence of God
And Jesus came up and spoke to them, saying, "All authority has been given to Me in heaven and on earth." (Matt. 28:18)
All things came into being through Him, and apart from Him nothing came into being that has come into being. (John 1:3)
Worthy are You, our Lord and our God, to receive glory and honor and power; for You created all things, and because of Your will they existed, and were created. (Rev. 4:11)

Theologians too often try to place constraints on he who has no constraints on his power, authority, and mercy. They try to determine what God can or cannot do. They try to set limits on who God can or cannot love. They try to create rules about who God can or cannot forgive. In the parable of the prodigal son, it did not seem fair or logical to the son who had been faithful to his father and stayed at home to work on the farm, when his father welcomed his wayward brother back home with a feast (Luke 15:11–32). In the parable of the workers, it did not seem fair or logical to the workers who had labored in the field since early morning, when their employer paid them the same wages as those workers who had only worked a few hours at the end of the day (Matt. 20:1–16). It did not seem fair or logical to Asaph that the wicked often prosper (Ps. 73:3) or to Job that God had seemingly repaid his faithfulness with the destruction of his household (Job 19:6). It did not seem fair or logical to Jonah when God decided to spare the city of Nineveh from destruction (Jonah 4:1–3). It may not seem fair or logical to us that the thief who was dying on a cross should be forgiven of his sins at the very end of his life, but Jesus forgave him (Luke 23:40–43). To all who question the decisions of the One whose power has no limits, he responds in the parable of the Laborers in the Vineyard: "Is it not lawful for me to do what I wish with what is my own? Or is your eye envious because I am generous?" (Matt. 20:15). Rather than question the fairness or logic of the decisions our omnipotent Creator makes, we should thank Him that his thoughts and ways are indeed so much higher than our own. Otherwise, we would all perish, as we so rightly deserve, because of our sins.

Scientists are very familiar with the law of cause and effect in the physical universe. As Isaac Newton once stated in his third law of motion, for every action, there is an opposite and equal reaction. Because modern science is based on induction, scientists make observations of the natural world before trying to develop explanations for what they see. As a result, scientists usually identify effects before they identify causes. For example, scientists find marine fossils on the continents, then they develop theories as to what may have caused ancient sea levels to rise. Scientists find the bones of dinosaurs scattered across the world, then they develop theories as to what caused dinosaurs to go extinct. Scientists witness an eclipse of the sun, then they develop theories as to what caused this temporary darkening of the sun. Scientists always assume that for every physical effect, there is a physical cause. Non-scientists are also very familiar with the law of cause and effect. If we find a watch or a coin (the effect) out in a field, we automatically assume that someone (the cause) has made these items. Moreover, we also assume that physical effort has gone into transforming natural materials into these humanly made items. However, because of God's omnipotence, he does not have to make things from pre-existing things. Instead, he simply brings them into existence by his will with no intermediate steps. As Charles Hodge has explained:

> We, beyond very narrow limits, must use means to accomplish our ends. With God means are unnecessary. He wills, and it is done. He said, Let there be light; and there was light. He, by a volition created the heavens and the earth. At the volition of Christ, the winds ceased, and there was a great calm. By an act of the will He healed the sick, opened the eyes of the blind, and raised the dead. This simple idea of the omnipotence of God, that He can do without effort, and by a volition, whatever He wills, is the highest conceivable idea of power, and is that which is clearly presented in the Scriptures.(1995:407)

When scientists try to explain the origin of the heavens and earth, they always have to start with pre-existing things, such as virtual particles in the vacuum of space, a *singularity* (a single point in space with infinite density), the rebound of a pre-existing universe, etc. God, however, creates the heavens and earth *ex nihilo* (out of nothing). As the writer of Hebrews (11:3) proclaimed, "By faith we understand that the worlds were prepared by the word of God, so that what is seen was not made out of things which are visible." Such power is so foreign to the everyday experiences of both scientists and theologians that it is almost unimaginable, except at the level of fantasy. Nevertheless, the Scriptures tell us that, by the words of his mouth, he speaks the universe into existence: "By the word of the LORD the heavens were made, And by the breath of His mouth all their host" (Ps. 33:6). By the words of his mouth, he calls light into existence: "Then God said, 'Let there be light'; and there was light" (Gen. 1:3). By the words of his mouth, he preserves that which he has created: "And He is the radiance of His glory and the exact representation of His nature, and upholds all things by the word of His power" (Heb. 1:3). By the words of his mouth, he calls the dead back to life: "…even God, who gives life to the dead and calls into being that which does not exist" (Rom. 4:17). This same powerful word was spoken through the prophets in the Old Testament (Heb. 1:1) and through the apostles and disciples in the New Testament (Rom. 1:16; 2 Tim. 3:16). Therefore, when theologians or laymen, like ourselves, read the Scriptures, we come face-to-face with the omnipotence of God. Consequently, when we study the Bible, we should always do so with humility, with fear and trembling, lest we wrongly divide the word of truth and not only imperil our own salvation, but that of others with whom we share our understanding and interpretations.

Conclusion

The logical limitations that scientists face in attempting to understand God's world are great, but the logical limitations that theologians encounter when trying to understand and interpret God's Word are even greater. Scientists confine their work to natural entities that can be apprehended with the physical senses, but theologians are dealing with a spiritual being whose throne is the heavens and whose footstool is the earth. Scientists are studying things that are made out of the same substances (atoms, elements, minerals) of which they themselves are made, but theologians are trying to understand a being whose holiness is totally foreign to their fallen, sinful natures. Scientists gather facts about the world and universe like children gathering shells along the sea shore, but theologians must try to understand the One who knows all things. Scientists are able to manipulate the materials that already exist upon the earth to generate or release power, but theologians must try to comprehend an all-powerful God who has called the heavens and earth into existence by his will and through the words of his mouth. Scientists' quest for absolute truth about God's world is impaired by the logical limitations imposed by Hume's Problem of Induction and Gödel's Incompleteness Theorem. Theologians' quest for absolute truth about God's Word, however, has even greater logical limitations to overcome due to the asymmetry between man's sinfulness, ignorance, and weakness, and God's holiness, omniscience, and omnipotence. If humility is a virtue for scientists who are trying to understand the natural realm, it should be an absolute requirement for theologians who are trying to comprehend God and his Word.

THE CULTURAL
LIMITATIONS OF
THEOLOGICAL TRUTH

INTRODUCTION

A third weakness that theological truth shares with scientific truth is cultural bias. Theologians, like scientists, are strongly influenced by the culture in which they live and work. When a Christian attempts to understand the Word of God, he or she sets about that task with a set of language skills, cultural knowledge, and personal beliefs that are already firmly in place. Even monks and hermits don't start out their lives living in a monastery or cave. They grow up as normal children surrounded by family, friends, and neighbors who teach them how to speak and behave based on the culture into which they are born. An individual's understanding of the world around them is initially acquired, largely from the people with whom they are in contact. Only gradually do they also begin to learn from their own experiences, but their understanding and interpretation of those experiences will still be strongly influenced by the culture in which they live. Therefore, when we, or a theologian, sit down to read the Bible, our minds are not like clear sheets of glass through which the light of God's Word can clearly shine. Instead, our minds are already deeply etched with information acquired from our cultures, as well as our own personal experiences. This previously acquired knowledge can, and often does, bias our interpretations of God's Word. As Paul said, "For now we see in a mirror dimly" (1 Cor. 13:12).

Cultural bias also plays a significant role in determining which scriptural passages and theological truths theologians will focus upon during the course of their lives. Theologians will naturally attempt to find answers in the Scriptures to the questions that their fellow humans are asking. These questions will not only vary from culture to culture, but from one time period to the next. The theological problems of one age are not the same as another age. Old questions may get answered, but new questions always arise. Therefore, the theological issues that are relevant to theologians will not only vary from culture to culture, but from one time period to another. Moreover, a culture's understanding of the natural world at one time period is not the same as at a later time period. Thus, the tools we have at our disposal to interpret the Bible, especially those scriptural passages concerning the physical world and universe that God has created, will change through time as our cultural and scientific knowledge and understanding of the natural world changes. In conclusion, both scientific truths and theological truths are cumulative because our understanding of God's world and God's Word are constantly being enriched, not only by our own efforts, but by the labors of those around us, as well as those who came before us.

I. THEOLOGY & SCIENCE IN THE FIRST MILLENNIUM A.D.

A.D. 1–499: God & Christ

One of the primary theological issues that dominated Christianity during the first half of the first millennium A.D. was centered on the nature of God and Christ (the Trinitarian Controversy and the Christological Controversy). Born of a virgin but conceived through the Holy Spirit, Christ was both the Son of Man and the Son of God. As foretold by the prophets, he was of the lineage of David, but also of divine nature: "And His name will be called Wonderful Counselor, Mighty God, Eternal Father, Prince of Peace" (Isa. 9:6). This was the stumbling block that many of the Jews could not get around: How could a man also claim divinity? Christ's physical parentage was well known to the Jews: "Therefore the Jews were grumbling about Him, because He said, 'I am the bread that came down out of heaven.' They were saying, 'Is not this Jesus, the son of Joseph, whose father and mother we know? How does He now say, "I have come down out of heaven"?'" (John 6:41–42). This same issue continued to be a stumbling block that was perpetuated by false prophets in the early church, as the apostle John admonishes his fellow believers: "By this you know the Spirit of God: every spirit that confesses that Jesus Christ has come in the flesh is from God; and every spirit that does not confess Jesus is not from God; this is the spirit of the antichrist, of which you have heard that it is coming, and now it is already in the world" (1 John 4:2–3).

Among these early false prophets in the Church who rejected the apostles teaching that Christ was both God and man were the Ebionites, a movement which first arose among Jewish Christians in Palestine in the latter part of the first century. They taught that Jesus was initially only a man born of a physical father and mother; he did not become the Messiah until the Spirit descended upon him when he was baptized by John the Baptist. They also taught that the Mosaic Law was a universal law and should still be followed by Christians. The Gnostics of the second century took the opposite position. Because they believed that all matter was evil, they taught that Christ could only have been a spiritual being— his physical body was just an illusion. Another false prophet was Mani who lived in Persia in the third century. He incorporated the dualistic ideas of Zoroastrianism into Christian beliefs, taught that the apostles had corrupted Christ's message, and also argued that Christ's physical body was illusionary. His teachings became known as Manichaeism and spread widely across the ancient world. In the fourth century, Arius, a priest in Alexandria, Egypt, developed a new heresy that spread widely throughout the church. Arius asserted that Christ was created by God at some point in time and therefore could not be equal with God—instead, he was the first created being. This doctrine of Arianism contradicted Jesus's own statements about himself: "Truly, truly, I say to you, before Abraham was born, I am" (John 8:58), "I and the Father are one" (John 10:30), and "He who has seen Me has seen the Father" (John 14:9), as well as the apostle John's own testimony: "In the beginning was the Word, and the Word was with God, and the Word was God" (John 1:1). In the fifth century, Nestorius, who became Patriarch of Constantinople, introduced a new heresy into the church. Nestorianism taught that the Word (Logos) indwelt the person of Jesus, making him a god-bearing man, rather than the God-man (Walton 1986: Charts 9, 15, & 16).

In addition to the five false doctrines mentioned above, there were many other attempts during the first five centuries of the Christian era to explain away the fact that Christ was both God and man, including Monarchianism, Sabellianism, Semi-Arianism, Apollinarianism, Eutychianism, Monophysitism, and Monothelitism (Walton 1986: Charts 15 & 16). This theological controversy led to several major church councils, including the First Council of Nicaea which was convened by the Roman Emperor Constantine I in A.D. 325, the First Council of Constantinople convened by the Roman Emperor Theodosius I. in A.D. 381, the First Council of Ephesus convened by the Byzantine Emperor Theodosius II in A.D. 431, the Second Council of Ephesus convened by Theodosius II in A.D. 449, and the Council of Chalcedon convened by the Byzantine Emperor Marcian in A.D. 451. Out of these councils a doctrinal statement was formulated concerning the nature of Christ, as well as the other members of the Trinity—the Nicene Creed. As the Old Testament prophets had foretold, the Messiah, Christ, was indeed: "true God from true God, begotten, not made, of one substance [homoousion] with the Father" (Latourette 1953:155). This creed has been accepted by all the major branches of Christianity, including Roman Catholic, Greek Orthodox, and most major branches of Protestantism. Thus, it took the theologians and the church nearly five hundred years to reach consensus on a single theological problem that had been an issue since the beginning of Christ's earthly ministry.

Theological problems concerning the heavens and earth that God had created were much simpler during this same five-hundred-year period. The science of the cultures surrounding the Mediterranean Sea in the first half of the first millennium A.D. did not present any major challenges to Christianity. Following Alexander the Great's conquest of much of the known world in the fourth century B.C., and the subsequent Hellenization of lands throughout the eastern Mediterranean following the fragmentation of his empire, Greek culture and science were pervasive. This was particularly true in the lands where Christianity first took root: Palestine, Egypt, Syria, Turkey, Greece, and Italy.

Although the Romans completed their conquest of Greece in 146 B.C. at the Battle of Corinth, this seemed to have only strengthened the influence the Greeks had on Roman culture. As the Roman poet Horace noted in his *Epistles* 2.1.156: "Graecia capta ferum victorem cepit et artis intulit agresti Latio (Greece, the captive, made her savage victor captive, and brought the arts into rustic Latium)" (Fairclough 1932:408). The Greek impact on Roman culture, however, may have had much deeper roots. According to ancient tradition, Greek survivors from the fall of Troy (c. 1000 B.C.) were the actual founders of the Roman race. The Roman poet Virgil begins the *Aeneid* with these lines:

> I tell about war and the hero who first from Troy's frontier,
> Displaced by destiny, came to the Lavinian shores,
> To Italy—a man much travailed on sea and land
> By the powers above, because of the brooding anger of Juno,
> Suffering much in war until he could found a city
> And march his gods into Latium, whence rose the Latin race,
> The royal line of Alba and the high walls of Rome.
>
> (Lewis 1952:13)

Based on archaeological, linguistic, and genetic evidence, we know that Greek colonists began to settle in Sicily and southern Greece

(Magna Graecia) around the eighth century B.C., a period when other Greek colonies were being established from southern France in the west to the Black Sea in the east. Therefore, Roman culture had deep interconnections with the Greek culture and borrowed heavily from them in areas of architecture, art, literature, philosophy, religion, and rhetoric. The Romans also sent some of their best and brightest sons to Greece to study, such as Cicero and Julius Caesar. They also brought Greek tutors to Italy.

During the first half of the first millennium A.D., therefore, Greek science dominated the lands of both the Greek and Roman Empires. The science of this time period that was to have the greatest influence on later cultures was astronomy. In Alexandria, an Egyptian city built by the Greeks, Claudius Ptolemy, a Greco-Egyptian astronomer and mathematician with Roman citizenship, composed his famous book, *Almagest*, in the second century A.D. The geocentric model of the universe that he developed in this book was based on the intellectual foundation of other Greek scholars dating back to Aristotle and his predecessors. Ptolemy's model would dominate astronomy for the next 1,200 years. Theologians in the early church were able to easily incorporate Ptolemy's geocentric model of the heavens into their theological interpretations because the biblical account of creation and nature was also totally earth-centered. The limited numbers of other scientific advances during this five-hundred-year period were largely confined to medicine, geography, and mathematics—practical sciences that, in their current state of development, posed no significant challenges to the theological interpretations of the time.

500–999 A.D.: Faith and Works

During the latter part of the previous five-hundred-year period, some theologians had begun to turn their attention away from the nature of God and Christ, and toward the nature of man and the issue of faith versus works/spirit versus flesh. One of the first indications of this change in theological focus was the Pelagian Controversy, which arose between Saint Augustine and Pelagius in the fourth century. Pelagius believed that human free will included the freedom not to sin whereas Augustine argued that all humans are tainted by Adam's sin and have lost the freedom not to sin. "Humans now sin habitually in that they act according to their sinful nature, inherited from their origins as human beings" (McKim 1988:73). Although the Second Council of Ephesus in A.D. 431 settled this issue in favor of Augustus, confusion over the relative importance of faith versus works/spirit versus flesh would remain an enduring problem in the church.

One approach that some Christians took to ensure that their thoughts and deeds were pure was to isolate themselves from the sinful world. Asceticism (the rejection of worldly comforts and pleasures) appeared quite early in the church and may have been inspired by the lifestyle of John the Baptist in the wilderness of Judea with his garment of camel's hair and diet of locusts and wild honey, although Jesus began his ministry by spending forty days fasting in the wilderness. One of the early *hermit monks* who sought sanctuary in the Egyptian desert (~A.D. 270) was Saint Anthony the Great. He is often regarded as the father and founder of desert monasticism. Over the next seven decades, thousands of monks and nuns would follow his example by seeking a more spiritual life in the desert. In 318, Saint Pachomius, another Egyptian hermit monk, decided to organize his many followers into the first Christian communal monastery. Instead of living in isolation as hermits, spiritually minded individuals could band together to collectively seek God in wilderness settings. Over the next two centuries, similar monasteries based on communal living were established throughout the eastern half of the Roman Empire. Perhaps the most famous of these monasteries was Saint Catherine's Monastery in the Sinai Peninsula. It was established by order of Emperor Justinian I and was built between A.D. 548 and 565 near the traditional site of Mount Sinai.

During the first half of the sixth century, monasteries also began to spread across the western half of the Roman Empire. Benedict of Nursia established a dozen communities for monks in the vicinity of Rome before creating the great monastery at

Monte Cassino in the mountains of southern Italy in A.D. 529. He is often regarded at the founder of Western monasticism due to his creation of the *Rule of Saint Benedict,* which provided a standardized set of rules for monks in a monastery to follow. These rules were adopted by many religious orders across Europe during the Middle Ages. Here again we see the striving for spiritual perfection through works of the flesh, both by isolating oneself from the world as a monk or nun in a monastery, and by following a prescribed set of rules. With the collapse of the Roman Empire and the descent of Western Europe into the Dark Ages, however, these monasteries also served another purpose—as repositories for the Scriptures and other ancient texts, as well as centers of learning and scholarship that preceded the establishment of universities across Europe during the latter part of the Middle Ages.

During the second half of the first millennium, there were no real scientific discoveries that posed any challenges to existing theological interpretations of the Bible concerning the physical universe. These being the Dark Ages in Europe, very little scientific research was being conducted other than the compilation of a few encyclopedias on nature, the arts and sciences, and medicine, as well as the discovery of the Faroe Islands, Iceland, Greenland, and Nova Scotia by Viking explorers. Even the scientific knowledge of the Greeks was eventually lost after the schism between Western and Eastern Christianity. Instead, during this period it was in Arab countries where significant work was being done in the sciences, including astronomy, chemistry, geography, mathematics, medicine, and physics. The development of many of these sciences, however, was still in a formative state and would not present any significant challenges for theologians until much later in time. For instance, the discovery of nebulae (clouds of dust and gas in outer space), first mentioned in the Arab astronomer Al Sûfi's *The Book of Fixed Stars* in A.D. 963 (Grun 1979:117) would not have theological significance until a thousand years later when telescopes had grown large and powerful enough to reveal that some of these clouds were actually composed of stars, thereby proving the existence of other galaxies beyond our own Milky Way Galaxy. Advances in mathematics and medicine were also occurring in India, as well as printing in China and Japan, although knowledge of most of these discoveries and technological advances was unavailable to the majority of people living in Europe at this time (Grun 1979:32–125).

II. THEOLOGY & SCIENCE IN THE SECOND MILLENNIUM A.D.

1000–1499 A.D.: *Faith & Reason*

A number of new religious orders came into existence in the early part of the second millennium, including the Cistercians in France (1098), the Dominicans in Spain (1216), and the Franciscans in Italy (1223). The monks in these monasteries played a significant role in the development of theology during the Middle Ages, especially the Dominicans, Franciscans, and Augustinians (McGrath 2011:27). Each of these orders developed their own distinctive theological approach to the Scriptures and each order also built schools to advance these ideas. As noted previously, the Benedictines were the first religious order to establish monasteries in Europe, beginning in Italy. It is not surprising, therefore, that the first university in Europe was at Salerno, Italy in A.D. 850. Located about 30 miles south of Naples, the initial focus of studies at this institution was not only theology, but also medicine. The area around Salerno had long been known for its mild climate, and the sick often came here to recuperate. One of the good works that the monks in Benedictine monasteries regularly performed was the care and healing of the sick. Thus, among the ancient texts preserved and copied in monasteries like Monte Cassino, were Greek, as well as Arab, medical texts. The preservation of ancient Greek texts, as well as the retention of the ability to read them, was facilitated by the strong Greek heritage in southern Italy, dating back to at least the eighth century B.C. By the end of the eleventh century A.D., Salerno had become known as the *Town of Hippocrates* and both those desiring to be healed, and those desiring to learn how to heal, came to the university from all over Europe, the Near East, and Africa. Over the next three centuries, a host of other cities would also found universities, including: Bologna, Italy (1119), Paris, France (1150), Oxford, England (1167), Cambridge, England (1200), Siena, Italy (1203), Vicenza, Italy (1204), Salamanca, Spain (1217), Naples, Italy (1224), Toulouse, France (1229), Montpellier, France (1289), Lisbon, Portugal (1290), and Rome, Italy (1303) (Grun 1979:96–183).

These universities were initially established as schools of theology for training the monks, nuns, and priests. As their curriculums expanded, however, some universities began to specialize: Paris and Oxford became centers for theological study and attracted some of the greatest scholars of the day. For example, "The University of Paris soon established itself as a leading center of theological speculation, with such scholars as Peter Abelard, Albert the Great, Thomas Aquinas, and Bonaventure" (McGrath 2011:28). Some of these universities, however, began to attract scholars and students for other specializations, such as medicine at Salerno, or church and civil law at Bologna (Walker 1959:242).

As the number of subjects being taught at these universities continued to grow, the church needed a way to bring all these disciplines and ideas under the umbrella of a Christian worldview. In an attempt to achieve this goal, the medieval scholars developed a methodology called Scholasticism that utilized dialectical reasoning to present and defend theological truths: "scholasticism is best regarded as the medieval movement, flourishing in the period 1200–1500, which placed emphasis upon the rational justification of religious belief and the systematic presentation of those beliefs. 'Scholasticism' thus does not refer to a *specific system of beliefs*, but to a particular way of doing and organizing theology—a highly developed method of presenting material, making fine distinctions, and attempting to achieve a comprehensive view of theology" (McGrath 2011:29). Scholasticism also attempted to show the rational connections between the theological truths of Christianity and the philosophical truths of Greek and other ancient cultures. The greatest of the scholastic scholars was Thomas Aquinas, who was also well versed in the works of Aristotle. Aquinas argued that both faith and reason are from God and are thus both roads to truth, although he also noted that some truths can only be apprehended through faith. As Kenneth Scott Latourette has noted in his *A History of Christianity,* "The great achievement of Thomas Aquinas was setting forth the relation of reason and faith in such a fashion that those to whom the Aristotelian philosophy was definitive could feel that they might consistently remain Christians" (1953:510). In a broader context, however, scholasticism was also an attempt by medieval scholars to bring all branches of knowledge and learning under the banner of Christ. As Alister McGrath points out in his book *Christian Theology,* scholasticism should be seen "as an attempt to create a bold and brilliant synthesis of Christian ideas, capable of undergirding every aspect of life. It can be thought of as a 'cathedral of the mind' (Etienne Gilson)—an attempt to do with ideas what the great medieval masons did with stones, as they constructed some of the most admired and visited buildings the world has ever known. At its best, scholastic theology is to the world of ideas what those cathedrals are to the world of architecture" (2011:28).

Unfortunately, although some of the scholastic scholars, such as Thomas Aquinas in his multi-volume *Summa Theologica* (1948), may have been at least partly successful in harmonizing the truths of Christianity with the philosophical truths of the ancient world, medieval theologians would not be nearly as successful in their attempt to harmonize some of the popular theological truths of the Middle Ages with discoveries about to be made in the sciences. During the eleventh century, Arab scholars continued to dominate the sciences in disciplines such as astronomy (e.g. Hakimite Tables and the Toledan Table) and physics, although Europeans, following the establishment of the University of Salerno in Italy, began to make a growing number of contributions and discoveries in medicine. Beginning in the twelfth century, Europeans began laying the foundations for the future explosive growth of science by establishing universities in many of their major cities. The increasing opportunity to study a variety of topics, besides theology, at these universities, as well as the arrival in Western Europe of Greek scholars with copies of ancient Greek texts following the fall of Constantinople to the Ottoman Turks in 1453, led to the Renaissance in the fourteenth century with its focus on man rather than God. Nevertheless, the primary contribution that Europeans would make to science during this five-hundred-year period was in geography, with the great sea voyages of exploration that dominated the Fourteenth and Fifteenth centuries and culminated in the discovery of the New World. The discovery of new peoples and races on these new continents and islands did present somewhat of a challenge to theologians of the time, and many debates occurred over whether many of these exotic peoples, particularly Native Americans, were true descendants of Adam and Eve with real souls. This issue was not settled until 1537 when Pope Paul III issued a papal bull, *Sublimis Deus*, declaring that Native Americans were indeed human beings with souls that could be saved.

Perhaps the most important events that occurred during the first half of the second millennium, which would be relevant to the future of science, was the birth of four individuals: Roger Bacon (1214), Johannes Gutenberg (1396), Leonardo da Vinci (1452), and Nicolaus Copernicus (1473). Roger Bacon was both an English philosopher and a Franciscan friar and is often credited with being the founder of the modern scientific method which utilizes induction rather than deduction in its study of the heavens and earth. Johann Gutenberg, with his development of the movable type printing press, made the dissemination of knowledge both rapid and efficient and thereby helped fuel both the Renaissance (A.D. 1300–1700) and the Protestant Reformation (1517–1648). For example, by the beginning of the sixteenth century, approximately 35,000 books had been printed, totaling some 10 million copies (Grun 1979:223). Leonardo da Vinci, the archetype of the *Renaissance Man,* made significant contributions in both the arts and the sciences. One of his discoveries in the field of geology was that a stream in flood stage loses velocity as its waters rise up out of its channel and spread across the valley floor.

This change in speed reduces the carrying capacity of the stream and results in the deposition of the sediments that it is carrying. This geologic observation would have theological significance two centuries later when Bishop Ussher and some of his fellow theologians suggested that the biblical chronologies showed that the earth was only about 6,000 years old. In the sixteenth century, Nicolaus Copernicus would challenge theologian's long-held belief that the earth was the center of the universe—a belief based on the scientific works of both Ptolemy and Aristotle.

1500–1999 A.D.: Faith & Scripture

At the beginning of the second half of the second millennium, the focus of Christian theologians would change once again as the culture around them was changing and new problems presented themselves. Johannes Gutenberg's printing press, as well as the increasing number of translations of the Bible from Latin into the vernacular languages, had made the Bible available to the laity as well as the clergy. Moreover, Renaissance ideals concerning the importance of man had emboldened many Christians to both read and interpret the Scriptures for themselves, rather than being told what to believe by the priests and monks. What they frequently found was a contemporary church that was often wildly out of sync with the moral standards and practices of the early church as recorded in the New Testament. Dissatisfaction with church practices and leaders had been growing throughout the Middle Ages and had been manifested in an increasing number of dissenting and heretical groups, such as the Paulicians, Bogomils, Cathari, Waldensians, Lollards, and Hussites (Walton 1986: Chart 28). These tensions came to a head with the posting of Martin Luther's Ninety-five Theses on the door of the Wittenberg Church in 1517.

The Protestant Reformation, in its attempt to restore the church to a state more in line with that found in the Scriptures, would result in the splintering of the church into smaller and smaller fragments over the next five hundred years, each with its own unique theological perspective and proof-texts that supported its beliefs and practices. The Renaissance ideal of *man as the measure of all things* didn't work out very well when it came to scriptural interpretation. As in the days of the Judges when Israel had no king, "every man did what was right in his own eyes" (Judg. 17:6). Although the main branches of Christianity—Roman Catholic, Greek Orthodox, Protestants—retained similar beliefs concerning the great doctrines of the Bible, such as God, creation, sin, and salvation, unity was lost in the theological minutia. Truly, as the old saying goes, "The devil is in the details." The Scriptures became a battleground for competing theologies in the second half of the second millennium.

Into this confused theological setting, science was about to introduce a host of new discoveries that would challenge theological interpretations that had been built on old scientific theories. Some of those scientific theories, such as Ptolemy's geocentric model of the universe, dated back a thousand years or more. However, the extremely slow pace of scientific discovery that had characterized most of human antiquity was about to become supercharged, with new information about the heavens and earth beginning to flow in from all directions as humans turned their attention to better understanding and controlling the natural world. Moreover, the development of new technologies, from telescopes to microscopes, would greatly enhance humanity's ability to study the physical universe. As Carlo Rovelli (2017:46) has noted: "Scientific instruments began to open the myopic eyes of humankind, onto a world more vast and varied than it had as yet been able to conceive of."

Near the beginning of the sixteenth century, Copernicus published *Commentariolus* (1512), in which he first presented evidence that the planets orbit around the sun (the heliocentric model), rather than around the earth (the geocentric model), as both Aristotle and Ptolemy had believed. In the following century, Galileo would prove Copernicus was correct with his observations of Jupiter and Venus (1610) using the newly invented telescope. This was just the initial shot across the bow of medieval theology, whose interpretations of scriptural passages concerning God's creation of the heavens and earth were firmly tied to ancient cultural and scientific models that were doomed to soon be proven wrong. During the sixteenth century, the early foundations of modern geology were also being laid by the German scholar Georgius Agricola, who published the first treatise on mineralogy (1530) and initiated the study of physical geology (1544). Geologists would later prove that the earth was not just a few thousand years old, as many Christians and non-Christians had long assumed, but billions of years old, based on a host of absolute dating techniques. The study of medicine by monks and scholars in the early universities would eventually expand into the study of life in general (i.e. biology), a field that, like astronomy, had long been dominated by the work of ancient Greeks such as Aristotle. It would not be until the eighteenth century, however, that a solid foundation of modern biology would be established by the Swedish scholar Carolous Linnaeus with the publication of his *Systema Naturae* (1735). Another century would pass before the publication of Charles Darwin's *On the Origin of Species* (1859). (Perhaps it is the fact that modern biology has a more recent origin than either astronomy or geology that has made it so difficult for Christian theologians to incorporate evolution into their theological interpretations.)

These three sciences, astronomy, geology, and biology, which arose in the latter half of the second millennium, have given us a very different view of the heavens and earth than that held by our forefathers in the Patristic Age, the Dark Ages, or the Late Middle Ages. A plethora of galaxies filled with stars now stretch out across the night sky for billions of light years with the earth nothing more than a pale blue dot (Sagan 1997) drifting in the darkness of outer space. God's creation of life upon the earth was apparently not a simple process accomplished in a few minutes, hours, or days. As geologists and biologists reconstructed the history of life on the earth from the fossils embedded in the rocks, they found that whole worlds and ecosystems had been created and destroyed, over and over again, before humans had finally appeared on the scene, just a few hundred thousand years ago. God had apparently not been constrained by human ideas and time-frames, but had slowly and carefully fashioned his creation in a series of logical and increasingly complex stages in order to finally bring into existence intelligent, self-aware beings in his own image. Therefore, theologians in the modern era were challenged with understanding and interpreting Scripture in terms of this flood of new information about the physical universe. The Scriptures themselves were not changing, but our cultural and scientific understanding of some of the passages in the Bible about creation, time, and life certainly were changing—or should have been changing. However, each new discovery was accompanied by a lot of theological foot dragging. Old scientific theories had been so tightly woven into theological interpretations of Scripture that some of these interpretations had literally become dogma and were often given the same divine status as the Scriptures themselves. This situation should remind us of one of the warnings Christ gave to the scribes and Pharisees: "You hypocrites, rightly did Isaiah prophesy of you: 'THIS PEOPLE HONORS ME WITH THEIR LIPS, BUT THEIR HEART IS FAR AWAY FROM ME. BUT IN VAIN DO THEY WORSHIP ME, TEACHING AS DOCTRINES THE PRECEPTS OF MEN'" (Matt. 15:7–9).

Scientific models of the physical universe are precepts of men; they are not divine revelations, they change through time as our understanding of nature changes and (hopefully) improves. Aristotle's model of the universe was replaced by Ptolemy's model, which was replaced by Isaac Newton's model, which was replaced by Albert Einstein's model, etc. Our scientific debates between science and religion are frequently just debates between older scientific models (such as that of Ptolemy), and newer scientific models (such as those of Copernicus and Galileo). One of the great limitations of theological truth is that theological interpretations of Scripture, especially those passages dealing with the heavens and earth, are often based on older cultural and scientific knowledge about nature that has subsequently been disproved. Over the past two thousand years, human knowledge about the physical universe has grown exponentially. Our understanding and interpretation of the Scriptures over the centuries, especially those passage dealing with creation and nature, should also be growing deeper and richer—but have sometimes failed to do so.

CONCLUSION

In this chapter we have seen that theological truth is often limited by the cultural and scientific background of the theologians who study Scripture. Each age has its own unique problems and questions that theologians attempt to answer from the Scriptures. In the first half of the first millennium (A.D. 1–499), one of the major issues was trying to understand the three-fold nature of God and the divine/human nature of Christ. After several church councils, consensus among most theologians was reached by the issuing of the Nicaean Creed. In the second half of the first millennium (A.D. 500–999), more and more theologians turned their attention to man and the relation between faith and works/spirit and flesh. As Western Europe descended into the Dark Ages following the fall of Rome, monasteries became sanctuaries for the more spiritually minded who wanted to escape from the chaos and worldliness of that time period. These monasteries also became the repositories of Scriptures and other ancient texts, although much of the knowledge of classical antiquity was lost. In the first half of the second millennium (A.D. 1000–1499), the focus of theology shifted once again. As universities were founded in various cities across Europe, knowledge of the Greek and Roman classics was recovered or revived, and the Renaissance further shifted human attention away from God and onto Man. Many theologians of this age, especially the Scholastics, now became concerned with faith and reason and tried to present their theological arguments in a logical, systematic manner. They also tried to harmonize the philosophical truths of ancient scholars, such as Aristotle and Plato, with theological truths derived from the Scriptures. In the second half of the second millennium (A.D. 1500–1999), as Gutenberg's printing press, as well as new vernacular translations, made the Bible more and more assessable to Christians across Western Europe, theologians turned their attention to reforming the church in an attempt to bring it more into line with the original church as recorded in the pages of the New Testament.

In this chapter we have also seen how theologians and their interpretations of Scripture are dependent on the cultural and scientific knowledge of the age in which they live. This is particularly true of passages in the Bible that deal specifically with the creation of the heavens and earth, or nature in general. Theologians interpret passages about the natural world on the basis of what they already know about nature. During the first half of the first millennium (A.D. 1–499) there was no major disagreement between theological truth and scientific truth. In astronomy, Ptolemy's geocentric model of the heavens was easily harmonized with the earth-centered account of the heavens found in Genesis. No major new scientific theories in biology or geology were being introduced at this time. During the second half of the first millennium (A.D. 500–999), Europe entered the Dark Ages and scientific learning and discoveries came to a virtual standstill in Christian countries. In the first half of the second millennium (A.D. 1000–1499), universities were founded across Europe. The initial fruits of this new emphasis on learning, however, were in practical areas, such as medicine or the great sea voyages of discovery that began near the end of this period. It was during the second half of the second millennium (A.D. 1500–1999) that scientific knowledge of the natural world would go through an explosive expansion, beginning in the Renaissance and accelerating as the centuries passed, on into the third millennium.

In conclusion, theology and the theologians who work within this human discipline are limited by the culture and time period in which they live. The problems they focus upon will, in large part, be determined by the questions and issues that are relevant to the majority of people in their culture at that particular time period. Moreover, the tools they have at hand to use in their interpretation of the Scriptures will also vary from place to place and time to time. This is particularly true with regard to a culture's current scientific knowledge about the physical universe.

Chapter 5

The Spatial Limitations of Theological Truth

Introduction

Although scientific truth is based on information acquired through observation of the physical universe, discoveries made in the twentieth century revealed that there are places that scientists cannot go and things that scientists cannot know. This is true at both the macro-scale and the micro-scale; the physical universe is both too large and too small for scientists to have total or, in some cases, even partial access to what God has made. Albert Einstein's Special Theory of Relativity showed us that it is impossible to know what is simultaneously happening throughout the universe at even a single point in time because time moves at different rates in different places. This is because the passage of time is based on the velocity or gravity of an object, be it a galaxy, star, planet, or person. What a person perceives as the present moment is forever confined to his or her own individual frame of reference. For example, time moves at a slightly different rate for individuals at different elevations on the earth because of variations in earth's gravity (the closer you are to the center of the earth, the slower time passes). It also varies between people sitting in a room, versus traveling in a car or plane (the faster you are moving, the slower time passes) (Rovelli 2017:85–86).

When scientists turn their eyes from the earth and heavens, to the atom, they find another blind spot that even their most sophisticated equipment will not help them overcome. Besides Einstein's Theory of Relativity, quantum mechanics was the other great scientific advance of the twentieth century. Its focus of study is the atoms and subatomic particles out of which the physical universe is made. Werner Heisenberg's Principle of Indeterminacy revealed that scientists cannot simultaneously know the position and momentum of even one subatomic particle. These particles are so small that any form of electromagnetic radiation that scientists use to *see* these particles will either alter the particle's position or its velocity. Thus, whether scientists are studying the stars and galaxies or atoms and subatomic particles, there are barriers that they cannot cross, limitations that they cannot overcome (Brush 2005:137–164).

When scientists try to merge these two great theories of the twentieth century, relativity and quantum mechanics, they find that one way to do so, mathematically, is by assuming that the physical universe has far more dimensions that the four we are familiar with: length, width, height, and time. These other dimensions, if they exist, are embedded within the present universe but they are invisible and therefore inaccessible to scientific study. Even more disturbing is the discovery of dark matter and dark energy. Dark matter has now been documented through several means, including the orbital velocity of stars within galaxies. Dark energy was identified when it was discovered that the expansion of the universe is accelerating. It is now estimated that 85 percent of the matter in the universe is dark matter and 70 percent of the energy in the universe is dark energy (Randall 2015:2, 8). Thus, even if multiple hidden dimensions do not exist, scientists still only have direct access to a very small percentage of the matter and energy that actually makes up the physical universe.

Scientific attempts to explain the origin of this physical universe have also encountered similar roadblocks to human inquiry. Based on his observation of galaxies with the 100-inch Hooker Tele-scope at Mount Washington in California, Edwin Hubble discov-ered that the universe was expanding: galaxies in every direction were moving away from each other at speeds that increased with distance. This observation provided one of the proofs for the Big Bang Theory, which postulates that the universe had a beginning some 13.8 billion years ago when it arose out of a singularity (a dimensionless point in space). As scientists attempt to explain the origin of the universe by following its history back through time to the singularity, however, they encounter the Planck Boundary at 10^{-43} second after creation when the universe was just 10^{-33} cm in diameter. These units of time (one Planck Time at 10^{-43} second) and length (one Planck Length at 10^{-33} cm) are the smallest units of time and length that have any meaning. Before this time, as the universe continues to contract back into a singularity, the laws of physics cease to operate and the universe enters the realm of Heisenberg's Principle of Indeterminacy which characterizes all subatomic particles—or a universe the size of a subatomic particle. Scientists simply cannot see back to the beginning of the universe.

Scientists can *speculate*, however, about how the universe came into existence. One popular theory is that space is not empty at the quantum scale but is literally bubbling with vacuum fluc-tuations out of which virtual particles appear and disappear at random. Many scientists suggest that one of these virtual parti-cles became the singularity that inflated into the present physical universe. The problem is, if one virtual particle could inflate into a universe, why not others? Perhaps there is an infinite number of universes that arose from these vacuum fluctuations? If so, scien-tific truth would face its ultimate limitation since most scientists think it would be impossible to travel to, or obtain any informa-tion from, these other universes. Thus our scientific knowledge about the totality of reality, no matter how extensive it becomes with regard to our universe, would forever remain just a fragment of the truths that would surely exist in such a multiverse.

Therefore, the scientific discoveries made and the scientific theories developed in the twentieth century have revealed some rather severe spatial limitations on what scientists can actually study. As Lisa Randall points out in her book, *Dark Matter and the Dinosaurs* : "The big lesson of physics over the centuries is how much is hidden from our view" (2015:5). Indeed, scientific discoveries that change our understanding of the heavens and earth have not been limited to the twentieth century. In his small but very useful book, *Seven Brief Lessons on Physics*, Carlo Rovelli also affirms this point: "Ever since we discovered that Earth is round and turns like a mad spinning-top, we have understood that reality is not as it appears to us: every time we glimpse a new aspect of it, it is a deeply emotional experience. Another veil has fallen" (2016:6). In another book, entitled *Reality Is Not What It Seems*, Rovelli traces these common-sense-shattering discoveries all the way back to Thales, Anaximander, and Hecataeus on the Greek isle of Miletus in the sixth century B.C. (2017:16–18). During the nearly three thousand years of philosophical and scientific investigation since that time, scholars have found many doors that opened into this hidden world and revealed truths that were not previously obvious to us. Other doors, however, have remained firmly closed. The same has been true of our theological investigations that date back at least four thousand years to the time of Abraham. Like our understanding of the heavens and earth, our understanding of God and the supernatural realm has also continued to expand and deepen, although theologians have also found closed doors, places where we, as humans, cannot go and things that we cannot know. In this chapter, we will examine some of the spatial limitations of theological truth.

I. THE SUPERNATURAL REALM

Given the many obstacles scientists have encountered in their quest to understand the physical universe, imagine the barriers facing the theologian whose focus of study, God, dwells in the supernatural realm! *Webster's New Collegiate Dictionary* (Woolf 1981:1161) defines the supernatural as: "of or relating to an order of existence beyond the visible observable universe." In the supernatural realm, 100 percent of what is there is hidden from our view, unless God chooses to reveal himself, or the beings in that realm, to us. The impetus lies totally with God. We can't force God to reveal himself to us, nor can we devise microscopes or telescopes, drones or satellites that will provide us a peek into the heavenly realm. The dwelling place of God is both beyond and outside the physical realm; that's why we call it the *super*natural realm.

There is a door between the natural and the supernatural realm, but it only opens one way. This door allows beings from the heavenly realm to visit the earth and interact with humans, but it does not allow humans access into the heavenly realm, except through death or by special dispensation, such as Elijah and Enoch. On rare occasions, however, it is recorded that God has allowed one of his servants to see through the door, but not to enter. In the book of Acts (7:55) we read that Stephen, the first recorded martyr to die for Christ's sake, "being full of the Holy Spirit, he gazed intently into heaven and saw the glory of God, and Jesus standing at the right hand of God; and he said, 'Behold, I see the heavens opened up and the Son of Man standing at the right hand of God.'" Immediately following this event, Stephen was taken outside the walls of the city by the Jews and stoned to death. Interestingly, Saul (Paul) was present at the stoning of Stephen and the witnesses to this execution laid their robes at his feet (Acts 7:58). Nevertheless, later in his life Paul was also granted the opportunity to look through this door into the supernatural realm: "I know a man in Christ who fourteen years ago—whether in the body I do not know, or out of the body I do not know, God knows—such a man was caught up to the third heaven. And I know how such a man—whether in the body or apart from the body I do not know, God knows—was caught up into Paradise and heard inexpressible words, which a man is not permitted to speak" (2 Cor. 12:2–4).

In the Old Testament, there are also instances where God has allowed his prophets to see into the supernatural realm. For example, the prophet Ezekiel records that: "Now it came about in the thirtieth year, on the fifth day of the fourth month, while I was by the river Chebar among the exiles, the heavens were opened and I saw visions of God" (Ezek. 1:1). The prophet Isaiah records a similar experience: "In the year of King Uzziah's death I saw the Lord sitting on a throne, lofty and exalted, with the train of His robe filling the temple. Seraphim stood above Him, each having six wings: with two he covered his face, and with two he covered his feet, and with two he flew. And one called out to another and said, 'Holy, Holy, Holy, is the LORD of hosts, The whole earth is full of His glory'" (Isa. 6:1–3).

Most of the accounts in the Bible concerning the interaction between the supernatural realm and the natural realm involve angels (God's messengers) or the Angel of the Lord (God's special representative) who abruptly appear and disappear, apparently moving back and forth between these two realms with ease. The key word in many of these encounters between humans and angels is *appeared*. Occasionally angels are described as actually *moving* between these two realms, such as Jacob's dream of angels who were ascending and descending a ladder between the earth and heaven (Gen. 28:12) or Matthew's account of an angel descending from heaven and rolling away the stone from the tomb on the morning of Christ's resurrection (Matt. 28:2). More frequently, however, an angel simply appears out of nowhere, and as rapidly disappears. For example: an angel of the Lord appeared to Zacharias at the altar of incense (Luke 1:11), an angel of the Lord suddenly stood before the shepherds in the fields (Luke 2:9), an angel from heaven appeared to Jesus on the Mount of Olives (Luke 22:43). After his resurrection, Jesus also displays this ability to freely move between the realm of the natural and the realm of the supernatural. In the village of Emmaus, Jesus broke bread with two of his disciples. As soon as the disciples recognized who Jesus was, however, "He vanished from their sight" (Luke 24:31). In Jerusalem, on the day of his resurrection, Jesus came and stood in the midst of his disciples, even though the doors were shut in the room where they had gathered (John 20:19). Eight days later, the disciples were again gathered together (this time with Thomas present) and the same thing happened again—doors were shut but Jesus suddenly stood in their midst (John 20:26). In this regard, one is reminded of quantum leaps at the subatomic level where electrons do not move across the space between different orbital levels as they absorb or emit energy, they simply disappear from one level and simultaneously appear in another level (Brush 2005:152–155). These quantum leaps seem to defy the law of cause and effect: electrons in orbit around an atom do not need to move across the space between points A and B, they are either in one place or another—never between those places. On the macro level, angels and the resurrected Christ also seem to be able to transcend this basic law of nature as they appear and disappear according to the will of God.

An even more interesting aspect of these interactions between the natural and supernatural realms is the evidence that angels and Christ do not really need to move from one realm to another because these two realms actually coexist. Angels do not need to come down from heaven and Christ does not need to enter a room where the doors are closed, because they are already present—we just can't *normally* see or interact with them. The scriptural justification for this rather surprising conclusion can be found in the following accounts where God must first open a person's eyes before they can see the supernatural beings near or around them (see Table 11):

Table 11: Scriptures concerning the Nearness of the Supernatural Realm
Then the Lord opened the eyes of Balaam, and he saw the angel of the Lord standing in the way with his drawn sword in his hand; and he bowed all the way to the ground. (Num. 22:31)
Now when the attendant of the man of God had risen early and gone out, behold, an army with horses and chariots was circling the city. And his servant said to him, "Alas, my master! What shall we do?" So he answered, "Do not fear, for those who are with us are more than those who are with them." Then Elisha prayed and said, "O LORD, I pray, open his eyes that he may see." And the LORD opened the servant's eyes and he saw; and behold, the mountain was full of horses and chariots of fire all around Elisha. (2 Kings 6:15–17)
When He [Jesus] had reclined at the table with them, He took the bread and blessed it, and breaking it, He began giving it to them. Then their eyes were opened and they recognized Him; and He vanished from their sight. (Luke 24:30–31)

Moreover, in Paul's sermon on Mars Hill to the Athenians, he also suggests that the supernatural and the natural realms are inter-mingled: "He made from one man every nation of mankind to live on all the face of the earth, having determined their appointed times and the boundaries of their habitation, that they would seek God, if perhaps they might grope for Him and find Him, though He is not far from each one of us; for in Him we live and move and exist" (Acts 17:26–28). A thousand years before Paul, King David was also aware of the all-pervasive presence of God:

> Where can I go from Your Spirit?
> Or where can I flee from Your presence?
> If I ascend to heaven, You are there;
> If I make my bed in Sheol, behold, You are there.
> If I take the wings of the dawn,
> If I dwell in the remotest part of the sea,
> Even there Your hand will lead me,
> And Your right hand will lay hold of me.
>   (Ps. 139:7–10)

The supernatural realm is not a far distant country. Instead, we seem to be immersed in it yet we cannot see it, nor can we enter it under our own volition. According to the Bible, on rare occasions we may be allowed to see into that realm, but only for a brief moment. Sometimes, men and women are visited by angels from that realm who abruptly appear or disappear.

Modern science provides some interesting insights as to how two realms could coexist. As noted earlier in this chapter, it is possible that the physical universe is composed of far more than four dimensions, but these other dimensions are not visible to us because they are rolled up and embedded in this universe. Also, there may be other parallel universes that coexist with ours. These parallel universes are all the offspring of vacuum fluctuations from which virtual particles inflated into separate universes. As our understanding of dark matter and dark energy continues to grow, it now appears that our visible universe is actually embedded in a much more extensive universe of dark matter (85 percent) and dark energy (70 percent) that we cannot see or interact with (except weakly through gravity). It has been suggested that a better name for dark matter would be *transparent matter,* since it doesn't interact with light. Instead, light passes right through it, therefore making it invisible (Randall 2015:5–7). It is tempting to suggest that the supernatural realm may be composed of this transparent matter while the natural realm is composed of regular matter, or that the supernatural realm exists as a parallel universe. It also seems possible that, rather than other dimensions being rolled up and embedded in our universe, it is our four dimensions that are embedded in a much larger multiple dimensional universe that is invisible to us. Indeed, the Christian astronomer, Hugh Ross, in his book *The Creator and the Cosmos,* has suggested that the transcendence of God may, in part, be explained in terms of his not being confined to the four dimensions of the space–time continuum that we experience in this physical universe (1993:157–161). Ross points out that some of the aspects of God that humans find so difficult to understand, such as his being three persons in one or his ability to be in all places at the same time, become more feasible if God dwells in multiple dimensions. In the second book of C. S. Lewis's space trilogy, *Perelandra,* the eldil (angels) seem to be described as multidimensional beings who are both present, but also elsewhere:

> They were perhaps thirty feet high. They were burning white like white-hot iron. The outline of their bodies when he looked at it steadily against the red landscape seemed to be faintly, swiftly undulating as though the permanence of their shape, like that of waterfalls or flames, co-existed with a rushing movement of the matter it contained. . . . They were not standing quite vertically in relation to the floor of the valley: but to Ransom it appeared (as it had appeared to me on Earth when I saw one) that the eldils were vertical. It was the valley—it was the whole world of Perelandra— which was aslant. He remembered the words of Oyarsa long ago in Mars, "I am not *here* in the same way you are *here*." It was borne

> in upon him that the creatures were really moving, though not moving in relation to him. This planet which inevitably seemed to him while he was in it an unmoving world—*the* world, in fact— was to them a thing moving through the heavens. In relation to their own celestial frame of reference they were rushing forward to keep abreast of the mountain valley. (Lewis 1944:198–99)

Such speculations concerning possible correlations between the supernatural realm and exotic entities from theoretical physics are certainly interesting and possibly useful in helping us understand God and heaven. Nevertheless, attempting to tie the nature of God too closely with these physical entities may also lead us into the old trap of pantheism by confusing the Creator with that which he has created. The apostle John tells us that "All things came into being through Him, and apart from Him nothing came into being that has come into being" (John 1:3). Thus, if such things as other dimensions, multiple universes, and dark matter/dark energy do exist as a part of this present physical universe, they are also things that God has created. Although God may choose to use these created things to partially reveal himself to us, even as he clothes himself in light (Ps. 104:2) or takes on human flesh in the incarnation (John 1:14), he is not confined, defined, or limited to these things that he has created.

Thus, aside from the hints that the Scriptures give us about the supernatural realm, or the interesting examples of other possible invisible realms that modern science can provide, theologians are very limited in what they know, or can learn, about the dwelling place of God. The supernatural realm, being separate from the natural realm, is not amenable to study through the senses of either scientists or theologians. Consequently, a theologian's time might be better spent writing imaginative fiction about the heavens, as C. S. Lewis has done, in *Perelandra* (1944) rather than trying to use the Scriptures to build rigid doctrines about that supernatural realm. It is a realm which cannot be apprehended by the physical senses. It is a realm which God has chosen only to reveal to a few of his servants, and then, for only a few brief moments.

II. BEFORE THE BEGINNING OF TIME

Another severe spatial limitation that theologians face is trying to understand what happened before God created the heavens and the earth. As God said to Job: "Where were you when I laid the foundation of the earth?" (Job 38:4). Some theologians think that the book of Job may be the oldest book in the Bible. Job, however, was not present at Creation, and neither were all the later generations of theologians. What happened in that time before time, "When the morning stars sang together And all the sons of God shouted for joy" (Job 38:7), is a great mystery. Scientists have certainly found that this period of time—actually non-time—is apparently forever beyond their reach because the laws of physics cease to operate as they approach the beginning of the universe. For example, if, in our minds, we run the Big Bang backwards in time, the presently expanding universe reverses direction and begins to contract. It eventually shrinks back into a singularity: a single dimensionless point with infinite mass that contains all the matter and energy of the present universe. Before this occurs, however, a shroud of darkness descends on this process at precisely 10^{-43} second before the Big Bang. At this point in time, the universe is only 10^{-33} cm in diameter and disappears from sight as it descends into the realm of quantum uncertainty and finally forms a singularity. The Big Bang (i.e. the point of creation) and the moments immediately thereafter are simply not accessible to science or to the theologian.

According to modern science, the entire history of the present heavens and earth can be encompassed by a mere 13.8 billion years. It is rather surprising that the universe is not a great deal older than this. This figure of 13.8 billion is much smaller than the number of dollars in many billionaires' bank accounts. It is a number much, much smaller than America's present national debt of around 20 trillion dollars. Even these figures, however pale into insignificance in comparison to really large numbers that we can imagine, such as a googol (10^{100}) which is a 1 followed by 100 zeros or a googolplex (10^{googol}) which is a number so large that, if it were written out on a piece of paper, there would not be enough room in the visible universe to contain it (Sagan 1980:219–220). But who can imagine the endless expanse of eternity stretching out before God created the present heavens and earth? As children, we are often frightened when our parents try to explain heaven and eternity. We ask, *How long does it last? Forever!*, they explain. So we try again. *But when does it end? Never!*, they respond. As the old gospel song by John Newton goes: "When we've been there ten-thousand years…. We've no less days to sing God's praise Than when we'd first begun" (Jorgenson 1937:337). Even if we inserted a googolplex into the first verse of this hymn—When we've been there a googolplex years, the second verse would remain the same—"We've no less days to sing God's praise Than when we've first begun." As Carl Sagan has noted in his book *Cosmos*: "And yet these numbers, the googol and the googolplex, do not approach, they come nowhere near, the idea of infinity [eternity]. A googolplex is *precisely* as far from infinity as is the number one" (1980:220). God is the great "I Am" (Exod. 3:14) who was eternally present. He was present before Abraham (John 8:58), He was present before Adam (Gen. 1:26–27), He was present before the earth (v. 2), He was present before the heavens (v. 1), He was present before the angels (Col. 1:16), He was *always* present (Ps. 90:2; Isa. 57:15).

How does a man or woman who only lives for a few decades, ever fully understand this God who dwells in eternity? We stand before the fearful void of eternity and feel the chill winds blowing out of the timeless darkness and our knees knock together and our teeth chatter. In short, we are deathly afraid and our imaginations fail us when we try to imagine the unimaginable. We do not want to die but we are so used to the temporal nature of things, that thinking too deeply about eternity—about something that will never, never end—awakens panic in our hearts and makes our minds half sick with dread of the unknown. Yet the God we seek to understand is the embodiment of eternity. Scientists sometimes talk about *the great abyss of time* when discussing the 4.6 billion years of earth history or the 13.8 billion years since the Big Bang. Theologians, however, must face the truly great abyss of *timelessness* that separates created beings from their Creator. This gulf between the temporal and eternal creates an impassable barrier for theologians trying to fully understand the nature of God.

In the Bible, God has not chosen to explain to humankind what he was doing in the eternity before he created the present heavens and earth. From the book of Job, we do know that the angels were present when God created the earth. Moreover, they shouted for joy as they witnessed this act of creation (Job 38:7), even as they would later do when they were present to witness the birth of God's Son (Luke 2:13–14). Based on the book of Genesis, we may *assume* that Satan had rebelled against God before God created the earth. In the third chapter of Genesis, we find him waiting in the garden of Eden, in the form of a Serpent, to tempt Adam and Eve. However, the exact timing of Satan's rebellion against God, as well as that of some of the other angels who joined him, is not clear. The passage from Job also tells us that the stars were already present when God created the earth: "Where were you when I laid the foundation of the earth?.... When the morning stars sang together And all the sons of God shouted for joy?" (38:4, 7). It is obvious, then, that the stars were not formed on the fourth day of creation (Gen. 1:14–19) as some theologians have suggested. Instead their creation is alluded to in Genesis 1:1: "In the beginning God created the Heavens and the Earth." Stars, the sun, and the moon are *specifically* mentioned for the first time on the fourth day of creation and they are assigned specific functions at this time: "Then God said, 'Let there be lights in the expanse of the heavens to separate the day from the night, and let them be for signs and for seasons and for days and years; and let them be for lights in the expanse of the heavens to give light on the earth'; and it was so. God made the two great lights, the greater light to govern the day, and the lesser light to govern the night; He made the stars also" (vv. 14–16).

When considering the eternity that existed before God created the heavens and earth, theological arguments about the age of this present creation seem inconsequential and silly. Time is irrelevant to this God who dwells in eternity. Attempting to limit his acts of creation to a few days, or the age of the heavens and earth to a few thousand years, is the perspective and preoccupation of time-bound humans. Time is not a matter of consequence to God. He makes a promise to Abraham that is not fully fulfilled until two thousand years later: "And in you all the families of the earth will be blessed" (Gen. 12:3). King David prophesied about Christ's suffering on the cross, which would not occur until a thousand years had passed: "My God, my God, why have You forsaken me?" (Ps. 22:1). Jesus promised his disciples: "If I go and prepare a place for you, I will come again and receive you to Myself, that where I am, there you may be also" (John 14:3). More than two thousand years have now elapsed since Christ made that promise and we are still awaiting his return for us. God's timescale is not in sync with man's short tenure upon the earth. Yet, many still believe that God crammed the creation of the heavens and earth into a brief period of only 144 hours. Perhaps we should ask ourselves why was God in such a hurry to make the heavens and earth when other accounts of his activities in the Old and New Testaments show him acting as though he had all the time in the world—which he does. Theologians are obviously limited in their understanding of this God who was here before the beginning of the earth, the beginning of the heavens, and the beginning of time.

III. After the End of Time

Another great barrier to our understanding of God is the eternity that stretches out after he brings this present heaven and earth to an end: "But the day of the Lord will come like a thief, in which the heavens will pass away with a roar and the elements will be destroyed with intense heat, and the earth and its works will be burned up" (2 Peter 3:10). The Scriptures provide us with more information about what comes after the end of the world than what came before it was created. Nevertheless, since we are talking about eternity, a few verses from the Old and New Testament are not a great deal to build upon. It is enough, however, to give us hope and to increase our longing for Christ's return. As the apostle John concludes at the end of his revelation, "He who testifies to these things says, 'Yes, I am coming quickly.' Amen. Come, Lord Jesus" (Rev. 22:20).

In the book of Revelation (21:1–22:7), we are told that there will be a new heaven and a new earth. We are not told anything about the physical characteristics of this new heaven. We don't know if it will contain a sun or moon since the New Jerusalem will not need any external source of light (v. 23). The glory of God will illuminate the city, and perhaps the entire earth: "The nations will walk by its light, and the kings of the earth will bring their glory into it. In the daytime (for there will be no night there) its gates will never be closed...." (v. 24). We don't know if this new earth will be part of a solar system or galaxy, or even if such entities will exist anymore. The only thing we are told about the new earth is that there is no ocean (v. 1). This, in itself, will make earth a very different place, since 71 percent of the current earth's surface is covered by oceans. Earth's climate and weather is also largely the product of the interaction between sunlight and the waters of the ocean, so many of the cycles we have identified in nature will, apparently, no longer be functioning on the new earth.

The Scriptures also tell us that we will have new bodies. Jesus taught that we will be like the angels (Matt. 22:30; Luke 20:36). Both John and Paul tell us that our new bodies will be like that of the resurrected Christ (1 John 3:2; Phil. 3:21). Therefore, our bodies will not be subject to death, they will be immortal (Luke 20:36; 1 Cor. 15:42, 53; Rev. 21:4). Like Christ, our new bodies will also be endowed with power (1 Cor. 15:43) and glory (Dan. 12:3; Matt. 13:43; 1 Cor. 15:43). Our new bodies will be spiritual (1 Cor. 15:44, 48), but also physical, with flesh and bones, like that of the resurrected Christ (Luke 24:39; John 20:27). Since our new bodies will be like the angels and the risen Christ, we can assume that we, like they, will not be constrained by time and space but will be able to move freely and instantaneously from one place to another (Luke 24:31; John 20:19, 26).

The dwelling place that Jesus promised his disciples that he would prepare for them (John 14:3), is a city, the New Jerusalem: "And I saw the holy city, new Jerusalem, coming down out of heaven from God, made ready as a bride adorned for her husband" (Rev. 21:2). John tells us that an angel measured the city with a golden rod. The city is laid out as a square, 1,500 miles long, 1,500 miles wide, and 1,500 miles high (about 300 miles less than the distance between New York and Denver). It is built on twelve foundations of precious stones and its walls are 216 feet thick with 12 gates, each made from a giant pearl (vv. 15–21). Since the tallest building on earth today is only about half a mile high, the laws of physics and the restraints of engineering on the new earth are not the same as on the present earth. On the present earth, the tallest mountain is only about 5½ miles in height, but there is not enough oxygen at that height for most humans to survive there for more than 15–30 minutes. At 1,500 miles on the present earth, you would be in outer space. Most American and Russian satellites orbit the earth at a distance of some 200 miles, with a few out to 400 miles, so a city 1,500 miles high is simply unimaginable from the perspective of the present heaven and earth with its many physical constraints.

The most unique aspect of the New Jerusalem, however, is that it will become the tabernacle of God (vv. 3–4). There on his throne, with Christ at his right hand, God will dwell with his people—"a great multitude which no one could count, from every nation and all tribes and peoples and tongues" (Rev. 7:9)—and "they will reign forever and ever" (Rev. 22:5). From his throne, a river of the water of life will flow, and on each side of the river the Tree of Life will provide twelve kinds of fruit, as well as its leaves for the healing of the nations (vv. 1–2). In this city will also dwell the angels and the other heavenly beings, such as the cherubim and seraphim: "Then I looked and I heard the voice of many angels around the throne and the living creatures and the elders; and the number of them was myriads of myriads, and thousands of thousands, saying with a loud voice, 'Worthy is the Lamb that was slain to receive power and riches and wisdom and might and honor and glory and blessing'" (Rev. 5:11–12). Given these multitudes of angels and humans, it is good that the New Jerusalem is a very large city with an area of 2,250,000 square miles and a volume of 3,375,000,000 square miles. But didn't Jesus promise that "In My Father's house are many dwelling places; if it were not so, I would have told you; for I go to prepare a place for you" (John 14:2)? Yet, having been told this and even given information about the size and composition of the New Jerusalem, we can hardly imagine it, let alone the new earth and the new heaven.

Conclusion

As scientists try to expand and deepen their understanding of the physical universe that God has created, they have encountered major areas at both the microscopic and macroscopic level into which they cannot peer. In addition, some of the fabric out of which the universe seems to be constructed, such as multiple dimensions and dark matter/energy, is invisible or largely invisible to human eyes and human instruments. As theologians try to more fully understand the nature of God, they are spatially limited to the physical universe. They simply cannot see into the supernatural realm, except by direct revelation from God. Theologians are also spatially bound to the present. Except for a few scriptural verses, they have no way of obtaining information about what God was doing before he created the heavens and earth, or what he will be doing after he brings this creation to an end. Of course, even this concept is flawed because we are speaking in terms of past and future tense, but the God who dwells in eternity stands outside the space/time continuum; there are no *befores* and *afters*.

Today it is rather shocking to realize that our scientific understanding of the physical universe is based on only that 15 percent of matter and 30 percent of energy that is visible to us—the other 85 percent of matter is dark matter; the other 70 percent of energy is dark energy. It would, no doubt, be even more shocking if we could compute the minuscule amount of information upon which our theological understanding of the supernatural realm is built. Even more daunting would be the great chasm that exists between a theologian's understanding of things that have occurred, are occurring, or will occur in the future, versus things that occur in eternity. Theologians are even more limited than scientists in the places they can go and the things they can know.

Chapter 6

THE EMPIRICAL LIMITATIONS OF THEOLOGICAL TRUTH

INTRODUCTION

The final limitations that theologians share with scientists are empirical limitations. As I noted in *The Limitations of Scientific Truth*: "Modern science is built on empirical observations of nature but empirical observations must be interpreted by the human mind before they have any meaning. Therefore, the weakest links in this dialogue between scientists and nature is the human mind itself. Although scientists can strive for objectivity in their analysis and interpretation of empirical observations, they are never entirely free from the subjective influence of their backgrounds, experiences, educations, beliefs, hopes, fears, theories, and biases" (Brush 2005:202). Science is often set apart from theology because it is based on empirical observations of the physical universe rather than supernatural revelation. Theologians, however, must interact with God's revelation through their senses, either by hearing the Word of God being spoken by preachers and teachers, or seeing the Word of God as they read the Scriptures. As Paul noted: "So faith comes from hearing, and hearing by the word of Christ" (Rom. 10:17). Therefore, in order to study and understand the Scriptures, supernatural revelation must pass through the mind via the avenue of the human senses. But, "empirical observations must be interpreted by the human mind before they have any meaning" (Brush 2005:202).

As was noted in Chapter 1 of this present book, theology, like science, is a human discipline, and all human disciplines are flawed because of the sinful nature of the humans who practice these disciplines. The flaws in humans that practice these academic disciplines include human ignorance, human error, and human bias. Therefore, a theologian trying to understand supernatural revelation shares the very same empirical limitations that a scientist does who is trying to understand the natural world.

I. THEOLOGIANS' IGNORANCE

A. *Ignorance of Nature*

Down through the ages, theologians have based their understanding and interpretations of God's Word, especially those passages dealing with creation and the natural world, on what they and their cultures knew about nature. One first has to learn the meaning of different words before one can learn to speak or read. As children, we initially acquire this knowledge from our parents and those around us. Our understanding of the meaning of words, however, may grow and deepen over time, based on our observations and continued education. This transformation of meaning occurs, not only during the course of an individual's lifetime, but also throughout human history as new discoveries are made and new insights are gained. Therefore, Aristotle's understanding of the word *heavens* was very different from that of Ptolemy, Copernicus, Newton, Einstein, or Stephen Hawking. Indeed, each of these individuals, representing different time periods, had their own unique understanding of the heavens. This fact should not be threatening to Christians; it simply means that, over time, as our understanding of the word *heavens* is expanded and enriched, so is our understanding of those passages in God's Word that speak of the heavens. No doubt our understanding of the heavens, even today, is minimal in comparison to what God knows the heavens to be, but at least we have been given ever-richer glimpses of its grandeur.

Unfortunately, theologians often assume that their current understanding of a word like the heavens, or the understanding of earlier theologians and scholars concerning that word, is the final, ultimate interpretation. History, however, has shown that this is not so, especially with regard to our understanding of nature and the physical universe. Therefore, when we intentionally exclude current scientific knowledge from our interpretations of Scripture, we are engaging in willful ignorance. We are shutting our eyes and putting our hands over our ears and crying, "No! No! No!" to any new information. We are discarding the opportunity to learn deeper truths in favor of the security of older, well-trodden pathways of understanding. Such preferred pathways of thought, just like many of the teachings of the Pharisees, can easily become *traditions of men* that eventually lose their connection with any scriptural passages on which they may have originally been based. The growing rejection of current scientific knowledge by many churches across America today is evidence that we have fallen into this trap. The living Word of God that is sharper than any two-edged sword has become dulled by mixing the Scriptures with old, now outdated human traditions and interpretations. If we truly believe that the Bible is the Word of God, then we have nothing to fear in learning new and deeper truths about the heavens and earth which he has created. All we will lose is the baggage of older human interpretations of some scriptural passages about nature, interpretations that have subsequently been proven to be flawed or totally wrong. It is not what the Scriptures say about Creation and the natural world, but the theologian's knowledge of those subjects which is incomplete and subject to revision.

B. Ignorance of Scriptures

A second area where a theologian's knowledge is often incomplete is with regard to the Scripture itself. Paul tells Timothy, "Be diligent to present yourself approved to God as a workman who does not need to be ashamed, accurately handling the word of truth" (2 Tim. 2:15). The Scriptures do not contradict themselves; they form a seamless cloth of revelation that God has woven through his servants down through the ages. Yet, many theological interpretations of the Scriptures not only contradict each other, but also other scriptural passages. Although Jesus prayed for unity among his followers, the church has been splintered into smaller and smaller fragments over theological controversies. As we saw in Chapter 4, debates within the church over seminal issues, such as the nature of Christ or faith and works, have sometimes gone on for centuries. Clearly, theologians have not been successful in their handling of the word of truth, and their failures have been writ large across the pages of history. Jesus promised his followers that the Holy Spirit would be sent to guide them into all truth (John 16:13). Unfortunately, many of Jesus's followers in later generations seem to have resisted that guidance.

In the time of Jesus, the Pharisees were the acknowledged guardians and interpreters of the Old Testament. They were also fervent in their expressed desire to see the coming of the Messiah. Nevertheless, when Christ came, they did not recognize who he was, despite all the prophecies scattered throughout the pages of the Old Testament. Jesus even challenged them: "You search the Scriptures because you think that in them you have eternal life; it is these that testify about Me; and you are unwilling to come to Me so that you may have life" (John 5:39–40). The Pharisees were ignorant of those things about which they should have been most knowledgeable. It is one thing to be ignorant of truths that may originate in other disciplines, but to be ignorant of the truths in your own discipline calls into question your competence and right to be called a practitioner of that subject. Tragically, many Christian theologians have followed the example that the Pharisees set in New Testament times, "'BUT IN VAIN DO THEY WORSHIP ME, TEACHING AS DOCTRINES THE PRECEPTS OF MEN'" (Mark 7:7).

Like scientists, theologians are also subject to the limitations that all humans share, including not having access to all the facts.

Thus, a theologian's interpretation of the Scriptures is only as good as his or her knowledge of the Scriptures. Holes in a theologian's scriptural knowledge may result in faulty interpretations of certain passages of Scripture. Failure to take into account "the whole purpose of God" (Acts 20:27) may result in theological interpretations of one passage of Scripture that directly contradict other passages of Scripture. The theologian, as well as the layman, will often limit their knowledge of the Scriptures to certain key passages or favorite proof-texts that are used over and over again, rather than considering the whole counsel of God that is found in the Bible. It has often been said, no doubt with justification, that one can find at least one passage in the Scriptures to justify any type of behavior. It is probably equally true that the more ignorant one is of the Scriptures, the easier it is to come up with theological interpretations that are out of sync with "the faith which was once for all handed down to the saints" (Jude 1:3).

C. Ignorance of God

Strangely enough, a theologian may also be ignorant of the God whose revelation he or she is studying. People are drawn to the various professions for many different reasons, not all of which are sound or logical. An individual who becomes a theologian is usually presumed to know more about God and his Word than the average follower of Christ. Therefore, individuals who dedicate themselves to the study of God share, by association, some of the honor and respect that people have for God. This status may be a strong enticement for some to become theologians. Some may be attracted to the discipline of theology because they did not have the necessary social skills for a full-time ministry and preferred a more academic lifestyle. Others, with a proclivity for the mystic or supernatural, may be drawn to theology more for its spirituality, rather than its focus on the one, true God. Given the various possible motives that individuals have for entering this discipline, it may be naive to assume that every theologian is also a lover of God.

There are certainly examples in the Bible of religious scholars who seemed to be ignorant of who God was and what he required of them. Indeed, God speaking through the prophet Isaiah, said: "THIS PEOPLE HONORS ME WITH THEIR LIPS, BUT THEIR HEART IS FAR AWAY FROM ME" (Matt. 15:8). Such a mindset was apparently true of many of the Jewish theologians of Jesus's day: "But woe to you, scribes and Pharisees, hypocrites, because you shut off the kingdom of heaven from people; for you do not enter in yourselves, nor do you allow those who are entering to go in" (Matt. 23:13). How ironic that some of the religious leaders who daily studied the Word of God used it, not for the salvation of souls, but instead, for their eternal destruction. Unfortunately, with a little reflection, it is rather easy to compile a list of heretical interpretations and damnable ideas which first arose in the minds of famous theologians who were working in prestigious seminaries, individuals who were really wolves dressed in shepherd's clothing. Some of these so-called theologians went so far as to champion interpretations of Scripture that denied the divinity of Christ, his sinless life, his death on the cross, and his resurrection from the dead. The fruit that these individuals produced poisoned the minds of countless men and women and no doubt led to the destruction of many souls. Although outwardly professing to be seekers after a deeper understanding of God and his Word, they had actually learned their craft by sitting at the feet of the father of lies. Men and women who truly knew God, would not have been led so far away. As Jesus said, "My sheep hear My voice, and I know them, and they follow Me; and I give eternal life to them, and they will never perish; and no one will snatch them out of My hand" (John 10:27–28).

II. THEOLOGIANS' MISTAKES

A. Personal Mistakes

Even men and women who know God and are personally committed to him sometimes make mistakes in their theological understanding, interpretations, or practices. The apostle Peter was the leader of the early church. The Spirit of God sent Peter to the household of Cornelius, a Gentile, to preach the gospel and bring salvation to his household (Acts 10:1–48). When he entered Cornelius' home, Peter explained: "You yourselves know how unlawful it is for a man who is a Jew to associate with a foreigner or to visit him; and yet God has shown me that I should not call any man unholy or unclean" (v. 28). Nevertheless, several years later, at the Council at Jerusalem, Paul opposed Peter because: "prior to the coming of certain men from James, he used to eat with the Gentiles; but when they came, he began to withdraw and hold himself aloof, fearing the party of the circumcision" (Gal. 2:12). Now if even an apostle of Peter's stature was wrong in his actions and stood in need of correction, surely all theologians need to walk with humility and circumspection, lest they, too, be found in error.

When we examine the lives and works of the great leaders of the church who followed Peter over the next 2,000 years, Saint Augustine, Saint Aquinas, Luther, John Calvin, etc., we see that these men also had feet of clay; none of them was infallible. Although the modern church has been greatly strengthened and spiritually enriched by the work of such individuals, their writings are not without taint of error. There are no doubt scriptural interpretations in the work of each of these giants of the faith that even the average Christian in the pew today might find fault with, on the basis of a better understanding of the Scriptures with which centuries or millennia of continued study by other Christian scholars have endowed us. Future generations will just as likely find errors in the theological work being done today, but each generation has the opportunity to correct the theological mistakes of the past and, hopefully, lay an even firmer foundation for the future.

B. Communal Mistakes

Like scientists, theologians do not work in a vacuum; they are members of larger communities, both religious and academic. The major divisions of Christianity—Eastern Orthodox, Catholic, and Protestant—all have their schools and seminaries for training theologians in the history, beliefs, and practices of their particular traditions. These major divisions are themselves often subdivided into more specialized groups. For example, in Catholicism there are large groups such as the Benedictines, Dominicans, Franciscans, and Jesuits, as well as many, many other orders and communities for men or women. In Protestantism, larger groups include Baptist, Congregational, Lutheran, Methodist, Pentecostal, and Presbyterian, as well as a plethora of smaller groups and subgroups. Although all of these various orders, communities, and denominations share a common belief in Christ, each has its own unique theology which focuses on certain, often highly specific, aspects of faith and practice that set it apart from the other groups. Consequently, to be a member in good standing within one of these Christian groups, a theologian must, in general, adhere to the doctrines and scriptural interpretations of that particular group to which he or she belongs. Deviate too much from the consensus of belief within your particular group and you may find yourself being asked to leave the group, or you may be inspired to join a different group, or even found a new group.

Now, the unique beliefs and practices of these many different religious groups cannot all be correct, since some of the beliefs held by the various groups will contradict each other. It is quite likely that none of these groups has managed to arrive at absolute truth concerning God and the Scriptures. Instead, like all human disciplines, their theologies probably contain a mixture of truths, partial truths, and falsehoods, as well as many ideas that are neither good nor bad, just different from those of other groups. As a result, some of the theological mistakes that theologians make are *collective* or *communal* mistakes that are intrinsic to the order, community, or denomination to which they belong. These types of theological mistakes are often very difficult to correct. In the first place, such mistakes are incorporated into the foundational beliefs of the group and are, therefore, not commonly questioned; they are simply taken for granted. Secondly, one's acceptance of these beliefs is continually reinforced by one's colleagues in the group. Finally, any questioning of these beliefs may result in one's ejection from the group.

C. Cultural Mistakes

Theologians sometimes inadvertently make personal mistakes in their interpretation of Scriptures. Theologians also often share any theological mistakes that are incorporated into the foundational beliefs of the order, community, or denomination to which they belong. In addition, all theologians are vulnerable to the prevailing beliefs, right or wrong, of the culture or age in which they live. These theological mistakes often transcend any religious boundaries, and are shared by the majority of Christians living in that particular culture or age.

Culture-wide theological mistakes are the most difficult to correct or even identify. They are so deeply embedded in the background of our lives that we simply take them for granted; they are not obvious to us; no other interpretation seems possible. For instance, most southerners in the Deep South saw nothing wrong with slavery. It was simply a part of the natural order of things. Some races were inferior to other races and needed the guidance and direction of the superior races. Scriptures were interpreted to validate this viewpoint. Thus, to many people living in the South, the whole system of slavery seemed to be ordained by God. Science was called upon to provide empirical proof of racial inequality and scientists were able to deliver the desired results by various means, such as measuring the cranial capacity of the different races. Moreover, slavery made good economic sense. The owner of a large plantation could not harvest all the crops by himself, nor could he afford to hire enough laborers to do the work. Because of Noah's curse on Ham's son Canaan, God had provided an answer to this problem—the descendants of Ham were meant to be slaves.

Other cultures in other ages had similar blind spots when it came to certain interpretations of Scripture that we now know to be false. For thousands of years it was obvious to all that the earth was located at the center of the heavens. The sun, moon, and stars all rotated around the earth. This was a fact of nature that could be observed by everyone on earth, either by day or by night. Anyone who said otherwise was either a fool or a heretic. Theologians argued that the Bible confirmed the privileged position of the earth at the very center of creation. After all, the sun, moon, and stars were not even created until the fourth day of creation. Even Galileo, with his improved telescope, could not convince the church fathers otherwise.

III. THEOLOGIANS' BIASES

A. *Bias of Pride*

Theologians make mistakes in their interpretation of the Scriptures, not only through ignorance and unintentional mistakes, but also because of their own personal biases. They sometimes only see what they want to see and hear what they want to hear in the Scriptures, as Jesus said: "while seeing they do not see, and while hearing they do not hear, nor do they understand" (Matt. 13:13). Perhaps the primary reason for such spiritual blindness is human pride. Like all humans, theologians may magnify the importance of their own opinions to the point where they cannot accept instruction from the Scriptures. Instead of trying to understand the Scriptures, they use the Scriptures to justify their own favorite ideas or theories.

Theologians may be particularly prone to pride because of the exalted position they occupy. Like ministers, priests, or teachers, they stand in the gap between God and his people. They are often called upon to interpret and explain difficult passages in the Scriptures. Their success or failure at this task may have eternal consequences for those whom they are educating and influencing. Scientists, on the other hand, sometimes stand between their discipline and the general public, and attempt to interpret and explain scientific discoveries and theories, but their work is far less likely to have eternal consequences. Scientists are working with material things while theologians are dealing with spiritual matters; scientists are studying rocks, bones, and plants while theologians are handling the Word of God. It is little wonder that some theologians may be overawed by the status of the position to which they have ascended. However, Jesus warns that: "From everyone who has been given much, much will be required; and to whom they entrusted much, of him they will ask all the more" (Luke 12:48). James also warned: "Let not many of you become teachers, my brethren, knowing that as such we will incur a stricter judgment" (James 3:1).

Sadly, the scribes and Pharisees in Jesus's day provided many object lessons in the danger of being an interpreter of the law, and pride was one of their greatest stumbling blocks. Indeed, Jesus used these religious leaders in many of his parables; for example:

> Two men went up into the temple to pray, one a Pharisee and the other a tax collector. The Pharisee stood and was praying this to himself: "God, I thank You that I am not like other people: swindlers, unjust, adulterers, or even like this tax collector. I fast twice a week; I pay tithes of all that I get." But the tax collector, standing some distance away, was even unwilling to lift up his eyes to heaven, but was beating his breast, saying, "God, be merciful to me, the sinner!" I tell you, this man went to his house justified rather than the other; for everyone who exalts himself will be humbled, but he who humbles himself will be exalted. (Luke 18:10–12)

The scribes and Pharisees, however, were not humble. They chose to elevate their interpretations over the law that God had given to Moses (Matt. 15:9). They were even willing to argue with the Son of God concerning the will of his Heavenly Father. When Jesus would not concede to their teachings, they condemned Him to death.

Like the Pharisees in New Testament times, many of the church leaders and theologians during the Inquisition, as well as in the later Protestant Reformation, were proud men. They had such strong convictions about the rightness of their understanding and interpretation of the Scriptures that they were willing to put men and women to death who disagreed with their teachings—just as the scribes and Pharisees had done with Christ. Jesus taught his disciples that "Greater love has no one than this, that one lay down his life for his friends" (John 15:13). He called upon his disciples to follow his example: "If anyone wishes to come after Me, he must deny himself, and take up his cross daily and follow Me" (Luke 9:23). Christians were the ones who must be willing to die for their faith; they were the ones who should be giving up their lives for others. How did this clear teaching of Christ become so perverted that men thought they had the right to kill others in his name? There are still individuals in the church today who have such hatred for fellow Christians with whom they disagree they would no doubt be willing to put them to death, if the opportunity arose. Such a mindset is clearly in direct opposition to the teaching of Jesus: "A new commandment I give you, that you love one another, even as I have loved you, that you also love one another. By this all men will know that you are My disciples, if you have love for one another" (John 13:34–35). The bias of pride is a very potent spiritual poison for the theologian. All who succumb to this toxin are willfully ignorant of the fact that "There are six things which the Lord hates, Yes, seven which are an abomination to Him: Haughty eyes, a lying tongue, And hands that shed innocent blood" (Prov. 6:16–17), or "GOD IS OPPOSED TO THE PROUD, BUT GIVES GRACE TO THE HUMBLE" (James 4:6).

B. Bias of Power

Some theologians also fall victim to the lust for power. They covet the opportunity to tell others what to think or believe, whether or not they believe and do these things themselves. Once again the religious leaders and theologians of Jesus's time provide a cautionary tale of how not to think and act:

> The scribes and the Pharisees have seated themselves in the chair of Moses; therefore all that they tell you, do and observe, but do not do according to their deeds; for they say things and do not do them. They tie up heavy burdens and lay them on men's shoulders, but they themselves are unwilling to move them with so much as a finger. But they do all their deeds to be noticed by men; for they broaden their phylacteries and lengthen the tassels of their garments. They love the place of honor at banquets and the chief

seats in the synagogues, and respectful greetings in the market places, and being called Rabbi by men. (Matt. 23:6)

One of the reasons that these men were willing to put Jesus to death was that they were afraid his teachings and popularity would jeopardize their own privileged position with the Roman authorities. After Jesus raised Lazarus from the dead, "the chief priests and the Pharisees convened a council, and were saying, 'What are we doing? For this man is performing many signs. If we let Him go on like this, all men will believe in Him, and the Romans will come and take away both our place and our nation'" (John 11:47–48). The power the Roman rulers had given them over the Jewish people was more important to them than submitting to the one who had power over death itself. Talk about exchanging your birthright for a bowl of porridge! The desire to control the actions and thoughts of others is an ever-present temptation to mankind, especially those who are already in positions of authority. We are only too ready to take on a dictatorial role in the lives of our fellow humans and assume power that even God has chosen not to assume in order to grant humanity the gift of free will.

In New Testament times, Rome was the secular center of the ancient Mediterranean world. As the Roman Empire began to collapse in the fourth century A.D., the church stepped in to take its place. The Roman Catholic Church became the religious center for much of the world over the next thousand years, and the various popes often assumed the role of an emperor, or at least as the arbitrator between emperors and kings. The position of pope offered ambitious men the ultimate pathway to power, not only over the mundane affairs of the faithful, but even (presumably) over their eternal destinies through the power of excommunication. All the paraphernalia of power were also assumed by the religious leaders of the church, from costly and richly decorated robes and cloaks, to golden cups and utensils, as well as lavish palaces and churches, decorated with paintings and carvings by the world's greatest artists. What a contrast to their Savior who was born in a stable, raised by a peasant carpenter, crucified on a cross, and buried in the tomb of another man. As Lord Acton once noted, "Power tends to corrupt and absolute power corrupts absolutely" (Oxford 1979:1).

The lust for power has been particularly obvious in recent years in America as more and more religious leaders have become involved in politics. As has often been noted, politics is a dirty business. It should not be surprising then that the church has not been able to avoid staining its white robe as many of its leaders have descended into the political pit. Many ministers have abandoned a life of contemplation and prayer for the glamor of the political arena. They have been only too happy to escape from the relative obscurity of a local church or seminary to a position of power on the national stage. They love being photographed next to congressmen, senators, and presidents, thereby bathing in their fame (or notoriety), and embracing their causes—whether or not those causes are Christian, or even rational. Instead of taking the government captive for Christ—as they avowed they would do—they themselves have been taken captive by the world. Their moral duplicity is plain for all to see and they have become an object of ridicule by the unsaved and an embarrassment to many of their Christian brothers and sisters. Truly, the salt has lost its savor! Can the scriptural interpretations of such men and women be trusted when the driving force behind their lives seems to be their desire for the acquisition of power?

C. Bias of Profit

During Jesus's ministry on the earth, we have an example of a man consumed by his desire for world possessions in the person of Judas Iscariot, one of Christ's disciples. We first encounter Judas in Luke 6:16 and Matthew 10:4 where he is listed among the twelve apostles. In that same verse Luke also notes that Judas was he "who became a traitor" and Matthew says that he is "the one who betrayed Him". In his gospel, John first introduces Judas after Peter's confession to Jesus that "You are the Holy One of God" (John 6:69). Jesus then responds, "Did I Myself not choose you, the twelve, and yet one of you is a devil?" (v. 70). John goes on to explain: "Now he meant Judas the son of Simon Iscariot, for he, one of the twelve, was going to betray Him" (v. 71). Judas's later betrayal of Jesus has become permanently entwined with his name. We next see Judas with the disciples in the home of Mary, Martha, and Lazarus, about a week before the Passover. Mary knelt before Jesus and anointed his feet with costly perfume and wiped them with her hair. Judas disapproved of this show of devotion and asked why the perfume was not sold and the money given to the poor (John 12:1–5). John, however, tells us: "Now he said this, not because he was concerned about the poor, but because he was a thief, and as he had the money box, he used to pilfer what was put into it" (v. 6). Judas's love of money is so great that he even uses his decision to betray Christ to the Jewish authorities as an opportunity to enrich himself: "Then one of the twelve, named Judas Iscariot, went to the chief priests and said, 'What are you willing to give me to betray Him to you?' And they weighed out thirty pieces of silver to him. From then on he began looking for a good opportunity to betray Jesus" (Matt. 26:14–16). Through these actions, Judas not only becomes known forever after as the betrayer of Christ, he also provides one of the most infamous examples of what the love of money can drive a person to do: "For the love of money is a root of all sorts of evil, and some by longing for it have wandered away from the faith and pierced themselves with many griefs" (1 Tim. 6:10).

Following the death, resurrection, and ascension of Christ into heaven, the love of money continued to be a problem in the early church. Simon, a man from Samaria, who had formerly won the acclaim of the local population through his magical tricks, eventually became a Christian through the preaching of Philip. However, when Peter and John came to Samaria and laid their hands on the believers so that they too might receive the Holy Spirit, Simon saw this and offered the apostles money if they would give him the authority to also do this. Peter responded: "May your silver perish with you, because you thought you could obtain the gift of God with money! You have no part or portion in this matter, for your heart is not right before God. Therefore repent of this wickedness of yours, and pray the Lord that, if possible, the intention of your heart may be forgiven you" (Acts 8:20–22). Another example of followers of Christ in the early church whose desire for money was greater than their love for God, was a married couple:

> But a man named Ananias, with his wife Sapphira, sold a piece of property, and kept back some of the price for himself, with his wife's full knowledge, and bringing a portion of it, he laid it at the apostles' feet. But Peter said, "Ananias, why has Satan filled your heart to lie to the Holy Spirit and to keep back some of the price of the land? While it remained unsold, did it not remain your own? And after it was sold, was it not under your control? Why is it that you have conceived this deed in your heart? You have not lied to men but to God." And as he heard these words, Ananias fell down and breathed his last; and great fear came over all who heard of it. (Acts 5–1–5)

In his teachings, Jesus was very clear about the danger of loving and trusting in money, rather than God. Although a rich young ruler came to Jesus seeking eternal life, he declined to become a disciple of Christ because Jesus asked him to, "'go and sell all you possess and give to the poor, and you will have treasure in heaven; and come, follow me.' But at these words he was saddened, and he went away grieving, for he was one who owned much property" (Mark 10:21–22). Jesus then went on to explain to his disciples that "It is easier for a camel to go through the eye of a needle than for a rich man to enter the kingdom of God" (v. 25). As Jesus had noted on another occasion: "where your treasure is, there your heart will be also" (Matt. 6:21). The rich young ruler had to give up his possessions because they were dearer to him than God: "No one can serve two masters; for either he will hate the one and love the other, or he will be devoted to one and despise the other. You cannot serve God and wealth" (v. 24).

Despite the clear teachings of Jesus, many churches across America today are awash with theologians, preachers, teachers, and laymen who glory in their love of money and material possessions. This is especially true of formerly conservative and evangelical churches that have embraced the various versions of one of the great heresies of the present age: the prosperity gospel. These people believe that wealth is a sign of God's favor and the greater the wealth, the greater the favor. Someone has well said that only in materialistic America could such a perversion of the gospel arise and prosper. Leaders of these churches have even devised methods for enlisting God's help in their quest for wealth: through monetary donations, faith visualization, or the power of the spoken word (name it and claim it). How very different from the Jesus who told the rich young ruler to sell all his worldly possessions and then come follow him, who himself had no place to lay his head at night (Luke 9:58), and who, in death, left no worldly treasures behind, but only the garments he was wearing (Matt. 27:35). This same Jesus who commanded his disciples: "Do not store up for yourselves treasures on earth, where moth and rust destroy, and where thieves break in and steal. But store up for yourselves treasures in heaven, where neither moth nor rust destroys, and where thieves do not break in or steal; for where your treasure is, there your heart will be also" (Matt. 6:19–21).

Where then does this new gospel, this prosperity gospel, come from? It comes from pastors of megachurches who are not content with a few tens of thousands in their congregation, but crave a larger audience; megachurches whose members apparently have so little knowledge of the Bible that they are easily taken in by this sideshow of affluence. It comes from television evangelists who constantly harangue their listeners to send donations and faith pledges. They promise that, by this means, the donors will not only ensure their salvation, but also their prosperity here on the earth. Of course, the one sure thing is that these donations will enhance the coffers of the pastor or televangelist. Indeed, many of these so-called pastors and evangelists live lavish lifestyles to emphasize how much God is blessing them. Occasionally we are treated to pictures of their multi-room mansions, their jets, their newest offices and broadcasting complexes, or the biblical theme park they are currently building—all for the glory of God, of course. This whole tawdry structure is founded on a theological foundation that sits on a bed of sand. Prosperity theologians have managed to twist and cobble enough Scriptures together to at least give the appearance of a sound biblical base, just like the Pharisees did for the false religion of traditions which they created. In other words, many churches today are very similar to the church of Laodicea (Rev. 3:14) in John's time. Therefore, Jesus's admonition to that church may be equally valid today: "Because you say, 'I am rich, and have become wealthy, and have need of nothing,' and you do not know that you are wretched and miserable and poor and blind and naked, I advise you to buy from Me gold refined by fire so that you may become rich, and white garments so that you may clothe yourself, and that the shame of your nakedness will not be revealed; and eye salve to anoint your eyes so that you may see" (vv. 17–18). The bias of profit, the love of money, the desire for the things of the world, are still very much with us today and strongly influencing some of our interpretations of Scripture. Neither the theologian, nor the apostle, disciple, megachurch pastor, or televangelist, is apparently immune from this deadly desire. It is so powerful that, like the bias of pride or power, it can warp our understanding and interpretation of the Scriptures.

Conclusion

As with science, the empirical limitations of theology are considerable. All these limitations are directly tied to the humans who practice this discipline. Theologians, like scientists, do not have perfect knowledge of the things they study, and their ignorance may affect their understanding and interpretations. In particular, theologians sometimes have only limited knowledge in areas critical to their studies, including nature, the Scriptures, and God. Being human, theologians are also prone to make mistakes with the information they do have. These mistakes may be on a personal level, but they also may be communal or culture-wide. Theologians, like all men and women, also have their own personal biases, especially in areas involving their pride or their desire for power or profit. Therefore, they may bend or distort scriptural passages in order to make them fit their own personal beliefs. Christians must always approach the Scriptures, not only with reverence, but also humility. We may not always know as much as we think we know. We must always remain open to the guidance of the Holy Spirit, rather than presume that our theology is perfect because God's Word is perfect. The human discipline of theology sometimes distorts or gets in the way of the Spirit guiding us into a deeper understanding of the Scriptures. One of my seminary professors used to say that, if we are saved, it will be in spite of our theology, rather than because of it. The Bible itself is the ultimate source of truth, not our theological interpretations of the Scriptures: "There is a theology in and of the NT which is both bigger and better than our distinctive theological systems, indeed that biblical theology calls those systems to account and says 'it is in your distinctives that you are least faithful to the Word, not most faithful'" (Witherington 2005:254).

PART 3

THEOLOGICAL MISTAKES
CONCERNING THE MESSIAH

Chapter 7

The Pharisees' Theological Mistake Concerning the Messiah's Place of Birth

Introduction: The Pharisees

In the New Testament we are provided with a number of clear examples of the limitations of theological truth. In Chapter 2, we focused on the temporal limitations of theological truth as exemplified by the apostles' slowly developing understanding of who Jesus was and the nature of his mission upon the earth. The Pharisees provide an even better example of the limitations of theological truth. Jesus drew his apostles from the lower classes in Israel; from relatively unlearned men, such as fishermen and tax collectors. The Pharisees, on the other hand, were from the middle class; their numbers included many merchants and tradesmen. Unlike the Sadducees, the Pharisees were not born into the aristocracy. Instead, through their own efforts, they had achieved positions of respect and authority. Moreover, because of their devotion to the Scriptures and ritual purity, the Pharisees were held in high esteem by the common people as the *experts* on the law of Moses and its interpretation.

Many of the Jews in the Intertestamental Period, including the Pharisees, believed (quite correctly) that the fall of Jerusalem in 586 B.C. and the 70 years of captivity in Babylon were the direct result of their neglect or abandonment of the law of Moses. As a consequence, their physical return to Jerusalem and the Promised Land in 538 B.C. was also accompanied by a renewed interest in studying the law of Moses and trying to adhere to its moral precepts. So great was their fear of departing from the law and again being subjected to the wrath of God, many Jewish scholars attempted to build a hedge of oral rules and traditions around the law of Moses, which, if strictly adhered to, would prevent them from even coming close to disobeying God's laws. Unfortunately, over time these oral traditions came to be viewed on a par with Scripture, assuming the same importance as the law of Moses. On a practical level, one might argue that, among the Pharisees and their followers, these oral traditions became even more important than the law of Moses. If one faithfully adhered to these oral rules and traditions, they need not worry about the law of Moses since they would never be in danger of breaking those laws. Unfortunately, in building this hedge around the law of Moses, they lost sight of the actual laws and, in effect, created their own religion. This is one of the reasons that Jesus often condemned the Pharisees:

> The Pharisees and the scribes asked Him, "Why do Your disciples not walk according to the tradition of the elders, but eat their bread with impure hands?" And He said to them, "Rightly did Isaiah prophesy of you hypocrites, as it is written: 'THIS PEOPLE HONORS ME WITH THEIR LIPS, BUT THEIR HEART IS FAR AWAY FROM ME. BUT IN VAIN DO THEY WORSHIP ME, TEACHING AS DOCTRINES THE PRECEPTS OF MEN.'" (Mark 7:5–8)

> Woe to you, scribes and Pharisees, hypocrites! For you tithe mint and dill and cumin, and have neglected the weightier provisions of the law: justice and mercy and faithfulness; but these are the things you should have done without neglecting the others. (Matt. 23:23)

A second reason that Jesus frequently condemned the Pharisees was that they had come to believe that if they carefully obeyed all these oral traditions to the letter, they could achieve righteousness and be justified before God. Unfortunately, their oral traditions were largely focused on outward actions rather than the inner condition of their hearts. They grew proud and arrogant over their great knowledge of the Scriptures and rigid adherence to all their oral traditions. But Jesus said to them:

> Woe to you, scribes and Pharisees, hypocrites! For you clean the outside of the cup and of the dish, but inside they are full of robbery and self-indulgence. You blind Pharisee, first clean the inside of the cup and of the dish, so that the outside of it may become clean also. Woe to you, scribes and Pharisees, hypocrites! For you are like whitewashed tombs which on the outside appear beautiful, but inside they are full of dead men's bones and all uncleanness. So you, too, outwardly appear righteous to men, but inwardly you are full of hypocrisy and lawlessness. (Matt. 23:25–28)

The greatest error of the Pharisees, however, was their failure to understand that the ultimate purpose of the law of Moses was not to provide a pathway by which men and women could achieve righteousness. Instead it was given to highlight humanity's fallen condition and inability to be like their Heavenly Father or obey his commands. As the apostle Paul explained:

> Is the Law then contrary to the promises of God? May it never be! For if a law had been given which was able to impart life, then righteousness would indeed have been based on law. But the Scripture has shut up everyone under sin, so that the promise by faith in Jesus Christ might be given to those who believe. But before faith came, we were kept in custody under the law, being shut up to the faith which was later to be revealed. Therefore the Law has become our tutor to lead us to Christ, so that we may be justified by faith. (Gal. 3:21–24)

Long before the time of the Pharisees, King David understood the limitations of fallen humanity and looked forward to the
coming of the Holy One who would save us from our sins, who
would justify us before God through his own righteousness: "The
LORD has looked down from heaven upon the sons of men To see
if there are any who understand, Who seek after God. They have all
turned aside, together they have become corrupt; There is no one
who does good, not even one. . . . Oh, that the salvation of Israel
would come out of Zion! When the LORD restores His captive
people, Jacob will rejoice, Israel will be glad" (Ps. 14:2–3, 7). A thousand years after the time of King David, the Pharisees still looked
forward to the coming of the Messiah. Indeed, through their efforts
to achieve righteousness by perfectly obeying the law of Moses,
they believed that they could actually hasten his coming. Yet, the
Messiah they longed for was not the Savior that King David foretold, not a Redeemer who would save his people from their sins.
The Pharisees wanted a Messiah who would finally bring an end to
the long reign of foreigners over the land of Israel: the Babylonians,
the Persians, the Greeks, and now the hated Romans. They wanted
a Messiah who would restore the autonomy and glory of ancient
Israel, usher in a glorious period of peace and prosperity, and, no
doubt, elevate the Pharisees to the positions of power and honor
that they believed they deserved. In believing these things, they
were stacking one theological mistake after another on top of each
other. Although, in their day, the Pharisees were the acknowledged
experts on the law of Moses and its interpretation, their theology—
their understanding of both the purpose and promise of the law—
was badly flawed. Indeed, when the Messiah finally arrived, the
Pharisees did not even recognize him as such. Instead, after many
discussions and arguments with him, they finally ended up calling
for his death. As the apostle John noted: "He came to His own, and
those who were His own did not receive Him" (John 1:11). Jesus
ended his condemnation of the scribes and Pharisees in Matthew
chapter 23 with a cry of anguish for them and all the Jews: "Jerusalem, Jerusalem, who kills the prophets and stones those who are
sent to her! How often I wanted to gather your children together,

the way a hen gathers her chicks under her wings, and you were unwilling" (Matt. 23:37).

I. HISTORICAL CONTEXT: THE TIME OF THE PHARISEES

Merrill Tenney has noted that: "The roots of the Pharisees can be traced to the 'Hasidim' of the 2nd cent.—those 'pious men' of Israel whose loyalty to their covenant relationship with Yahweh impelled them to resist the increasing pressure toward Helleniza- tion" (1976:745). He also points out that the name *Pharisee* is prob- ably derived from a Hebrew word that means *to separate*, although who they were to be separate from is somewhat unclear: the Gentiles, the Jewish aristocracy (Hasmonean rulers), or the common people (ibid.). Outside the New Testament, one of the earliest references to the Pharisees is found in the writings of Flavius Josephus (A.D. 37–100). In his book *The War of the Jews* (Book 1 Chapter 5, Verse 2), which was written c. A.D. 75, Josephus recorded:

> And now the Pharisees joined themselves to her [Salome Alex- andra] (141–67 BCE)] to assist her in the government. These are a certain sect of the Jews that appear more religious than others, and seem to interpret the laws more accurately. Now, Alexandra hearkened to them to an extraordinary degree, as being herself a woman of great piety towards God. But these Pharisees artfully insinuated themselves into her favour by little and little, and became themselves the real administrators of the public affairs: they banished and reduced whom they pleased; they bound and loosed [men] at their pleasure; and, to say all at once, they had the enjoyment of the royal authority, whilst the expenses and the diffi- culties of it belonged to Alexandra. She was a sagacious woman in the management of great affairs, and intent always upon gather- ing soldiers together; so that she increased the army the one half, and procured a great body of foreign troops, till her own nation became not only very powerful at home, but terrible also to foreign potentates, while she governed other people, and the Pharisees governed her. (1970a:434)

Josephus also mentioned the Pharisees in his book, *The Antiquities of the Jews* (Book 13, Chapter 5, Verse 9), which was written c. A.D. 94. In this book he noted that:

> At this time there were three sects among the Jews, who had different opinions concerning human actions; the one was called the sect of the Pharisees, another the sect of the Sadducees, and the other the sect of the Essens. Now for the Pharisees, they say that some actions, but not all, are the work of fate, and some of them are in our own power, and that they are liable to fate, but are not caused by fate. But the sect of the Essens affirm, that fate governs all things, and that nothing befalls men but what is according to its determination. And for the Sadducees, they take away fate, and say there is no such thing, and that the events of human affairs are not at its disposal; but they suppose that all our actions are in our power, so that we are ourselves the causes of what is good, and receive what is evil from our own folly. However, I have given a more exact account of these opinions in the second book of the Jewish War. (1970b:274)

In Josephus's first account we see a rather unflattering picture of the Pharisee's activities in the Hasmonean Court, one not inconsistent with what we would expect from reading the New Testament accounts: the Pharisees using religion to advance their own prestige and power.

Josephus was writing about events that occurred in the second and first centuries B.C.. By this time, the Great Babylonian Empire, which had reached its zenith under King Nebuchadnezzar, was just a distant memory, as was the Persian Empire under Cyrus the Great and his successors. In their place had arisen the third kingdom of Daniel's vision by the Ulai Canal in Elam: The Greek Empire under Alexander the Great. Daniel tells us:

> Then I lifted my eyes and looked, and behold, a ram [Medeo-Persia] which had two horns was standing in front of the canal. Now the two horns were long, but one was longer than the other, with the longer one coming up last. I saw the ram butting west-

ward, northward, and southward, and no other beasts could stand
before him nor was there anyone to rescue from his power, but
he did as he pleased and magnified himself. While I was observing, behold, a male goat [Greece] was coming from the west over
the surface of the whole earth without touching the ground; and
the goat had a conspicuous horn between his eyes. He came up
to the ram that had the two horns, which I had seen standing in
front of the canal, and rushed at him in his mighty wrath. I saw
him come beside the ram, and he was enraged at him; and he
struck the ram and shattered his two horns, and the ram had no
strength to withstand him. So he hurled him to the ground and
trampled on him, and there was none to rescue the ram from his
power. Then the male goat magnified himself exceedingly. But as
soon as he was mighty, the large horn was broken; and in its place
there came up four conspicuous horns toward the four winds of
heaven. (Dan. 8:3–8)

The *notable horn* on the goat was Alexander the Great (356–323
B.C.). At the time of his death, Alexander's empire stretched from
Greece to India, and included both Egypt and Israel. Because
Alexander had failed to choose a successor before his untimely
death in the palace of Nebuchadnezzar II in Babylon when he was
only 32 years old, his generals began to fight for control of this
vast empire. These wars of succession became known as the Wars
of the Diadochi (322–275 B.C.). The victorious generals in these
wars eventually divided up Alexander's empire into four parts: (1)
the earlier Antipatrid and later Antigonid dynasties in Macedo-
nia, (2) the Kingdom of Pergamon in Asia Minor, (3) the Ptolemaic Kingdom in Egypt, and (4) the Seleucid Empire in Syria,
which included much of the Near East and Asia. This division of
Alexander the Great's empire was also revealed to Daniel:

The ram which you saw with the two horns represents the kings
of Media and Persia. The shaggy goat represents the kingdom of
Greece, and the large horn that is between his eyes is the first king.
The broken horn and the four horns that arose in its place repre-

sent four kingdoms which will arise from his nation, although not
with his power. (Dan. 8:20–22)

In the first year of Darius the Mede, I [an angel] arose to be an
encouragement and a protection for him. And now I will tell you
the truth. Behold, three more kings are going to arise in Persia.
Then a fourth will gain far more riches than all of them; as soon
as he becomes strong through his riches, he will arouse the whole
empire against the realm of Greece. And a mighty king will arise,
and he will rule with great authority and do as he pleases. But as
soon as he has arisen, his kingdom will be broken up and parceled
out toward the four points of the compass, though not to his own
descendants, nor according to his authority which he wielded, for
his sovereignty will be uprooted and given to others besides them.
(Dan. 11:1–4)

After the fall of the Persian Empire to Alexander the Great
in 333 B.C., Palestine initially became a vassal state of Alexander's
Greek Empire and then, following Alexander's death in 323 B.C., the
Ptolemaic Kingdom in Egypt (323–30 B.C.). As a vassal state under
the previous Persian Empire, the Jews had largely been allowed to
govern their own affairs and practice their own religion. Similar
arrangements occurred under Alexander and then the Ptolemaic
Kingdom in Egypt. However, continued warfare between Alexander's generals, especially Seleucus I Nicator (who eventually
gained control over much of the Near Eastern and Asian portion
of Alexander the Great's empire), and Ptolemy I Soter (who gained
control of Egypt and parts of the eastern Mediterranean), as well
as the successors of these two generals, often put the land of Israel
squarely in the center of these conflicts. Caught between these
warring factions, the control of Jerusalem changed hands seven
times between 319 and 302 B.C.. The Ptolemaic Kingdom's claim
to Palestine would repeatedly be challenged over the next century
until the Seleucid king, Antiochus III (The Great) (r. 223–187 B.C.),
finally gained control of Palestine after the Battle of Panion which
was fought in the Jordan Valley in 198 B.C. Thus, Palestine passed

into the hands of the rulers of the Seleucid Empire (312 B.C. to 63 B.C.) who had their capitol in Syria.

All the rulers of those portions of Alexander's empire that lay outside of Greece attempted to maintain control of the local populations through the presence of Greek soldiers and colonists; by building Greek cities, temples, and gymnasiums; as well as enculturating (Hellenizing) the native peoples into Greek sports, Greek religious beliefs, etc. Perhaps the most enthusiastic propagators of Hellenization were the Seleucid rulers, since they controlled the largest and most diverse portion of Alexander's empire and therefore had the greatest need for means to integrate these different cultures into a cohesive political unit. Many of the Jews, however, were not about to abandon their belief in one God for the polytheistic beliefs of the Greeks, nor were they ready to lay aside their moral codes for such common Greek practices as nude wrestling or homosexuality.

Antiochus III was followed by Seleucus IV Philopator (r. 187–175 B.C.), who sent his general, Heliodorus, to Jerusalem to collect money from the temple to help pay a war-indemnity to the Romans that had been imposed on Antiochus III at the Treaty of Apamea in 188 B.C. Seleucus IV Philopator is probably another Greek king mentioned in the revelation to Daniel: "Then in his place one will arise who will send an oppressor through the Jewel of his kingdom; yet within a few days he will be shattered, though not in anger nor in battle. In his place a despicable person will arise, on whom the honor of kingship has not been conferred, but he will come in a time of tranquility and seize the kingdom by intrigue" (Dan. 11:20–21). After returning from Jerusalem, Heliodorus assassinated Seleucus IV Philopator and seized the throne for himself—but was subsequently ousted by Antiochus IV Epiphanes (r. 175–163 B.C.) who became the eighth king of the Seleucid Empire. Antiochus IV Epiphanes was likely the *vile person* previously mentioned in Daniel's revelation. He was the first Seleucid king to refer to himself as a god (Epiphanes means *God Manifest*), although many of his subjects referred to him as Epimanes (which means *The Mad*). Daniel prophesied that:

> Out of one of them [the four horns] came forth a rather small horn
> which grew exceedingly great toward the south, toward the east,
> and toward the Beautiful Land. It grew up to the host of heaven
> and caused some of the host and some of the stars to fall to the
> earth, and it trampled them down. It even magnified itself to be
> equal with the Commander of the host; and it removed the regular
> sacrifice from Him, and the place of His sanctuary was thrown
> down. (Dan. 8:9–11)

> Then the king will do as he pleases, and he will exalt and magnify
> himself above every god and will speak monstrous things against
> the God of gods; and he will prosper until the indignation is
> finished, for that which is decreed will be done. He will show no
> regard for the gods of his fathers or for the desire of women, nor
> will he show regard for any other god; for he will magnify himself
> above them all. (Dan. 11:36–37)

Unlike the Persians or Ptolemies, who had allowed the Jews to
follow their cultural and religious beliefs, Antiochus IV, considering himself to be God, had little respect for the Jewish religion or
culture. He attempted to force the Jews to adopt many Greek beliefs
and practices. In 167, after a rebellion of the Jews in Jerusalem over
his replacement of the high priest, Jason, with his own man, Mene-
laus, Antiochus IV retook Jerusalem and garrisoned it with Syrian
soldiers. Moreover, he banned all Jewish religious rites (such as
circumcision and the Sabbath), he erected an altar to Zeus in the
temple and sacrificed a pig on the altar; he also had sacrifices made
at the feet of an idol bearing his own image (Grainger 2012:5–6;
Sievers 1990:19–20; Tcherikover 1972:138–140).

The religious atrocities of Antiochus IV resulted in the Macca-
bean Revolt (167 to 160 B.C.). This revolt began when Mattathias
the Hasmonean rejected Antiochus's attempt to Hellenize the
Jewish faith and struck down a fellow priest who was about to offer
a sacrifice to an idol. Mattathias and his five sons then became the
driving force behind a guerrilla war against the occupying Syrians.
After his soldiers were defeated by the Maccabees in several small

battles, Antiochus IV raised a large Seleucid army to crush the rebels, but he died (160 B.C.) before this could be accomplished. The commander of this Seleucid army, Lysias, reached a compromise with the Maccabees that restored the Jews' religious freedom (Avi-Yonah 1972:162–164). After this, the Seleucid Empire largely turned its attention away from Palestine, as growing threats from the Romans on their western frontier and Parthians on their eastern frontier, gave them more important things to worry about. In 104 B.C., Judah Aristobulus I (140–103 B.C.), the great-grandson of Mattathias the Hasmonean, declared himself king of Judea and thereby founded the Hasmonean Dynasty, which ruled until 63 B.C., when the Romans arrived and annexed the land of Judea to their Empire.

Judah Aristobulus I, the first king of the Hasmonean Dynasty, was the husband of Salome Alexandra (141–67 B.C.) who was previously mentioned in Josephus's account of the Pharisees during the second century B.C. (1970a:434). Following the death of Judah Aristobulus I in 103 B.C., Salome Alexandra married his brother Alexander Jannaeus (127–76 B.C.). She governed Jerusalem while her husband was away at war but, after his death in 76 B.C., she ruled as queen over Judea (76–67 B.C.). Before his death, however, Alexander Jannaeus altered his approach to the Pharisees. As Abraham Schalit has noted: "Jannaeus finally tired of the civil war and of the unending struggle against the Pharisees and, according to the sources, advised his wife Salome before his death to compromise with the Pharisees. This appears very probable, since Jannaeus felt that the civil war was undermining the strength of the kingdom, which was bound to fall into the hands of its neighbors if the internal strife did not cease" (1972:296). Salome Alexandra followed her husband's advice in this matter concerning the Pharisees. Indeed, as Josephus recorded: "Now, Alexandra hearkened to them to an extraordinary degree, as being herself a woman of great piety towards God. But these Pharisees artfully insinuated themselves into her favour by little and little, and became themselves the real administrators of the public affairs" (1970a:434).

The Pharisees' favored position changed following Queen Salome's death in 67 B.C. when civil war broke out between her two sons, Hyrcanus II and Aristobulus II, for control of the kingdom. Before her death she had appointed her elder son, Hyrcanus II as both high priest and co-ruler with her. As Kenneth Atkinson notes in his book *Queen Salome: Jerusalem's Warrior Monarch of the First Century B.C.E.*: "Salome Alexandra's decision to name her eldest son as her political successor also meant that the Pharisees would continue to dominate the temple and the courts" (2012:222). Shortly before her death, however, Hyrcanus II began to persecute the Sadducees, thereby giving his brother Aristobulus II, who was a Sadducee, an excuse to try and overthrow him. Both sons, fighting against each other for control of the kingdom, sought the aid of the Romans, who were at that time solidifying their control over Syria and what remained of the Seleucid Empire. When the Romans threw their support behind Aristobulus II the Pharisees, realizing they might lose their control over the temple and court, encouraged the Romans to abolish the entire Hasmonean Dynasty. Schalit explains that:

> Provided they were allowed to do as they pleased, the Pharisees did not undermine the foundation of the Hasmonean kingdom. But the moment it seemed to them that their aims were in jeopardy, they did not hesitate to sacrifice the national state, so long as they would be in a position to strive for the Kingdom of the Messiah. This is how they acted during the quarrel of Jannaeus' two sons before Pompey. At that time the Pharisees feared that Aristobulus II, who resembled his father, would triumph. They therefore suggested to the Roman conqueror that he abolish the Hasmonean kingdom altogether, since it was not consonant with Jewish tradition. (1972:296–297)

The Romans were only too happy to follow the Pharisees' suggestion. They took over control of Judea and replaced the Hasmonean Dynasty with one of their own, the Herodian Dynasty. Thus, both because of their manipulations and quest for religious and political power, as well as their desire to be separate from the common people, the Greeks, and the Jewish aristocracy, the Pharisees were instrumental in helping bring about the fulfillment of Daniel's prophecy concerning a fourth kingdom, that would follow that of the Babylonian, Persian, and Greek Empires—the Roman Empire:

> You, O king, were looking and behold, there was a single great statue; that statue, which was large and of extraordinary splendor, was standing in front of you, and its appearance was awesome. The head of that statue was made of fine gold, its breast and its arms of silver, its belly and its thighs of bronze, its legs of iron, its feet partly of iron and partly of clay. You continued looking until a stone was cut out without hands, and it struck the statue on its feet of iron and clay and crushed them. Then the iron, the clay, the bronze, the silver and the gold were crushed all at the same time and became like chaff from the summer threshing floors; and the wind carried them away so that not a trace of them was found. But the stone that struck the statue became a great mountain and filled the whole earth. (Dan. 2:31–35)

> After this I kept looking in the night visions, and behold, a fourth beast, dreadful and terrifying and extremely strong; and it had large iron teeth. It devoured and crushed and trampled down the remainder with its feet; and it was different from all the beasts that were before it, and it had ten horns. (Dan. 7:7)

Ironically, in their rejection of earthly kingdoms and their desire for a messianic kingdom, the Pharisees helped bring into existence the Herodian Dynasty whose first king, King Herod the Great, would attempt to kill their long-awaited Messiah after learning from the wise men of his birth in Bethlehem. This is not so ironic when we consider the fact that their fellow Pharisees later plotted to kill the Messiah and eventually brought him before the Roman prefect, Pontius Pilate, and demanded that he be executed for blasphemy. Despite their expertise in the law of Moses and its interpretation, despite their longing for the coming of the Messiah, despite their efforts to speed his coming by trying to achieve righteousness through obedience to the law (or at least the oral traditions surrounding the law), they did not even recognize the Messiah when he arrived upon the earth. Instead, they were repeatedly involved in attempts to put the Messiah to death. How could they have made such a grave theological mistake?

II. PROPHECIES CONCERNING THE MESSIAH'S PLACE OF BIRTH

For more than one thousand years the Jews had been awaiting the coming of the Messiah. Indeed, as noted previously in Chapter 2, some theologians have suggested that the first mention of a future savior of mankind was made by God in the garden of Eden after Adam and Eve disobeyed God and ate from the Tree of Knowledge of Good and Evil: "And I will put enmity Between you and the woman, And between your seed and her seed; He shall bruise you on the head, And you shall bruise him on the heel" (Gen. 3:15). Be that as it may, a somewhat clearer prophecy concerning the blessing that a future redeemer will bring is found in a promise given first to Abraham, and then to his descendants Isaac (Gen. 26:4) and Jacob (Gen. 28:14): "Now the LORD said to Abram, 'Go forth from your country, And from your relatives And from your father's house, To the land which I will show you; And I will make you a great nation, And I will bless you, And make your name great; And so you shall be a blessing; And I will bless those who bless you, And the one who curses you I will curse. And in you all the families of the earth will be blessed'" (Gen. 12:1–3). This promise was fulfilled at the birth of he who was to become the Savior of both the Jews and the Gentiles; it was through a direct line of decent from Abraham, through Isaac, Jacob, Boaz, Jesse, and David. In the fullness of time, the promised Savior was born in Bethlehem (Matt. 1:1–17). Moreover, Abraham's willingness to sacrifice his son on Mount Moriah was a prefigurement of the sacrifice that God would himself later make with his own Son at Golgotha. According to many Christian scholars, the place where God instructed Abraham to sacrifice his son Isaac, Mount Moriah, was the same location where Solomon built the temple, and near where Jesus was later crucified (see Table 12):

Table 12: Scriptures concerning Mount Moriah
He said, "Take now your son, your only son, whom you love, Isaac, and go to the land of Moriah, and offer him there as a burnt offering on one of the mountains of which I will tell you." (Gen. 22:2)
Then Solomon began to build the house of the LORD in Jerusalem on Mount Moriah, where the LORD had appeared to his father David, at the place that David had prepared on the threshing floor of Ornan the Jebusite. (2 Chron. 3:1)
They took Jesus, therefore, and He went out, bearing His own cross, to the place called the Place of a Skull, which is called in Hebrew, Golgotha. There they crucified Him, and with Him two other men, one on either side, and Jesus in between. (John 19:17–18)

It was not until a thousand years after the time of Abraham, however, and a thousand years before the birth of Christ, that those prophecies explaining exactly how God would bless all the families of the earth through the seed of Abraham, Isaac, and Jacob, came into clearer focus. Through his servant, David, God revealed that he was sending his only Son to redeem mankind from their sins. Indeed, the Psalms are filled with detailed prophecies concerning the Messiah; these prophecies begin in the second chapter:

> Why are the nations in an uproar And the peoples devising a vain thing? The kings of the earth take their stand And the rulers take counsel together Against the LORD and against His Anointed, saying, "Let us tear their fetters apart And cast away their cords from us!" He who sits in the heavens laughs, The Lord scoffs at them. Then He will speak to them in His anger And terrify them in His fury, saying, "But as for Me, I have installed My King Upon Zion, My holy mountain." "I will surely tell of the decree of the LORD: He said to Me, 'You are My Son, Today I have begotten You. Ask of Me, and I will surely give the nations as Your inheritance, And the very ends of the earth as Your possession. You shall break them with a rod of iron, You shall shatter them like earthenware.'" Now therefore, O kings, show discernment; Take warning, O

judges of the earth. Worship the LORD with reverence And rejoice with trembling. Do homage to the Son, that He not become angry, and you perish in the way, For His wrath may soon be kindled. How blessed are all who take refuge in Him! (Ps. 2:1–12)

After the time of David, God continued to send prophets to the kings of Judah and Israel. Through these prophets (Isa. 42:1–7, 53:1–12; Jer. 31:15; Ezek. 34:23–24; Dan. 2:44–45; Hos. 11:1; Mic. 5:2; Hag. 2:7; Zech. 9:9–10; Mal. 3:1), God provided even more precise details concerning his Son and the nature of his mission on the earth. Approximately 700 years before Mary gave birth to Jesus in Bethlehem, the prophet Micah (~737–696 B.C.) foretold that the Messiah would be born in this small Judean village in the hills some six miles south of Jerusalem:

> But as for you, Bethlehem Ephrathah, Too little to be among the clans of Judah, From you One will go forth for Me to be ruler in Israel. His goings forth are from long ago, From the days of eternity. Therefore He will give them up until the time When she who is in labor has borne a child. Then the remainder of His brethren Will return to the sons of Israel. And He will arise and shepherd His flock In the strength of the LORD, In the majesty of the name of the LORD His God. And they will remain, Because at that time He will be great To the ends of the earth. This One will be our peace. (Mic. 5:2–5)

Micah prophesied over a 53-year period during the reigns of three kings of Judah: Jotham (740–732 B.C.), Ahaz (732–716 B.C.), and Hezekiah (716–687 B.C.). At that time, the fall of Jerusalem (586 B.C.) to the Babylonians, was still about one hundred years in the future, the conquest of the Babylonian Empire by the Persians (539 B.C.) was about 150 years in the future, the fall of the Persian Empire to the Greeks (330 B.C.) was around 350 years in the future, and the annexation of Judea to the Roman Empire (63 B.C.) was about 650 years in the future. Nevertheless, God revealed to Micah the exact location where the Messiah would be born, in Bethlehem of Judea.

The earliest biblical record we have for the existence of Bethlehem is in Genesis, where it is recorded that Isaac's wife, Rachel, died near Bethlehem while giving birth to Benjamin (Gen. 35:16–20). After spending 400 years in Egypt, the children of Israel returned to Canaan and conquered it under the leadership of Joshua. Over the next 400 years, the Israelites were governed by a series of judges. It was during this period of the judges that Naomi, after the death of her husband in Moab, returned to Bethlehem with her daughter-in-law Ruth (Ruth 1:19–22). Finally, after the first king of Israel, Saul, disobeyed God, God sent Samuel to Bethlehem to anoint David, the son of Jessie, to be king over Israel (1 Sam. 16:1–13). Therefore, it seems altogether fitting that the Messiah, the Son of David, should be born in Bethlehem: the village near where Abraham's son's wife (Rachel) died and was buried, the village where Boaz and Ruth—other family members in the line leading to Christ— lived (Matt. 1:5), and the village where David was anointed king by Samuel.

III. FULFILLMENT OF PROPHECIES CONCERNING THE MESSIAH'S PLACE OF BIRTH

> But when the fullness of the time came, God sent forth His Son, born of a woman, born under the Law, so that He might redeem those who were under the Law, that we might receive the adoption as sons. (Gal. 4:4–5)

Micah's prophecy concerning the birthplace of the Messiah was fulfilled some 700 years later, in part because of the convergence of several lines in human history. Two of these lines were: (1) the 42 generations of Abraham's children, through which Joseph, the husband of Mary had descended, and (2) the four great kingdoms foreseen by the prophet Daniel (Babylonian, Medo-Persian, Greek, and Roman) which concluded with the annexation of Judea by the Romans in 63 B.C.. Because the Roman, Caesar Augustus, had issued a decree that a census be taken, Joseph, a descendant of the house and family of David who was living in Nazareth, had to return to Bethlehem in order to register for this census. It was while Joseph was in Bethlehem with his wife Mary (a virgin), that she gave birth to her firstborn child:

> Now in those days a decree went out from Caesar Augustus, that a census be taken of all the inhabited earth. This was the first census taken while Quirinius was governor of Syria. And everyone was on his way to register for the census, each to his own city. Joseph also went up from Galilee, from the city of Nazareth, to Judea, to the city of David which is called Bethlehem, because he was of the house and family of David, in order to register along with Mary, who was engaged to him, and was with child. While they were there, the days were completed for her to give birth. And she gave birth to her firstborn son; and she wrapped Him in cloths, and laid Him in a manger, because there was no room for them in the inn. (Luke 2:1–7)

Although some 700 years had passed since Micah had made his prophecy, the Jewish chief priests, scribes, Pharisees, and Sadducees were nevertheless quite familiar with its content. When the magi from the east came to King Herod in Jerusalem in search of he "who has been born King of the Jews," whose star they had seen in the east, the chief priests and scribes knew exactly where to look for the prophecy concerning the Messiah's place of birth:

> Now after Jesus was born in Bethlehem of Judea in the days of Herod the king, magi from the east arrived in Jerusalem, saying, "Where is He who has been born King of the Jews? For we saw His star in the east and have come to worship Him." When Herod the king heard this, he was troubled, and all Jerusalem with him. Gathering together all the chief priests and scribes of the people, he inquired of them where the Messiah was to be born. They said to him, "In Bethlehem of Judea; for this is what has been written by the prophet: 'AND YOU, BETHLEHEM, LAND OF JUDAH, ARE BY NO MEANS LEAST AMONG THE LEADERS OF JUDAH;

FOR OUT OF YOU SHALL COME FORTH A RULER WHO WILL SHEPHERD MY PEOPLE ISRAEL.'" (Matt. 2:1–6)

This King Herod (74–4 B.C.) was the very king whom the Romans had put on the throne in place of Salome Alexandra's son, Aristobulus II. When Herod came to realize that the magi were not going to return to him and report who the child was, as he had commanded them, he sent his soldiers to Bethlehem and killed all the male children who were two years old or younger, thereby inadvertently fulfilling another prophecy about the Messiah by a prophet who lived during the time of the Babylonian captivity: "Thus says the LORD, 'A voice is heard in Ramah, Lamentation and bitter weeping. Rachel is weeping for her children; She refuses to be comforted for her children, Because they are no more'" (Jer. 31:15). In his gospel, Matthew tells us of the fulfillment of this prophecy, "Then when Herod saw that he had been tricked by the magi, he became very enraged, and sent and slew all the male children who were in Bethlehem and all its vicinity, from two years old and under, according to the time which he had determined from the magi. Then what had been spoken through Jeremiah the prophet was fulfilled: 'A VOICE WAS HEARD IN RAMAH, WEEPING AND GREAT MOURNING, RACHEL WEEPING FOR HER CHILDREN; AND SHE REFUSED TO BE COMFORTED, BECAUSE THEY WERE NO MORE'" (Matt. 2:16–18). In the Old Testament, *Ramah* is a name given to several sites in ancient Israel. Ramah is also one of the cities given to the tribe of Benjamin (Josh. 18:25) and is one of the cities to which the sons of Benjamin returned after the Babylonian captivity (Neh. 11:31–33). Moreover, Bethlehem was the village where Benjamin was born to Rachel. The prophecy in Jeremiah (31:15) and its fulfillment in Matthew (2:16–18) neatly tie these four elements together: Bethlehem, Rachel, Benjamin, and Ramah.

The Pharisees who were present in Jerusalem during the visit of the magi would have certainly known of the magi's inquiry, since the Pharisees, being *experts* on the law of Moses and some of their number being scribes, were no doubt called upon to explain

to Herod where the King of the Jews was to be born. They also
would have heard about the ensuing slaughter of the children in
Bethlehem, since it was only six miles south of Jerusalem. Indeed,
this latter event no doubt gave the Pharisees even more reason for
hating the Romans, as well as King Herod whom the Romans had
chosen to rule over Judea in place of the Hasmonian Dynasty. We
might excuse the Pharisees for assuming that the magi's interpretation of the star was wrong, since Herod had killed all the children in Bethlehem who were born at that time, and God would
certainly not allow this to happen to the Messiah. Of course we
know that Joseph, being warned by God in a dream, had escaped
into Egypt with Mary and the baby before the massacre in Bethlehem had occurred. We also know that none of the Pharisees
had been invited by God to witness the birth of his Son, but only
the lowly shepherds and the angelic host. On the other hand, one
wonders if there was no stirring of memories about these events
some 30 years later, when a man of about 30 years of age began to
perform miracles and proclaim that "the Kingdom of Heaven is at
hand" (Mark 1:15) .

IV. MISUNDERSTANDING OF PROPHECIES
CONCERNING THE MESSIAH'S PLACE OF BIRTH

It is apparent that the Pharisees were both aware and interested in the ministry of Christ from its outset. Indeed, some of
their numbers, including Nicodemus, and later Paul, became
followers of Christ. The majority of the Pharisees, however,
soon found reason to reject his person and teachings. Christ not
only ignored the oral traditions which the Pharisees so rigor-
ously followed, but often chose to blatantly defy those traditions,
such as the prohibition against healing the sick on the Sabbath.
Even worse, he openly criticized their righteousness before the
masses and called into question their understanding of the law
of Moses.

If the Pharisees had any doubts about their justification for
rejecting the words of this man called Jesus, they no doubt soothed
their consciences with the fact that this teacher and healer was

Jesus of Nazareth, not *Jesus of Bethlehem.* Unlike Bethlehem, Nazareth is not even mentioned in the Old Testament; neither in the law nor the prophets is there any reference to this small village in Galilee. Instead of being associated with patriarchs or kings, like Bethlehem, Nazareth was looked down upon as a place one would rather not be from. As Nathanael said to Philip, upon learning that Jesus was from Nazareth: "Can any good thing come out of Nazareth?" (John 1:46). Thus, the prophecy in Micah concerning the Messiah's birthplace became a *proof text* for the Pharisees. This verse seemingly provided a solid scriptural foundation for rejecting Christ as the Messiah. It was repeatedly used against Jesus by his enemies and became a point of contention, both among the Pharisees, and even among the common people. During one of Jesus's trips to Jerusalem to observe the Feast of the Passover, his public teaching so angered the Pharisees and chief priests that they sent officers to arrest him:

> Some of the people therefore, when they heard these words, were saying, "This certainly is the Prophet." Others were saying, "This is the Christ." Still others were saying, "Surely the Christ is not going to come from Galilee, is He? Has not the Scripture said that the Christ comes from the descendants of David, and from Bethlehem, the village where David was?" So a division occurred in the crowd because of Him. Some of them wanted to seize Him, but no one laid hands on Him. The officers then came to the chief priests and Pharisees, and they said to them, "Why did you not bring Him?" The officers answered, "Never has a man spoken the way this man speaks." The Pharisees then answered them, "You have not also been led astray, have you? No one of the rulers or Pharisees has believed in Him, has he? But this crowd which does not know the Law is accursed." Nicodemus (he who came to Him before, being one of them) said to them, "Our Law does not judge a man unless it first hears from him and knows what he is doing, does it?" They answered him, "You are not also from Galilee, are you? Search, and see that no prophet arises out of Galilee." Everyone went to his home. (John 7:40–53)

Unlike the Pharisees, we know that Jesus was indeed born in Bethlehem, just as the prophet Micah had predicted. But, we also know from the gospel of Matthew (2:13–15) that Joseph and Mary took the babe to Egypt and thereby escaped Herod's massacre of the children in Bethlehem. By doing this, Joseph fulfilled another Old Testament prophecy: "When Israel was a youth, I loved him, And out of Egypt I called My son" (Hos. 11:1). Moreover, on their return from Egypt to Judea following Herod's death, Matthew (2:19–23) informs us that Joseph was afraid to return to Bethlehem after hearing that Herod's son, Archelaus, had now become king of Judea. More importantly, Joseph was warned by God in a dream, so he took Mary and Jesus back to his home in Nazareth.

CONCLUSION

Since the Gospels were not written until after the death, burial, and resurrection of Christ, the Pharisees did not have access to these clarifications as to where Christ had actually been born (Bethlehem), why he had been in Egypt, or how he had ended up in Nazareth. However, neither did the apostles or disciples have access to these written records. Nevertheless, there were eyewitnesses to these events who were still living at that time, including Mary, the mother of Jesus. The question naturally arises, if a tax-collector like Matthew and a doctor like Luke could have gained access to the fact that Jesus had been born in Bethlehem, just as Micah had prophesied, then why couldn't the scribes and Pharisees who were the scholars of the day, the experts in the law? Surely they understood that a person could be born in one place and raised in another? They probably knew of numerous instances where this had happened. Perhaps some of the Pharisees themselves had been born in one town and later raised in another because their father had changed jobs or moved the family's place of residence.

Since the Pharisees regularly talked and argued with Jesus, why didn't they simply ask him where he had been born, rather than assume it was Nazareth? Why didn't they seek out the mother of Jesus, or his brothers and sisters to answer this question? Why didn't they have deep conversations with the apostles and disciples about why they believed Jesus was indeed the Messiah? Why didn't they go to Bethlehem and talk to the innkeeper or go into the hills surrounding Bethlehem and find those shepherds who had witnessed the heavenly host announcing the birth of a Savior (Luke 2:8–20)? Why didn't they believe the testimony of Zacharias the priest and his wife Elizabeth (Luke 1:5–25, 57–80) or their son, John the Baptist (Matt. 3:13–17); devout Simeon of Jerusalem (Luke 2:25–35); or Anna the prophetess who was in the temple daily (vv. 36–38)? Why didn't they talk with their fellow scribes and Pharisees who had been in Jerusalem when the magi made their inquiries, or had been at the temple when a young boy of 12 had sat with the teachers in the temple "both listening to them and asking them questions" (v. 46)? As Paul noted when testifying of Christ before King Agrippa, "this has not been done in a corner" (Acts 26:26).

There were so many avenues of inquiry open to the Pharisees that would have resolved the question of Christ's birthplace, but none of them were taken. The reason for the Pharisees inattention to all these potential sources of information was, of course, because they weren't actively looking for information that would explain such seeming inconsistencies as Jesus being from Nazareth. Instead, most of the Pharisees had already made up their minds that Jesus wasn't the Messiah, or at least, not the type of Messiah for which they had been longing. Their biases immobilized them from seeking out any additional information about this Jesus of Nazareth. Even if they had stumbled across some of the information now found in the gospels, their preconceptions would probably have hindered them from understanding it. They had already arrived at conclusions with which they were happy. Two thousand years later, this same mindset helps explain why the majority of Jews living today still have not recognized who Jesus is, despite the availability of the Gospels which were written by their fellow Jews. This blindness among the Jews, however, will one day come to an end, as Zechariah prophesied concerning the last days: "I will pour out on the house of David and on the inhabitants of Jerusalem, the Spirit of grace and of supplica- tion, so that they will look on Me whom they have pierced; and they will mourn for Him, as one mourns for an only son, and they will weep bitterly over Him like the bitter weeping over a firstborn. In that day there will be great mourning in Jerusalem, like the mourning of Hadadrimmon in the plain of Megiddo" (Zech. 12:10–11).

In any event, Jesus bore the title, Jesus of Nazareth, throughout his ministry. During his triumphal entry into Jerusalem in the final week of his life upon the earth, his pedigree as the Son of David, born in Bethlehem, was still not recognized. "When He had entered Jerusalem, all the city was stirred, saying, 'Who is this?' And the crowds were saying, 'This is the prophet Jesus, from Nazareth in Galilee'" (Matt. 21:10–11). Even in death, the world still refused to recognize who it was that they were crucifying, contesting both his birthright and his kingship: "Pilate also wrote an inscription and put it on the cross. It was written, 'JESUS THE NAZARENE, THE KING OF THE JEWS.' Therefore many of the Jews read this inscription, for the place where Jesus was crucified was near the city; and it was written in Hebrew, Latin and in Greek. So the chief priests of the Jews were saying to Pilate, 'Do not write,' "The King of the Jews"; but that He said, "I am King of the Jews."' Pilate answered, 'What I have written I have written'" (John 19:19–22).

After Jesus's death, we read in the book of Acts (24:5) that the high priest and the elders referred to Paul as "a ringleader of the sect of the Nazarenes." In their minds, he was still "Jesus of Nazareth," not "Jesus of Bethlehem." How else could they possibly live with what they had done to the Son of God, without lying to themselves about who he was and where he was from? Although the Pharisees knew from the Scriptures where the Messiah would be born, their pride, sinful hearts, and strong biases kept them from recognizing that Christ was indeed that Messiah, born in Bethlehem, just as the prophet Micah had foretold some 700 years earlier. Instead, the prophecy in Micah 5:2 became a stumbling block to them, their ultimate scriptural justification for not believing that this Jesus was the promised Messiah! No greater theological mistake could have been made by the Pharisees than this.

Chapter 8

The Pharisees' Theological Mistakes Concerning the Messiah's Authority

Introduction

A second theological mistake that the Pharisees made concerning the Messiah was the authority he would wield while upon the earth. In Genesis, God promised Abraham, Isaac, and Jacob that their seed would be a blessing to the entire earth. This promise was made some 2,000 years before Christ was born in Bethlehem. More specific prophecies as to how this promise would be fulfilled were made by King David in the book of Psalms, one thousand years before the angel Gabriel announced to Mary that she would bear a son whose name would be called Jesus (Luke 1:26–31). God would continue to supply additional information about the coming Messiah through the major and minor prophets until the concluding prophecies were given through Malachi, only 400 years before John the Baptist began preaching in the wilderness of Judea saying: "Repent for the kingdom of heaven is at hand" (Matt. 3:1).

In addition to these prophecies concerning the coming Messiah, God had made it clear to the Children of Israel that they were a called-out people, a chosen nation. Out of all the peoples of the earth, God had chosen Abraham and his offspring as his own. To them he had revealed himself in special ways: through miracles and prophecies. To them he had entrusted the knowledge that there was only one true God. To them he had given the law of Moses. Through them, he had promised to send a King and Savior who would be a blessing to the entire world. Now out of this nation had arisen the sect of the Pharisees, who, at the time when the Messiah finally appeared, were the acknowledged experts on the law of Moses and its interpretation. They had chosen to separate themselves from worldly influences. They, in particular, longed for the coming of the Messiah and through their efforts to achieve righteousness, believed they could hasten his appearing. Yet, when the Messiah did appear, they knew him not. Their theological interpretations of the Scriptures had become so distorted that, instead of falling at the feet of this one whose coming they and their nation had so long desired and anticipated, they found fault with him, argued with him, and eventually demanded that he be put to death. How could this be?

From the very early years of his life upon the earth, even his parents did not fully comprehend who Christ was or the nature of his mission upon the earth. As a boy of 12 years of age, Jesus became separated from his parents while visiting Jerusalem during the feast of the Passover:

> Then, after three days they found Him in the temple, sitting in the midst of the teachers, both listening to them and asking them questions. And all who heard Him were amazed at His understanding and His answers. When they saw Him, they were astonished; and His mother said to Him, "Son, why have You treated us this way? Behold, Your father and I have been anxiously looking for You." And He said to them, "Why is it that you were looking for Me? Did you not know that I had to be in My Father's house?"

> But they did not understand the statement which He had made to them. (Luke 2:46–50)

This incident, when Jesus was just a boy, was to foreshadow his adult life and his conflicts with the spiritual and political leaders of the Jewish nation. With Jesus, it was always about what his Father in Heaven wanted, not what his earthly family wanted; not what the common people wanted; not what the scribes, Pharisees, Sadducees, or chief priests wanted; not what the Romans wanted; or even, what he himself wanted: "For I have come down from heaven, not to do My own will, but the will of Him who sent Me" (John 6:38). Even unto death, Jesus always submitted to the wishes of his Father, as he prayed in the garden of Gethsemane before his crucifixion: "Father, if You are willing, remove this cup from Me; yet not My will, but Yours be done" (Luke 22:42). Unfortunately, over the course of his ministry, it became painfully obvious that what the Jews wanted, particularly the Pharisees, was not what Christ's Heavenly Father wanted. Their interpretation of the Scriptures had become biased by their own hopes and desires. They wanted praise and honor from their fellow Jews; God, through his Son, gave them reproof and condemnation (John 5:44; Matt. 5:20). They wanted to achieve righteousness through their own actions; God wanted to give them righteousness through the sacrifice of his Son (Rom. 3:21–22, 4:5–7). They wanted an earthly king who would drive out the hated Romans; God gave them a ruler whose kingdom was not of this earth (John 18:36). None of these things fitted with the Pharisees' theological interpretation of the prophecies concerning the coming Messiah. Therefore, they were sorely disappointed with Jesus, and questioned not only his place of birth but also his words and actions—by what authority do you say and do the things you do? Jesus's response to these questions was always the same: "For I have come down from heaven, not to do My own will, but the will of Him who sent Me" (John 6:38).

Jesus was always going about his Heavenly Father's business. His desire was always to please his Father. What he did and said was always according to the wishes, example, and authority of his Father: "Truly, truly, I say to you, the Son can do nothing of Himself, unless it is something He sees the Father doing; for whatever the Father does, these things the Son also does in like manner" (John 5:19). How, then, could the Pharisees, who also claimed to love and worship God, find fault with the words and deeds of the Messiah, God's own Son? As Jesus pointed out to the Pharisees, they were also going about their father's business, but their father was not the Heavenly Father:

> Jesus said to them, "If God were your Father, you would love Me, for I proceeded forth and have come from God, for I have not even come on My own initiative, but He sent Me. Why do you not understand what I am saying? It is because you cannot hear My word. You are of your father the devil, and you want to do the desires of your father. He was a murderer from the beginning, and does not stand in the truth because there is no truth in him. Whenever he speaks a lie, he speaks from his own nature, for he is a liar and the father of lies." (John 8:42–44)

Their theology and interpretation of the Scriptures had been warped by their own sinful desires and by the one whom they served—who was the father of lies.

The citizens of one nation do not recognize the authority of a ruler in another nation because they are not his subjects. As long as a person stays within the boundaries of his own country, he is only bound by the laws and regulations of the rulers of that country. Because the Pharisees were serving Satan rather than God, they did not recognize the authority that the Father had given to his Son. As Jesus said to the unbelieving Jews, "But you do not believe because you are not of My sheep. My sheep hear My voice, and I know them, and they follow Me" (John 10:26–27). As a result, many of the Jews and Pharisees constantly found fault with what Jesus said and did. In the Gospels, there were four areas where the Pharisees repeatedly challenged Christ's authority: (1) over the Sabbath, (2) over sinners, (3) over the forgiveness of sin, and (4) over death.

I. THE MESSIAH'S AUTHORITY OVER THE SABBATH

For the Son of Man is Lord of the Sabbath. (Matt. 12:8)

In erecting a fence around the law of Moses, the Pharisees seem to have been particularly proud of the oral traditions they had created to keep from breaking the Sabbath, as God commanded in the Old Testament:

> Remember the sabbath day, to keep it holy. Six days you shall labor and do all your work, but the seventh day is a sabbath of the LORD your God; in it you shall not do any work, you or your son or your daughter, your male or your female servant or your cattle or your sojourner who stays with you. For in six days the LORD made the heavens and the earth, the sea and all that is in them, and rested on the seventh day; therefore the LORD blessed the sabbath day and made it holy. (Exod. 20:8–11)

Perhaps this was because the breaking of this law was the easiest to observe in public and, therefore, the easiest to enforce, which the Pharisees apparently loved to do. Many of these oral traditions which the Pharisees followed were eventually written down in the third century A.D. and became known as the Mishnah. In the Mishnah, there were no fewer than 39 classes of labor which were unlawful on the Sabbath (Danby 1933:106). These rules covered everything from how many steps you could take on a Sabbath journey to how you should respond if your house catches fire on the Sabbath.

The Pharisees repeatedly found Jesus in violation of their oral traditions concerning the Sabbath. On one occasion, they questioned him because his disciples were seen plucking heads of grain, removing the hull, and eating the seeds as they passed near a wheat field on the Sabbath (apparently a violation of oral rules concerning reaping and threshing). "At that time Jesus went through the grainfields on the Sabbath, and His disciples became hungry and began to pick the heads of grain and eat. But when the Pharisees saw this, they said to Him, 'Look, Your disciples do what is not lawful to do on a Sabbath'" (Matt. 12:1–2). Jesus pointed out to the Pharisees that hunger had driven David and his men to eat the consecrated bread in temple which was reserved for priest's alone (vv. 3–4). Moreover, he noted that even the priests in the temple do work on the Sabbath by offering sacrifice, as required by the law of Moses, but are nevertheless blameless (v. 5). Thus, if the temple could be violated in this manner without penalty, the one for whom the temple was built could likewise have mercy on the hungry since he was Lord, not only over the temple, but also the Sabbath (vv. 6–8). Moreover, Jesus pointed out on another occasion that: "The Sabbath was made for man, and not man for the Sabbath" (Mark 2:27). However, the Pharisees with their oral traditions often turned the Sabbath into a burden for man, rather than a blessing; hungry men could not be given food on the Sabbath, sick men could not be healed on the Sabbath.

It was the Messiah's repeated performance of miracles of healing on the Sabbath that most angered the Pharisees. There are no fewer than seven recorded instances in which Jesus healed someone on the Sabbath, often in the presence of the Pharisees, sometimes in the synagogue, and even within a Pharisee's house:

A. The Man with the Unclean Spirit

> They went into Capernaum; and immediately on the Sabbath He entered the synagogue and began to teach. They were amazed at His teaching; for He was teaching them as one having authority, and not as the scribes. Just then there was a man in their synagogue with an unclean spirit; and he cried out, saying, "What business do we have with each other, Jesus of Nazareth? Have You come to destroy us? I know who You are—the Holy One of God!" And Jesus rebuked him, saying, "Be quiet, and come out of him!"

Throwing him into convulsions, the unclean spirit cried out with a loud voice and came out of him. They were all amazed, so that they debated among themselves, saying, "What is this? A new teaching with authority! He commands even the unclean spirits, and they obey Him." Immediately the news about Him spread everywhere into all the surrounding district of Galilee. (Mark 1:21–28)

B. Simon's Wife's Mother

And immediately after they came out of the synagogue, they came into the house of Simon and Andrew, with James and John. Now Simon's mother-in-law was lying sick with a fever; and immediately they spoke to Jesus about her. And He came to her and raised her up, taking her by the hand, and the fever left her, and she waited on them. When evening came, after the sun had set, they began bringing to Him all who were ill and those who were demon-possessed. And the whole city had gathered at the door. And He healed many who were ill with various diseases, and cast out many demons; and He was not permitting the demons to speak, because they knew who He was. (Mark 1:29–34)

C. The Man with the Infirmity

Now there is in Jerusalem by the sheep gate a pool, which is called in Hebrew Bethesda, having five porticoes. In these lay a multitude of those who were sick, blind, lame, and withered, waiting for the moving of the waters; for an angel of the Lord went down at certain seasons into the pool and stirred up the water; whoever then first, after the stirring up of the water, stepped in was made well from whatever disease with which he was afflicted. A man was there who had been ill for thirty-eight years. When Jesus saw him lying there, and knew that he had already been a long time in that condition, He said to him, "Do you wish to get well?" The sick man answered Him, "Sir, I have no man to put me into the pool when the water is stirred up, but while I am coming, another steps down before me." Jesus said to him, "Get up, pick up your pallet and walk." Immediately the man became well, and picked up his pallet and began to walk. Now it was the Sabbath on that day. So the Jews were saying to the man who was cured, "It is the Sabbath, and it is not permissible for you to carry your pallet." But he answered them, "He who made me well was the one who said to me, 'Pick up your pallet and walk.'". . . For this reason the Jews were persecuting Jesus, because He was doing these things on the Sabbath. But He answered them, "My Father is working until now, and I Myself am working." For this reason therefore the Jews were seeking all the more to kill Him, because He not only was breaking the Sabbath, but also was calling God His own Father, making Himself equal with God. (John 5:2–11, 16–18)

D. *The Man with the Withered Right Hand*

Departing from there, He went into their synagogue. And a man was there whose hand was withered. And they questioned Jesus, asking, "Is it lawful to heal on the Sabbath?"—so that they might accuse Him. And He said to them, "What man is there among you who has a sheep, and if it falls into a pit on the Sabbath, will he not take hold of it and lift it out? How much more valuable then is a man than a sheep! So then, it is lawful to do good on the Sabbath." Then He said to the man, "Stretch out your hand!" He stretched it out, and it was restored to normal, like the other. But the Pharisees went out and conspired against Him, as to how they might destroy Him. (Matt. 12:9–14)

E. *The Blind Man*

As He passed by, He saw a man blind from birth. And His disciples asked Him, "Rabbi, who sinned, this man or his parents, that he would be born blind?" Jesus answered, "It was neither that this man sinned, nor his parents; but it was so that the works of God might be displayed in him. We must work the works of Him who sent Me as long as it is day; night is coming when no one can work. While I am in the world, I am the Light of the world." When He had said this, He spat on the ground, and made clay of the spittle, and applied the clay to his eyes, and said to him, "Go, wash in the pool of Siloam" (which is translated, Sent). So he went away and washed, and came back seeing. . . . They brought to the Pharisees the man who was formerly blind. Now it was a Sabbath on the day when Jesus made the clay and opened his eyes. Then the Pharisees also were asking him again how he received his sight. And he said to them, "He applied clay to my eyes, and I washed, and I see." Therefore some of the Pharisees were saying, "This man is not from God, because He does not keep the Sabbath." But others were saying, "How can a man who is a sinner perform such signs?" And there was a division among them. (John 9:1–7, 13–16)

F. The Woman with the Infirmity

And He was teaching in one of the synagogues on the Sabbath. And there was a woman who for eighteen years had had a sickness caused by a spirit; and she was bent double, and could not straighten up at all. When Jesus saw her, He called her over and said to her, "Woman, you are freed from your sickness." And He laid His hands on her; and immediately she was made erect again and began glorifying God. But the synagogue official, indignant because Jesus had healed on the Sabbath, began saying to the crowd in response, "There are six days in which work should be done; so come during them and get healed, and not on the Sabbath day." But the Lord answered him and said, "You hypocrites, does not each of you on the Sabbath untie his ox or his donkey from the stall and lead him away to water him? And this woman, a daughter of Abraham as she is, whom Satan has bound for eighteen long years, should she not have been released from this bond on the Sabbath day?" As He said this, all His opponents were being humiliated; and the entire crowd was rejoicing over all the glorious things being done by Him. (Luke 13:10–17)

G. *The Man with Dropsy*

> It happened that when He went into the house of one of the leaders
> of the Pharisees on the Sabbath to eat bread, they were watching
> Him closely. And there in front of Him was a man suffering from
> dropsy. And Jesus answered and spoke to the lawyers and Phari-
> sees, saying, "Is it lawful to heal on the Sabbath, or not?" But they
> kept silent. And He took hold of him and healed him, and sent him
> away. And He said to them, "Which one of you will have a son or
> an ox fall into a well, and will not immediately pull him out on a
> Sabbath day?" And they could make no reply to this. (Luke 14:1–6)

On the third recorded occasion of Jesus healing someone on the
Sabbath, we learn that the Jews are so incensed by his blatant disre-
gard for their oral traditions against healing on the Sabbath—as
well as his statement that he worked on the Sabbath, as did his
Father—that they began to plot to kill him. After Jesus's fourth
recorded healing on the Sabbath, the Pharisees actually held a
council with the Herodians to discuss how they might put him to
death. Jesus, however, was not bound by their theological errors
in this matter, nor was he deterred by their anger. He continued doing the will of his Father by healing on the Sabbath and
confronting the Pharisees over this issue.

It may well be that the Pharisees were particularly sensitive over
this matter of Christ performing miracles of healing on the Sabbath,
not only because they prided themselves with being the enforcers of
oral tradition on Sabbath law, but also because there was such a clear
contradiction between their oral traditions (which they believed
were given by God), and the miracles which Christ was performing on the Sabbath (which had always before been viewed as acts
of God). These two things could not be reconciled in their minds.
When humans are confronted with such dissonance in their thinking, they frequently respond with anger by lashing out at others. (We
often see the same frustration and anger on display in the modern
world when faulty theological positions come up against the rules of
logic or scientific evidence.) How could this man who was obviously

a sinner (since he was working on the Sabbath), perform such miracles as healing the sick and lame and giving sight to the blind (which required the power of God)? It was illogical. Therefore, the Pharisees came up with an alternate hypothesis: Christ was performing these miracles through the power of Satan rather than God:

> Then a demon-possessed man who was blind and mute was brought to Jesus, and He healed him, so that the mute man spoke and saw. All the crowds were amazed, and were saying, "This man cannot be the Son of David, can he?" But when the Pharisees heard this, they said, "This man casts out demons only by Beelzebul the ruler of the demons." (Matt. 12:22–24)

Jesus, however, responded to this charge with a dire warning: "Therefore I say to you, any sin and blasphemy shall be forgiven people, but blasphemy against the Spirit shall not be forgiven. Whoever speaks a word against the Son of Man, it shall be forgiven him; but whoever speaks against the Holy Spirit, it shall not be forgiven him, either in this age or in the age to come" (Matt. 12:31–32).

II. THE MESSIAH'S AUTHORITY TO ASSOCIATE WITH SINNERS

> I have not come to call the righteous but sinners to repentance. (Luke 5:32)

Another charge that the Pharisees frequently brought against Jesus was that he was friends with publicans and sinners, and, therefore, of questionable moral character. "Now all the tax collectors and the sinners were coming near Him to listen to Him. Both the Pharisees and the scribes began to grumble, saying, 'This man receives sinners and eats with them'" (Luke 15:1–2). Jesus responded to this criticism with three parables: (1) the man with a hundred sheep, who lost one; (2) the woman with ten pieces of silver, who lost one; and (3) the prodigal son. The very reason that

God had sent his only begotten Son into the world was to redeem the lost, to become their Savior. The Pharisees, however, had given little thought as to the need for a Savior since they believed they were achieving righteousness through their own actions and adherence to their oral traditions. Moreover, as pointed out previously, the Pharisees considered themselves to be the *separate ones*; they went out of their way to avoid physical or ritual pollution of any kind, including close physical contact with sinners. This behavior was both illustrated and condemned by Jesus in his parable of The Good Samaritan:

> A man was going down from Jerusalem to Jericho, and fell among robbers, and they stripped him and beat him, and went away leaving him half dead. And by chance a priest was going down on that road, and when he saw him, he passed by on the other side. Likewise a Levite also, when he came to the place and saw him, passed by on the other side. But a Samaritan, who was on a journey, came upon him; and when he saw him, he felt compassion, and came to him and bandaged up his wounds, pouring oil and wine on them; and he put him on his own beast, and brought him to an inn and took care of him. (Luke 10:30–34)

Besides the passage in Luke 15:1–2 that was noted previously, there are three other accounts where the Pharisees complain that Jesus was associating with *publicans and sinners*:

A. At Matthew's House

> As Jesus went on from there, He saw a man called Matthew, sitting in the tax collector's booth; and He said to him, "Follow Me!" And he got up and followed Him. Then it happened that as Jesus was reclining at the table in the house, behold, many tax collectors and sinners came and were dining with Jesus and His disciples. When the Pharisees saw this, they said to His disciples, "Why is your Teacher eating with the tax collectors and sinners?" But when Jesus heard this, He said, "It is not those who are healthy who need

a physician, but those who are sick. But go and learn what this means: 'I DESIRE COMPASSION, AND NOT SACRIFICE,' for I did not come to call the righteous, but sinners." (Matt. 9:9–13)

B. At Simon the Pharisee's House

Now one of the Pharisees was requesting Him to dine with him, and He entered the Pharisee's house and reclined at the table. And there was a woman in the city who was a sinner; and when she learned that He was reclining at the table in the Pharisee's house, she brought an alabaster vial of perfume, and standing behind Him at His feet, weeping, she began to wet His feet with her tears, and kept wiping them with the hair of her head, and kissing His feet and anointing them with the perfume. Now when the Pharisee who had invited Him saw this, he said to himself, "If this man were a prophet He would know who and what sort of person this woman is who is touching Him, that she is a sinner." And Jesus answered him, "Simon, I have something to say to you." And he replied, "Say it, Teacher." "A moneylender had two debtors: one owed five hundred denarii, and the other fifty. When they were unable to repay, he graciously forgave them both. So which of them will love him more?" Simon answered and said, "I suppose the one whom he forgave more." And He said to him, "You have judged correctly." (Luke 7:36–43)

C. At Zaccheus's House

He entered Jericho and was passing through. And there was a man called by the name of Zaccheus; he was a chief tax collector and he was rich. Zaccheus was trying to see who Jesus was, and was unable because of the crowd, for he was small in stature. So he ran on ahead and climbed up into a sycamore tree in order to see Him, for He was about to pass through that way. When Jesus came to the place, He looked up and said to him, "Zaccheus, hurry and come down, for today I must stay at your house." And he hurried and came down and received Him gladly. When they saw it, they all began to grumble, saying, "He has gone to be the guest of a man who is a sinner." Zaccheus stopped and said to the Lord, "Behold, Lord, half of my possessions I will give to the poor, and if I have defrauded anyone of anything, I will give back four times as much." And Jesus said to him, "Today salvation has come to this house, because he, too, is a son of Abraham. For the Son of Man has come to seek and to save that which was lost." (Luke 19:1–10)

From these three accounts we can plainly see that the Pharisees were right, Jesus did indeed associate with publicans and sinners. In the Roman world, publicans were *public contractors* who often acted as intermediaries between the Roman authorities and the general public. Their responsibilities often included providing provisions for the army, collecting fees at ports, or collecting taxes from the peoples over which the Romans ruled. Since publicans were often drawn from among the local peoples, they were often viewed as lackeys of the hated Romans. Two of the publicans mentioned in the previous biblical accounts, Jesus publicly called to follow him, and then went on to eat at their houses. Is it any wonder that other publicans and sinners were present at these meals? Moreover, one of these publicans, Matthew, Christ called to be an apostle (Luke 5:27), thereby putting his record-keeping and writing skills as a tax collector to better use as the author of the first gospel in the New Testament. The other publican became the topic of a song that we, as children in Sunday school and vacation Bible school, delighted in singing: "Zaccheus was a wee little man, a wee little man was he." Through associating with these publicans and sinners, Jesus was once again going about his Father's business, calling sinners to repentance and saving them, just as Isaiah the prophet said he would:

> The Spirit of the Lord GOD is upon me, Because the LORD has anointed me To bring good news to the afflicted; He has sent me to bind up the brokenhearted, To proclaim liberty to captives And freedom to prisoners; To proclaim the favorable year of the LORD And

> the day of vengeance of our God; To comfort all who mourn, To grant those who mourn in Zion, Giving them a garland instead of ashes, The oil of gladness instead of mourning, The mantle of praise instead of a spirit of fainting. So they will be called oaks of righteousness, The planting of the LORD, that He may be glorified. (Isa. 61:1–3)

Even though he was the Son of God, come down from Heaven, Jesus did not see it as being beneath his office (Phil. 2:6–7) to dine with publicans and sinners or have his feet washed with tears by the fallen woman at Simon the Pharisee's house. Since these men and women were also made in the image of God (Gen. 1:27), they were, potentially, brothers and sisters of Christ (Matt. 12:50), as well as sons and daughters of God (2 Cor. 6:18). Unfortunately, most of the Pharisees, because of their pride, flawed theology, and biased interpretations of the Scriptures, did not understand that Jesus was once again acting on the authority his Father had given him to seek and save the lost. They rejected both the preaching of John the Baptist, as well as that of Christ, and used various excuses for this rejection, as Jesus explained: "For John came neither eating nor drinking, and they say, 'He has a demon.' The Son of man came eating and drinking, and they say, 'Behold a gluttonous man and a drunkard, a friend of tax collectors and sinners'" (Matt. 11:18–19). As a result of their disbelief, Jesus gave this parable to the chief priests and the elders at the temple in Jerusalem:

> "But what do you think? A man had two sons, and he came to the first and said," 'Son, go work today in the vineyard.' And he answered, 'I will not'; but afterward he regretted it and went. The man came to the second and said the same thing; and he answered, 'I will, sir'; but he did not go. "Which of the two did the will of his father?" They said, "The first." Jesus said to them, "Truly I say to you that the tax collectors and prostitutes will get into the kingdom of God before you." (Matt. 21:28–31)

This condemnation was, no doubt, also applicable to the Pharisees.

III. THE MESSIAH'S AUTHORITY TO FORGIVE SIN

> ...the Son of Man has authority on earth to forgive sins. (Matt. 9:6)

The Father not only gave his Son authority over the Sabbath, as well as to seek and save the lost, but also to forgive the sins of those who were lost. This was his ultimate purpose for coming into the world. As John the Baptist said, "Behold, the Lamb of God, who takes away the sin of the world!" (John 1:29). It is quite logical, therefore, that, since Christ was to become the sacrifice for sin on the cross, his Father should grant him the power to forgive whomever he would. Of course the Pharisees, because of their theological errors and misunderstanding, had no idea why God should grant this *man* from Nazareth the authority to forgive sin. To them, such a claim was simply blasphemy, since only God could forgive sin. While we as individuals can forgive what others have done to us, we cannot forgive the trespasses that other individuals commit against their own family, friends, or enemies. Moreover, the sins we commit against each other are ultimately sins against the character and commands of our Creator. As a consequence, only God can truly forgive our sins, or give that authority to another. On an even deeper level, however, through the mystery of the Holy Trinity, Christ was our Creator: "In the beginning was the Word, and the Word was with God, and the Word was God. He was in the beginning with God. All things came into being through Him, and apart from Him nothing came into being that has come into being. In Him was life, and the life was the Light of men. The Light shines in the darkness, and the darkness did not comprehend it" (vv. 1–5). Therefore, from the standpoint of both creation and redemption, it was entirely justified that Christ, through his Heavenly Father, should be given authority over the forgiveness of sins.

There are four times in the Gospels where we see Jesus exercising his authority to forgive sins:

A. The Man Sick of Palsy in Capernaum

And they brought to Him a paralytic lying on a bed. Seeing their faith, Jesus said to the paralytic, "Take courage, son; your sins are forgiven." And some of the scribes said to themselves, "This fellow blasphemes." And Jesus knowing their thoughts said, "Why are you thinking evil in your hearts? Which is easier, to say, 'Your sins are forgiven,' or to say, 'Get up, and walk'? But so that you may know that the Son of Man has authority on earth to forgive sins"— then He said to the paralytic, "Get up, pick up your bed and go home." And he got up and went home. But when the crowds saw this, they were awestruck, and glorified God, who had given such authority to men. (Matt. 9:2–8)

B. The Sinful Woman at Simon the Pharisee's House

Turning toward the woman, He said to Simon, "Do you see this woman? I entered your house; you gave Me no water for My feet, but she has wet My feet with her tears and wiped them with her hair. You gave Me no kiss; but she, since the time I came in, has not ceased to kiss My feet. You did not anoint My head with oil, but she anointed My feet with perfume. For this reason I say to you, her sins, which are many, have been forgiven, for she loved much; but he who is forgiven little, loves little." Then He said to her, "Your sins have been forgiven." Those who were reclining at the table with Him began to say to themselves, "Who is this man who even forgives sins?" And He said to the woman, "Your faith has saved you; go in peace." (Luke 7:44–50)

C. The Woman Taken in Adultery

The scribes and the Pharisees brought a woman caught in adultery, and having set her in the center of the court, they said to Him, "Teacher, this woman has been caught in adultery, in the very act. Now in the Law Moses commanded us to stone such women; what then do You say?" They were saying this, testing Him, so that they

might have grounds for accusing Him. But Jesus stooped down
and with His finger wrote on the ground. But when they persisted
in asking Him, He straightened up, and said to them, "He who
is without sin among you, let him be the first to throw a stone at
her." Again He stooped down and wrote on the ground. When they
heard it, they began to go out one by one, beginning with the older
ones, and He was left alone, and the woman, where she was, in the
center of the court. Straightening up, Jesus said to her, "Woman,
where are they? Did no one condemn you?" She said, "No one,
Lord." And Jesus said, "I do not condemn you, either. Go. From
now on sin no more." (John 8:3–11)

D. The Thief on the Cross

One of the criminals who were hanged there was hurling abuse
at Him, saying, "Are You not the Christ? Save Yourself and us!"
But the other answered, and rebuking him said, "Do you not even
fear God, since you are under the same sentence of condemnation? And we indeed are suffering justly, for we are receiving what
we deserve for our deeds; but this man has done nothing wrong."
And he was saying, "Jesus, remember me when You come in Your
kingdom!" And He said to him, "Truly I say to you, today you shall
be with Me in Paradise." (Luke 23:39–43)

The earliest of these encounters occurred in Capernaum and
involved a man sick with palsy. Before healing this man, Jesus
first forgives him of his sins. Matthew and Mark tell us that
scribes witnessed this event, and Luke (5:17) mentions that there
were also Pharisees and teachers of the law present. Matthew
goes on to note that the scribes were offended by Jesus's words
and said that he was committing blasphemy by telling the man
his sins were forgiven. Jesus then asked them if it was easier
to tell the man his sins were forgiven, or to tell him to rise up
and walk. It was obvious that the scribes, with all their learning
and adherence to the law of Moses, could do neither. Christ's
inference was that, if God had given him the power to heal the

sick, he could also give him the power to forgive a person's sins; both were acts of God. Christ's works affirmed his claims. But the scribes, Pharisees, and doctors of the law were blind to this obvious connection. Because of their flawed theological interpretations of the Scriptures, they constantly came to the wrong conclusions.

To reaffirm his authority to forgive sins, Jesus publicly forgave a woman in the house of Simon the Pharisee, and later, a woman taken in adultery whom the scribes and Pharisees had brought to Jesus, asking whether she should be stoned as the law of Moses commanded. Then, at the very end of his ministry on earth, even as he was dying on the cross, he promised one of the two thieves who was being crucified with him that he would, that very day, be with him in Paradise. Now Paul tells us in Romans 6:23 that "the wages of sin is death" and Jesus, the Son of God, was about to pay that price on the cross to redeem all who believed in his name. Therefore, Jesus not only had the authority to forgive sins because: (1) his Father had given him that authority (as affirmed by the miracles which God also gave him the power to perform), (2) not only because he, as Creator, was redeeming his creation from the wages of sin on the cross, but in addition (3) because his Father had also given him authority over death itself which was the penalty for sin. "All authority has been given to Me in heaven and on earth" (Matt. 28:18).

IV. The Messiah's Authority over Death

> For the Father loves the Son, and shows Him all things that He Himself is doing; and the Father will show Him greater works than these, so that you will marvel. For just as the Father raises the dead and gives them life, even so the Son also gives life to whom He wishes. (John 5:20–21)

> Truly, truly, I say to you, he who hears My word, and believes Him who sent Me, has eternal life, and does not come into judgment, but has passed out of death into life. Truly, truly, I say to you, an

> hour is coming and now is, when the dead will hear the voice of
> the Son of God, and those who hear will live. For just as the Father
> has life in Himself, even so He gave to the Son also to have life in
> Himself; and He gave Him authority to execute judgment, because
> He is the Son of Man. (vv. 24–27)

The one thing that separates Christianity from all other world religions is that its founder was not just someone who sought God, had been given a revelation by God, or was the chosen prophet of God. Christianity's founder was God who authenticated his claim by his power to raise the dead from the grave—including himself. All other claims pale to insignificance in the searing light of this manifestation of true divinity. Why dedicate your life to a religion that is the result of another man's efforts to find God, when God himself has come down from Heaven to find us, to lay down his life to redeem us from our sins, and to raise us up from the dead, as he raised himself, and is now alive for evermore? "Do not be afraid; I am the first and the last, and the living One; and I was dead, and behold, I am alive forevermore, and I have the keys of death and of Hades" (Rev. 1:17–18).

There are four accounts in the Gospels where Jesus exercises his authority over death:

A. Widow of Nain's Son

> Soon afterwards He went to a city called Nain; and His disciples
> were going along with Him, accompanied by a large crowd. Now
> as He approached the gate of the city, a dead man was being carried
> out, the only son of his mother, and she was a widow; and a size-
> able crowd from the city was with her. When the Lord saw her, He
> felt compassion for her, and said to her, "Do not weep." And He
> came up and touched the coffin; and the bearers came to a halt.
> And He said, "Young man, I say to you, arise!" The dead man sat
> up and began to speak. And Jesus gave him back to his mother.
> Fear gripped them all, and they began glorifying God, saying, "A
> great prophet has arisen among us!" and, "God has visited His

people!" This report concerning Him went out all over Judea and in all the surrounding district. (Luke 7:11–17)

B. Daughter of Jairus

One of the synagogue officials named Jairus came up, and on seeing Him, fell at His feet and implored Him earnestly, saying, "My little daughter is at the point of death; please come and lay Your hands on her, so that she will get well and live." And He went off with him; and a large crowd was following Him and pressing in on Him.... While He was still speaking, they came from the house of the synagogue official, saying, "Your daughter has died; why trouble the Teacher anymore?" But Jesus, overhearing what was being spoken, said to the synagogue official, "Do not be afraid any longer, only believe." And He allowed no one to accompany Him, except Peter and James and John the brother of James. They came to the house of the synagogue official; and He saw a commotion, and people loudly weeping and wailing. And entering in, He said to them, "Why make a commotion and weep? The child has not died, but is asleep." They began laughing at Him. But putting them all out, He took along the child's father and mother and His own companions, and entered the room where the child was. Taking the child by the hand, He said to her, "Talitha kum!" (which translated means, "Little girl, I say to you, get up!"). Immediately the girl got up and began to walk, for she was twelve years old. And immediately they were completely astounded. And He gave them strict orders that no one should know about this, and He said that something should be given her to eat. (Mark 5:22–24, 35–43)

C. Lazarus

Jesus said to her, "Your brother will rise again." Martha said to Him, "I know that he will rise again in the resurrection on the last day." Jesus said to her, "I am the resurrection and the life; he who believes in Me will live even if he dies, and everyone who lives and believes in Me will never die. Do you believe this?" She said to

Him, "Yes, Lord; I have believed that You are the Christ, the Son of God, even He who comes into the world".... When Jesus therefore saw her weeping, and the Jews who came with her also weeping, He was deeply moved in spirit and was troubled, and said, "Where have you laid him?" They said to Him, "Lord, come and see." Jesus wept. So the Jews were saying, "See how He loved him!" But some of them said, "Could not this man, who opened the eyes of the blind man, have kept this man also from dying?" So Jesus, again being deeply moved within, came to the tomb. Now it was a cave, and a stone was lying against it. Jesus said, "Remove the stone." Martha, the sister of the deceased, said to Him, "Lord, by this time there will be a stench, for he has been dead four days." Jesus said to her, "Did I not say to you that if you believe, you will see the glory of God?" So they removed the stone. Then Jesus raised His eyes, and said, "Father, I thank You that You have heard Me. I knew that You always hear Me; but because of the people standing around I said it, so that they may believe that You sent Me." When He had said these things, He cried out with a loud voice, "Lazarus, come forth." The man who had died came forth, bound hand and foot with wrappings, and his face was wrapped around with a cloth. Jesus said to them, "Unbind him, and let him go." Therefore many of the Jews who came to Mary, and saw what He had done, believed in Him. (John 11:23–27, 33–45)

D. Jesus Himself

I am the good shepherd, and I know My own and My own know Me, even as the Father knows Me and I know the Father; and I lay down My life for the sheep. I have other sheep, which are not of this fold; I must bring them also, and they will hear My voice; and they will become one flock with one shepherd. For this reason the Father loves Me, because I lay down My life so that I may take it again. No one has taken it away from Me, but I lay it down on My own initiative. I have authority to lay it down, and I have authority to take it up again. This commandment I received from My Father. (John 10:14–18)

When the Sabbath was over, Mary Magdalene, and Mary the mother of James, and Salome, bought spices, so that they might come and anoint Him. Very early on the first day of the week, they came to the tomb when the sun had risen. They were saying to one another, "Who will roll away the stone for us from the entrance of the tomb?" Looking up, they saw that the stone had been rolled away, although it was extremely large. Entering the tomb, they saw a young man sitting at the right, wearing a white robe; and they were amazed. And he said to them, "Do not be amazed; you are looking for Jesus the Nazarene, who has been crucified. He has risen; He is not here; behold, here is the place where they laid Him. But go, tell His disciples and Peter, 'He is going ahead of you to Galilee; there you will see Him, just as He told you.'" They went out and fled from the tomb, for trembling and astonishment had gripped them; and they said nothing to anyone, for they were afraid. Now after He had risen early on the first day of the week, He first appeared to Mary Magdalene, from whom He had cast out seven demons. (Mark 16:1–9)

And they found the stone rolled away from the tomb, but when they entered, they did not find the body of the Lord Jesus. While they were perplexed about this, behold, two men suddenly stood near them in dazzling clothing; and as the women were terrified and bowed their faces to the ground, the men said to them, "Why do you seek the living One among the dead? He is not here, but He has risen. Remember how He spoke to you while He was still in Galilee, saying that the Son of Man must be delivered into the hands of sinful men, and be crucified, and the third day rise again." And they remembered His words, and returned from the tomb and reported all these things to the eleven and to all the rest. (Luke 24:2–9)

And they left the tomb quickly with fear and great joy and ran to report it to His disciples. And behold, Jesus met them and greeted them. And they came up and took hold of His feet and worshiped Him. Then Jesus said to them, "Do not be afraid; go and take word

to My brethren to leave for Galilee, and there they will see Me."
(Matt. 28:8–10)

But Mary was standing outside the tomb weeping; and so, as
she wept, she stooped and looked into the tomb; and she saw
two angels in white sitting, one at the head and one at the feet,
where the body of Jesus had been lying. And they said to her,
"Woman, why are you weeping?" She said to them, "Because they
have taken away my Lord, and I do not know where they have
laid Him." When she had said this, she turned around and saw
Jesus standing there, and did not know that it was Jesus. Jesus
said to her, "Woman, why are you weeping? Whom are you seeking?" Supposing Him to be the gardener, she said to Him, "Sir,
if you have carried Him away, tell me where you have laid Him,
and I will take Him away." Jesus said to her, "Mary!" She turned
and said to Him in Hebrew, "Rabboni!" (which means, Teacher).
(John 20:11–16)

In the first instance, the Widow of Nain's son was being carried
to the graveyard on a bier. In the second instance, the Daughter of
Jairus died while Jesus was on the way to her home. In the third
instance, Lazarus had been dead and in the tomb for four days.
Thus, it didn't matter what the circumstances were or how long
the person had been dead, when they were bidden to arise from
the dead by Jesus, they obeyed his command! Of all the miracles that Jesus performed, none were greater than these. Turning
water into wine; feeding the 5,000 and the 4,000 with a few loaves
and fishes; calming the storms on the Sea of Galilee; casting out
demons; healing the sick, the lame, the deaf, and the blind; these
were all of only transitory value to the people experiencing these
miracles. These people would all get thirsty and hungry again,
new storms would arise, and subsequent illness would inevitably crop up. But to give life to the dead, that was the one thing
that all humanity through all time had desired, but none could
obtain since having been driven out of the garden of Eden. It is the
one thing for which we would pay any price, for which we would

perform any labor, but our search outside the garden of Eden for another Tree of Life has been a long and futile one.

So how did the Pharisees respond to this greatest of miracles, this breach of natural law that God had only allowed three times before through all of Old Testament times: (1) Elijah raising the son of Zarephath's widow (1 Kings 17:17–24), (2) Elisha raising the son of the Shunammite woman (2 Kings 4:12–37), and (3) the dead man who was lowered into Elisha's sepulcher and accidentally came into contact with Elisha's bones (2 Kings 13:20–21)? Since Adam, Noah, Abraham, Moses, and King David had never been given the power to raise the dead, but only these two great prophets, Elijah and Elisha, the ability of Jesus to raise the dead would surely have come to the attention of the Pharisees? The raising of the Widow of Nain's son, as well as the raising of Lazarus, had been done in public and the account of these events had spread far and wide across the countryside. Indeed, an account of the raising of Lazarus had even reached the ears of the chief priests in Jerusalem. Their response was not only to ignore this miracle, but to suggest that the evidence for this miracle should be destroyed (i.e. Lazarus should be put *back* to death): "But the chief priests planned to put Lazarus to death also; because on account of him many of the Jews were going away and were believing in Jesus" (John 12:10–11). Sometimes, one gets the impression that the scribes and Pharisees, the Sadducees and chief priests must have each had four arms and four hands, two for putting over their ears and two for putting over their eyes, lest they recognize the errors of their theological interpretations, repent of their sins, and accept the Messiah whom their God had promised and subsequently sent to them: As Jesus said, "In their case the prophecy of Isaiah is being fulfilled, which says, 'YOU WILL KEEP ON HEARING, BUT WILL NOT UNDERSTAND; YOU WILL KEEP ON SEEING, BUT WILL NOT PERCEIVE; FOR THE HEART OF THIS PEOPLE HAS BECOME DULL, WITH THEIR EARS THEY SCARCELY HEAR, AND THEY HAVE CLOSED THEIR EYES, OTHERWISE THEY WOULD SEE WITH THEIR EYES, HEAR WITH THEIR EARS, AND

UNDERSTAND WITH THEIR HEART AND RETURN, AND I
WOULD HEAL THEM'" (Matt. 13:14–15).

In the fourth example of Jesus's authority over death, he
raised himself from the grave after his crucifixion. Jesus had been
crucified on a cross and then pierced with a spear to make sure he
was dead. The Romans were very good at this sort of thing; they
had had plenty of practice putting people to death. Those whom
the Romans killed in this manner stayed dead, but not Jesus. But
how can you put someone to death who has authority over death?
You can nail him to a cross, you can pierce him with a spear to
make sure he is dead, you can put him in a rock-hewn tomb and
block it with a heavy stone, you can even place a guard outside
the tomb, but it is all to no avail. The Pharisees simply had no idea
with whom they were dealing. They had no idea of the authority
that God had given to his Son, not only over the Sabbath, over
the seeking and saving of the lost, over the forgiveness of sins,
but also over death itself. Although Jesus was himself in a tomb
for three days and three nights, death could not hold him there,
just as David had prophesied a thousand years earlier, "I have
set the LORD continually before me; Because He is at my right
hand, I will not be shaken. Therefore my heart is glad and my
glory rejoices; My flesh also will dwell securely. For You will not
abandon my soul to Sheol; Nor will You allow Your Holy One to
undergo decay" (Ps. 16:8–10). The wages of sin had once and for
all been paid on the cross, the gates of hades had been breached,
"O DEATH, WHERE IS YOUR VICTORY? O DEATH WHERE
IS YOUR STING?" (1 Cor. 15:55).

If Christ had lingered longer upon the earth after his resurrection, it is likely that the Pharisees would have tried to do to Jesus what
the chief priests had plotted to do to Lazarus: put him back to death.
This was certainly the desire of their Father, the Devil. However, as
John saw in his great revelation, God had other plans for his Son:

> A great sign appeared in heaven: a woman clothed with the sun,
> and the moon under her feet, and on her head a crown of twelve
> stars; and she was with child; and she cried out, being in labor and

> in pain to give birth. Then another sign appeared in heaven: and
> behold, a great red dragon having seven heads and ten horns, and
> on his heads were seven diadems. And his tail swept away a third
> of the stars of heaven and threw them to the earth. And the dragon
> stood before the woman who was about to give birth, so that when
> she gave birth he might devour her child. And she gave birth to a
> son, a male child, who is to rule all the nations with a rod of iron;
> and her child was caught up to God and to His throne. Then the
> woman fled into the wilderness where she had a place prepared by
> God, so that there she would be nourished for one thousand two
> hundred and sixty days. (Rev. 12:1–6)

Even as Satan, through his henchman, King Herod, stood waiting to destroy the babe who was to be born in Bethlehem, so the
Pharisees, scribes, and chief priests, doing the business of their
father, Satan, would attempt to kill this now grown Son, whom
God had ordained to rule the nations. Instead, after his resurrection from the dead, Christ returned to Heaven to sit on the right
hand of his Father while Jerusalem was destroyed by the Romans
and the Jews were dispersed among the nations until the times of
the Gentiles should be fulfilled (Luke 21:24).

Sometimes we wonder why God has made faith such an
important part of his plan of salvation. Why doesn't he just
pull back the drapes of heaven and reveal himself to us so that
we would no longer have to live by faith? All would then see his
majesty and know that he exists, and unbelief would be impossible. Isn't seeing believing? The reality is that God did indeed
reveal himself to us through his beloved Son—but the end result
was not the conversion of the world, but the attempt of the world
to put the Son to death. Seeing is apparently not superior to faith.
When the rich man in hell begged Abraham to send Lazarus back
to his father's house so that Lazarus could warn his five brothers about the coming judgment and the place of torment where
he now found himself, Abraham replied: "If they do not listen to
Moses and the Prophets, they will not be persuaded even if someone rises from the dead" (Luke 16:31). One indeed did rise from

the dead. Nevertheless, many in the world, such as the scribes, Pharisees, and chief priests continued to believe what they wanted to believe. Seeing is not believing. Instead, God has ordained that "faith comes from hearing, and hearing by the word of Christ" (Rom. 10:17). If we do not allow ourselves to hear and obey God's voice, no amount of empirical evidence will ever make us believe. Just ask the Pharisees.

Chapter 9

THE PHARISEES' THEOLOGICAL MISTAKES CONCERNING THE MESSIAH'S DIVINITY

INTRODUCTION

In their theology, the Pharisees knew exactly where the Messiah was to be born. They were, however, willfully ignorant that Jesus had been born in Bethlehem. Although there were a number of family members, friends, and even strangers (such as the shepherds) still living in Judea at that time who could have attested to the circumstances surrounding Christ's birth, the Pharisees chose not pursue those lines of inquiry. Each move Joseph and Mary had made, from Nazareth to Bethlehem, from Bethlehem to Egypt, and from Egypt back to Nazareth, had been the result of a public pronouncement or event that was well known to the Jews living in Judea at that time: (1) the decree of Caesar Augustus that all the world should be taxed, (2) the command of Herod the King that all the babies born in Bethlehem who were two years old or less should be put to death, and (3) the accession of Archelaus to his father's throne in Judea. Despite the availability of such evidence, to the non-believing Pharisees Jesus would always be *Jesus of Nazareth*.

In their theology, the Pharisees were also familiar with the prophecies concerning the authority that God would impart to his chosen Messiah, the one who would rule the nations with a rod of iron. Nevertheless, they chose to ignore these inconvenient passages of Scripture. As a result, they constantly challenged Jesus's authority to: (1) heal the sick on the Sabbath, (2) associate with publicans and sinners, (3) forgive individuals of their sins, and (4) raise the dead. In part, the Pharisees were rejecting the Messiah's authority to do some of these things because he was infringing on their own authority. After all, they were the guardians of the sanctity of the Sabbath. They were the ones who had helped built a fence around the law of Moses with their oral traditions to keep their fellow Jews from sinning, and they were the ones who felt it was their duty to force the common people to obey these oral traditions—particularly the observance of the Sabbath. Moreover, in their attempt to justify themselves before God and achieve righteousness through their own actions, the Pharisees had also attempted to withdraw or separate themselves from all sources of ceremonial or physical impurity, including physical contact or association with sinners, such as publicans and harlots. In their minds, therefore, Jesus of Nazareth, who often dined at the house of publicans and sinners, and actually chose some of them to be his disciples or apostles, could not possibly be the Messiah, the Holy One of Israel.

In their theology, the Pharisees were no doubt also familiar with some of the prophecies in the Scriptures concerning the divinity of the Messiah because these passages are neither rare nor obscure in their meaning. Based on their actions, however, the Pharisees seem to have totally rejected these passages. While they apparently could accept the Messiah as being the Son of David, a member of their own lineage and ancestry, they could not accept a Messiah who was also the Son of God. After all, the Jews and Israelites were a called-out people who stood apart from all the nations of the earth with their central affirmation that there was only one God, and Jehovah was his name. Consequently, for any man to claim equality with God was the greatest of blasphemies. So strong was this belief among the Pharisees that most of them seemed to be impervious to the significance of the miracles which Jesus performed in their presence: from casting out demons; healing the deaf, the blind, the lame, and the sick; or even raising the dead. Yet, Christ's claim to divinity was affirmed by the power which his Heavenly Father gave him to do these things. As the man who had been blind from birth before being healed by Jesus testified before the Pharisees, "The man answered and said to them, 'Well, here is an amazing thing, that you do not know where He is from, and yet He opened my eyes. We know that God does not hear sinners; but if anyone is God-fearing and does His will, He hears him. Since the beginning of time it has never been heard that anyone opened the eyes of a person born blind. If this man were not from God, He could do nothing'" (John 9:30–33). The Pharisees, unfortunately, would not accept the blind man's testimony but cast him out of the synagogue. Indeed, so strong was the Pharisees' rejection of the divinity of the Messiah that later, when Jesus demonstrated that most awesome power of God, the raising of the dead, the Jews plotted not only to kill Jesus, but also the one whom he had raised from the dead. Was not this desire of the Jews a foreshadowing of that most Satanic of desires, to undo what Christ was about to accomplish on the cross, free mankind from the penalty of sin, from death itself? Such is the nature of theological mistakes: they can grow from misunderstanding certain scriptural passages, to willful ignorance of certain scriptural passages, to outright rejection of certain scriptural passages. At each stage, we become less and less like our Father in Heaven and more and more like Satan. The divinity of the Messiah became the final, fatal stumbling block for the Pharisees.

I. Prophecies concerning the Messiah's Divinity

The prophecies concerning the divinity of the Messiah are quite clear and go all the way back to the time of King David, around 1000 B.C.. Among the titles given to the coming King and future Messiah, are *the Son of God, Lord, God, the mighty God,* and *the everlasting Father*:

A. *The Son of God*

> But as for Me, I have installed My King Upon Zion, My holy mountain. "I will surely tell of the decree of the LORD: He said to Me, 'You are My Son, Today I have begotten You. Ask of Me, and I will surely give the nations as Your inheritance, And the very ends of the earth as Your possession. You shall break them with a rod of iron, You shall shatter them like earthenware.'" Now therefore, O kings, show discernment; Take warning, O judges of the earth. Worship the LORD with reverence And rejoice with trembling. Do homage to the Son, that He not become angry, and you perish in the way, For His wrath may soon be kindled. How blessed are all who take refuge in Him! (Ps. 2:6–12)

> He will cry to Me, "You are my Father, My God, and the rock of my salvation." I also shall make him My firstborn, The highest of the kings of the earth. My lovingkindness I will keep for him forever, And My covenant shall be confirmed to him. So I will establish his descendants forever And his throne as the days of heaven. (Ps. 89:26–29)

B. *Lord*

> The LORD says to my Lord: "Sit at My right hand Until I make Your enemies a footstool for Your feet." The LORD will stretch forth Your strong scepter from Zion, saying, "Rule in the midst of Your enemies. Your people will volunteer freely in the day of Your power; In holy array, from the womb of the dawn, Your youth are to You as the dew. The LORD has sworn and will not change His mind, You are a priest forever According to the order of Melchizedek. The Lord is at Your right hand; He will shatter kings in the day of His wrath. He will judge among the nations, He will fill them with corpses, He will shatter the

> chief men over a broad country. He will drink from the brook by the wayside; Therefore He will lift up His head." (Ps. 110:1–7)

C. God

> Your throne, O God, is forever and ever; A scepter of uprightness is the scepter of Your kingdom. You have loved righteousness and hated wickedness; Therefore God, Your God, has anointed You With the oil of joy above Your fellows. (Ps. 45:6–7)

D. Mighty God / Eternal Father

> For a child will be born to us, a son will be given to us; And the government will rest on His shoulders; And His name will be called Wonderful Counselor, Mighty God, Eternal Father, Prince of Peace. There will be no end to the increase of His government or of peace, On the throne of David and over his kingdom To establish it and to uphold it with justice and righteousness From then on and forever-more. The zeal of the Lord of hosts will accomplish this. (Isa. 9:6–7)

Such titles seem to leave little doubt that the Messiah will some-how share the divinity and attributes of God, but this was exactly the idea that the Jews and the Pharisees could not accept: "The Jews picked up stones again to stone Him. Jesus answered them, 'I showed you many good works from the Father; for which of them are you stoning Me?' The Jews answered Him, 'For a good work we do not stone You, but for blasphemy; and because You, being a man, make Yourself out to be God'" (John 10:31–33).

In these passages concerning the divinity of the Messiah, we see the mystery of the Trinity first beginning to clearly emerge. The three-fold nature of God was first foreshadowed in Genesis 1:26 where the plural tense was used concerning God's making of man: "Then God said, Let Us make man in Our image, according to Our likeness..." It has also been suggested that Melchizedek, *king of Salem* and *priest of God Most High* (Gen. 14:18), seems to have occupied a unique position relative to God. Abram offered a tithe to Melchizedek after defeating the confederation of kings who raided Sodom and Gomorrah and took Lot and his family captive (vv. 1–24). Later, King David, prophesying of the Messiah in one of the Psalms, said: "The Lord has sworn and will not change His mind, You are a priest forever according to the order of Melchizedek" (Ps. 110:4). In the New Testament, the writer of Hebrews also mentions Melchizedek in relation to the priesthood of Christ: "having become a high priest forever according to the order of Melchizedek" (Heb. 6:20). The Hebrew writer then goes on to explain: "For this Melchizedek, king of Salem, priest of the Most High God, who met Abraham as he was returning from the slaughter of the kings and blessed him, to whom also Abraham apportioned a tenth part of all the spoils, was first of all, by the translation of his name, king of righteousness, and then also king of Salem, which is king of peace. Without father, without mother, without genealogy, having neither beginning of days nor end of life, but made like the Son of God, he remains a priest perpetually" (Heb. 7:1–3). Because of these parallels between Christ and Melchizedek in Genesis, Psalms, and Hebrews, some have suggested that Melchizedek was a Christophany, a pre-incarnate appearance of Christ in Old Testament times.

Another possible hint as to the triune nature of God in the Old Testament is the Angel of the Lord. Normally, angels do not accept the worship of men (unless they are fallen angels). For example, John tells us that: "I, John, am the one who heard and saw these things. And when I heard and saw, I fell down to worship at the feet of the angel who showed me these things. But he said to me, 'Do not do that. I am a fellow servant of yours and of your brethren the prophets and of those who heed the words of this book. Worship God'" (Rev. 22:8–9). The Angel of the Lord, however, both speaks for God and accepts the worship of men:

> Now Moses was pasturing the flock of Jethro his father-in-law, the priest of Midian; and he led the flock to the west side of the wilderness and came to Horeb, the mountain of God. The Angel of the LORD appeared to him in a blazing fire from the midst of a bush;

> and he looked, and behold, the bush was burning with fire, yet the bush was not consumed. So Moses said, "I must turn aside now and see this marvelous sight, why the bush is not burned up." When the LORD saw that he turned aside to look, God called to him from the midst of the bush and said, "Moses, Moses!" And he said, "Here I am." Then He said, "Do not come near here; remove your sandals from your feet, for the place on which you are standing is holy ground." He said also, "I am the God of your father, the God of Abraham, the God of Isaac, and the God of Jacob." Then Moses hid his face, for he was afraid to look at God. (Exod. 3:1–6)

Prior to the time of Moses, the Angel of the Lord had also appeared to Hagar (Gen. 16:7–14), Abraham (Gen. 22:11–18), and Jacob (Gen. 31:11–13). Since the Angel of the Lord in all these instances speaks for God in the first person, using the pronoun *I*, it has been suggested by some theologians that these appearances of the Angel of the Lord were also Christophanes, the pre-incarnate Christ representing his Father.

Jesus testified to the Jews: "Truly, truly, I say to you, before Abraham was born, I am" (John 8:58). This was the same name, *I am*, which God used to identify himself when speaking to Moses out of the burning bush.

> Then Moses said to God, "Behold, I am going to the sons of Israel, and I will say to them, 'The God of your fathers has sent me to you.' Now they may say to me, 'What is His name?' What shall I say to them?" God said to Moses, "I AM WHO I AM"; and He said, "Thus you shall say to the sons of Israel, 'I AM has sent me to you.'" God, furthermore, said to Moses, "Thus you shall say to the sons of Israel, 'The LORD, the God of your fathers, the God of Abraham, the God of Isaac, and the God of Jacob, has sent me to you.' This is My name forever, and this is My memorial-name to all generations." (Exod. 3:13–15)

Now we know that Christ (the Word) was not only present before Abraham, but was also present at the beginning when "God created the heavens and earth" (Gen. 1:1). Indeed, John also tells us that: "In the beginning was the Word, and the Word was with God, and the Word was God. He was in the beginning with God. All things came into being through Him, and apart from Him nothing came into being that has come into being" (John 1:1–3). Therefore, many Christians would very much like to know more about the activities of our Lord between Creation and his incarnation in Bethlehem. Unfortunately, the Scriptures are largely silent about the activities of Christ during this long period, although it is possible that God *may* have been starting to reveal his triune nature to man through the activities of Melchizedek the priest and/or the Angel of the Lord. Nevertheless, the true relationship of Melchizedek and the Angel of the Lord to the Trinity is still a great mystery to us, and when we speculate about possible Christophanes in the Old Testament, we are not on very solid scriptural ground. The same has certainly been true of those who have attempted to fill in that much shorter, almost blank period between Christ's birth in Bethlehem and the beginning of his ministry some thirty years later. No doubt all will be made clear to us someday when we meet him face to face.

In any event, while there may be hints of the three-fold nature of God prior to the time of King David, there are much clearer indications of God's triune nature during and after the reign of David. In some of the prophecies which David makes concerning the coming Messiah, we see the divine interacting with the divine. In other words, God seems to be sharing his divine attributes and titles with another. For example, in Psalm 110:1: "The Lord says to my Lord, 'Sit at My right hand Until I make Your enemies a footstool for Your feet'" and in Psalms 45:7: "Therefore God, Your God, has anointed You With the oil of joy above Your fellows." The Lord speaking to the Lord, and God speaking to God, are certainly similar to the passage in Genesis from the sixth day of creation: "And God said, let us make man in our image, after our likeness" (Gen. 1:26). Indeed, when Jesus questioned the Pharisees as to whom they thought the Christ (the Messiah) was, he cited the previously mentioned passage from Psalms 110:1: "Now while the Pharisees were gathered together, Jesus asked them a question: 'What do you think about the Christ, whose son is He?' They said to Him, 'The son of David.' He said to them, 'Then how does David in the Spirit call Him 'Lord,' saying, 'THE LORD SAID TO MY LORD, SIT AT MY RIGHT HAND, UNTIL I PUT YOUR ENEMIES BENEATH YOUR FEET'? If David then calls Him 'Lord,' how is He his son?' No one was able to answer Him a word, nor did anyone dare from that day on to ask Him another question" (Matt. 22:41–46). Jesus was not *just* the Son of David, he was also the Son of God, but most of the Pharisees could not accept this.

II. Fulfillment of Prophecies concerning the Messiah's Divinity

Contrary to some ancient *and* modern theories, the divinity of Christ was never in doubt: it was not something he achieved by a life of good works, nor was it something that was appended to him by his loving disciples after his death. Instead, both before his inception and after his birth, the Scriptures are very clear concerning his divinity. Before his inception, the Angel Gabriel made this promise to Mary concerning her son: "Do not be afraid, Mary; for you have found favor with God. And behold, you will conceive in your womb and bear a son, and you shall name Him Jesus. He will be great and will be called the Son of the Most High; and the Lord God will give Him the throne of His father David; and He will reign over the house of Jacob forever, and His kingdom will have no end" (Luke 1:30–33). On the night of his birth, angels once more affirmed his lordship: "In the same region there were some shepherds staying out in the fields and keeping watch over their flock by night. And an angel of the Lord suddenly stood before them, and the glory of the Lord shone around them; and they were terribly frightened. But the angel said to them, 'Do not be afraid; for behold, I bring you good news of great joy which will be for all the people; for today in the city of David there has been born for you a Savior, who is Christ the Lord'" (Luke 2:8–11).

At the beginning of Christ's ministry, John the Baptist affirmed that Jesus was the Messiah, the promised one. As a result, several of John's disciples (Andrew and John) left him, and began to follow Jesus. At the beginning of Christ's ministry, and twice throughout its course, God vocally affirmed that Christ was his beloved Son in whom he was well pleased. At the beginning of Christ's ministry, and throughout its course, Jesus himself testified that he was the Son of God. Throughout Christ's ministry, God the Father would also continue to affirm that Christ was his Son by giving him the power to perform miracles, from calming the sea to raising the dead. Eventually, the Jews put Christ to death for claiming to be the Son of God

A. *The Testimony of God*

Three times God spoke from heaven to affirm that Jesus was indeed his Son: (1) at the river Jordan when Jesus was baptized by John, (2) on the Mount of Transfiguration where Jesus appeared in glory with Elijah and Moses, and (3) after Jesus's Triumphal Entry into Jerusalem near the end of his earthly ministry.

1. At the River Jordan

Then Jesus arrived from Galilee at the Jordan coming to John, to be baptized by him. But John tried to prevent Him, saying, "I have need to be baptized by You, and do You come to me?" But Jesus answering said to him, "Permit it at this time; for in this way it is fitting for us to fulfill all righteousness." Then he permitted Him. After being baptized, Jesus came up immediately from the water; and behold, the heavens were opened, and he saw the Spirit of God descending as a dove and lighting on Him, and behold, a voice out of the heavens said, "This is My beloved Son, in whom I am well-pleased." (Matt. 3:13–17)

2. On the Mount of Transfiguration

Six days later Jesus took with Him Peter and James and John his brother, and led them up on a high mountain by themselves. And He was transfigured before them; and His face shone like the sun, and His garments became as white as light. And behold, Moses and Elijah appeared to them, talking with Him. Peter said to Jesus, "Lord, it is good for us to be here; if You wish, I will make three tabernacles here, one for You, and one for Moses, and one for Elijah." While he was still speaking, a bright cloud overshadowed them, and behold, a voice out of the cloud said, "This is My beloved Son, with whom I am well-pleased; listen to Him!" When the disciples heard this, they fell face down to the ground and were terrified. (Matt. 17:1–6)

For we did not follow cleverly devised tales when we made known to you the power and coming of our Lord Jesus Christ, but we were eyewitnesses of His majesty. For when He received honor and glory from God the Father, such an utterance as this was made to Him by the Majestic Glory, "This is My beloved Son with whom I am well-pleased"—and we ourselves heard this utterance made from heaven when we were with Him on the holy mountain. (2 Peter 1:16–18)

3. After Christ's Triumphal Entry into Jerusalem

"Now My soul has become troubled; and what shall I say, 'Father, save Me from this Hour'? But for this purpose I came to this hour. Father, glorify Your name." Then a voice came out of heaven: "I have both glorified it, and will glorify it again." So the crowd of people who stood by and heard it were saying that it had thundered; others were saying, "An angel has spoken to Him." Jesus answered and said, "This voice has not come for My sake, but for your sakes. Now judgment is upon this world; now the ruler of this world will be cast out. And I, if I am lifted up from the earth, will draw all men to Myself." (John 12:27–32)

Now the first and third of God's proclamations from heaven were made in public, whereas during the second, only Peter, James, and John were present. We also do not know if all the people who were present at Jesus's baptism, heard—and understood—the voice of God, or only a select few, such as John the Baptist and some of his disciples. In the third instance, after Jesus's Triumphal Entry into Jerusalem, John notes that when God spoke, some of the people thought they heard thunder while others believed an angel had spoken to Jesus. Those who thought they heard thunder obviously didn't understand the message; it is unclear whether those who thought an angel spoke to Jesus understood what was said to him. To hear the voice of God, even when he speaks directly from Heaven, often appears to require a heart and mind that is actively seeking God.

B. The Testimony of John the Baptist

Whether or not all those present at Jesus's baptism understood what God had proclaimed from heaven about his Son, John the Baptist, being the one sent to prepare the way of the Lord (Mal. 3:1, 4:5; Luke 1:16–17, 76), was faithful in his testimony as to whom Jesus was:

1. After the baptism of Christ

The next day he saw Jesus coming to him and said, "Behold, the Lamb of God who takes away the sin of the world! This is He on behalf of whom I said, 'After me comes a Man who has a higher rank than I, for He existed before me.' I did not recognize Him, but so that He might be manifested to Israel, I came baptizing in water." John testified saying, "I have seen the Spirit descending as a dove out of heaven, and He remained upon Him. I did not recognize Him, but He who sent me to baptize in water said to me, 'He upon whom you see the Spirit descending and remaining upon Him, this is the One who baptizes in the Holy Spirit.' I myself have seen, and have testified that this is the Son of God." (John 1:29–34)

C. The Testimony of Jesus

In addition to the testimony of his Heavenly Father and John the Baptist, Jesus himself repeatedly affirmed that he was the Messiah, the Son of God:

1. After the healing of the impotent man by the Pool of Bethesda in Jerusalem

The man went away, and told the Jews that it was Jesus who had made him well. For this reason the Jews were persecuting Jesus, because He was doing these things on the Sabbath. But He answered them, "My Father is working until now, and I Myself am working." For this reason therefore the Jews were seeking all the more to kill Him, because He not only was breaking the Sabbath, but also was calling God His own Father, making Himself equal with God. (John 5:15–18)

2. At the beginning of his Galilean ministry

And He came to Nazareth, where He had been brought up; and as was His custom, He entered the synagogue on the Sabbath, and stood up to read. And the book of the prophet Isaiah was handed to Him. And He opened the book and found the place where it was written, "THE SPIRIT OF THE LORD IS UPON ME, BECAUSE HE ANOINTED ME TO PREACH THE GOSPEL TO THE POOR. HE HAS SENT ME TO PROCLAIM RELEASE TO THE CAPTIVES, AND RECOVERY OF SIGHT TO THE BLIND, TO SET FREE THOSE WHO ARE OPPRESSED, TO PROCLAIM THE FAVORABLE YEAR OF THE LORD." And He closed the book, gave it back to the attendant and sat down; and the eyes of all in the synagogue were fixed on Him. And He began to say to them, "Today this Scripture has been fulfilled in your hearing".... And all the people in the synagogue were filled with rage as they heard these things; and they got up and drove Him out of the city, and led Him to the brow of the hill on which their city had been built, in order to throw Him down the cliff. But passing through their midst, He went His way. (Luke 4:16–21, 28–30)

3. At the end of his sermon in Judea on the light of the world

"Your father Abraham rejoiced to see My day, and he saw it and was glad." So the Jews said to Him, "You are not yet fifty years old, and have You seen Abraham?" Jesus said to them, "Truly, truly, I say to you, before Abraham was born, I am." Therefore they picked up stones to throw at Him, but Jesus hid Himself and went out of the temple. (John 8:56–59)

4. After Peter's good confession at Caesarea Philippi

For the Son of Man is going to come in the glory of His Father with His angels, and WILL THEN REPAY EVERY MAN ACCORD-ING TO HIS DEEDS. (Matt. 16:27)

5. At the Feast of Dedication in Jerusalem

The Jews then gathered around Him, and were saying to Him, "How long will You keep us in suspense? If You are the Christ, tell us plainly." Jesus answered them, "I told you, and you do not believe; the works that I do in My Father's name, these testify of Me. But you do not believe because you are not of My sheep. My sheep hear My voice, and I know them, and they follow Me; and I give eternal life to them, and they will never perish; and no one will snatch them out of My hand. My Father, who has given them to Me, is greater than all; and no one is able to snatch them out of the Father's hand. I and the Father are one." The Jews picked up stones again to stone Him. Jesus answered them, "I showed you many good works from the Father; for which of them are you stoning Me?" The Jews answered Him, "For a good work we do not stone You, but for blasphemy; and because You, being a man, make Yourself out to be God." (John 10:24–33)

6. During his last public ministry in Jerusalem

Now while the Pharisees were gathered together, Jesus asked them a question: "What do you think about the Christ, whose son is He?" They said to Him, "The son of David." He said to them, "Then how does David in the Spirit call Him 'Lord,' saying, 'THE LORD SAID TO MY LORD, SIT AT MY RIGHT HAND, UNTIL I PUT YOUR ENEMIES BENEATH YOUR FEET'? If David then calls Him 'Lord,' how is He his son?" No one was able to answer Him a word, nor did anyone dare from that day on to ask Him another question. (Matt. 22:41–46)

7. During his Farewell Discourse after the Last Supper

"If you had known Me, you would have known My Father also; from now on you know Him, and have seen Him." Philip said to Him, "Lord, show us the Father, and it is enough for us." Jesus said to him, "Have I been so long with you, and yet you have not come to know Me, Philip? He who has seen Me has seen the Father; how can you say, 'Show us the Father'?" (John 14:7–9)

8. During his the trial before Caiaphas the high priest

The high priest stood up and said to Him, "Do You not answer? What is it that these men are testifying against You?" But Jesus kept silent. And the high priest said to Him, "I adjure You by the living God, that You tell us whether You are the Christ, the Son of God." Jesus said to him, "You have said it yourself; nevertheless I tell you, hereafter you will see THE SON OF MAN SITTING AT THE RIGHT HAND OF POWER, and COMING ON THE CLOUDS OF HEAVEN." Then the high priest tore his robes and said, "He has blasphemed! What further need do we have of witnesses? Behold, you have now heard the blasphemy; what do you think?" They answered, "He deserves death!" (Matt. 26:62–66)

9. During his trial before the Sanhedrin

When it was day, the Council of elders of the people assembled, both chief priests and scribes, and they led Him away to their council chamber, saying, "If You are the Christ, tell us." But He said to them, "If I tell you, you will not believe; and if I ask a question, you will not answer. But from now on THE SON OF MAN WILL BE SEATED AT THE RIGHT HAND of the power OF GOD." And they all said, "Are You the Son of God, then?" And He said to them, "Yes, I am." Then they said, "What further need do we have of testimony? For we have heard it ourselves from His own mouth." (Luke 22:66–71)

Concerning his authority to heal on the Sabbath, Jesus said that he worked, even as his Father continued to work. In the synagogue of his hometown, Nazareth, he publicly read Isaiah 61:1–2 which is one of the beautiful prophecies concerning the coming Messiah. He then sat down and calmly proclaimed that this prophecy was, that very day, fulfilled. Later, in Jerusalem, he proclaimed that he had existed before Abraham and that Abraham had actually looked forward to the day of his appearance. Outside Caesarea Philippi, he promised his disciples that he would one day return to earth in glory and with the angels to judge the world. At the Feast of Dedication in Jerusalem he proclaimed that he and his Father were one. Near the end of his ministry he pointed out that, even though the

Messiah was the Son of David, David had addressed him as Lord. After the Last Supper with his Disciples, he told Phillip that they which had seen him, had seen the Father. During his trial before Caiaphas the high priest, and later, the Sanhedrin, he promised his judges that they would subsequently see him setting on the right hand of God's throne. These statements were neither the wild fantasies of an egotistical maniac nor the incoherent ramblings of a mentally ill person, but rather, the calm, assured voice of the Son of God who knew from whence he had come, why he was here, and to whom he would return. The only man who ever walked on the earth and claimed that he was divine, who was not out of his mind, was the Son of God who was divine, who had been with the Father from the beginning of the heavens and earth, and whom the Father acknowledged as his beloved son.

D. The Testimony of the Works of Jesus

In addition to verbally acknowledging his Son from heaven, the Father also showed his approval of his Son by granting him power and authority to perform miracles, including the raising of the dead. Jesus repeatedly pointed out to the scribes and Pharisees that, if they didn't believe his testimony as to who he was, the Messiah, the Son of God, they should believe his works, since the mighty miracles he was performing could only be done through the power of God. The works (miracles) were proof that God approved of what Jesus was saying. Jesus repeatedly explained how his works validated his claims on many occasions:

1. After the healing of the impotent man by the Pool of Bethsaida in Jerusalem

But the testimony which I have is greater than the testimony of John; for the works which the Father has given Me to accomplish— the very works that I do—testify about Me, that the Father has sent Me. And the Father who sent Me, He has testified of Me. You have neither heard His voice at any time nor seen His form. You do not have His word abiding in you, for you do not believe Him whom He sent. You search the Scriptures because you think that in them you have eternal life; it is these that testify about Me; and you are unwilling to come to Me so that you may have life. (John 5:36–40)

2. After his discourse on John the Baptist

Then He began to denounce the cities in which most of His miracles were done, because they did not repent. "Woe to you, Chorazin! Woe to you, Bethsaida! For if the miracles had occurred in Tyre and Sidon which occurred in you, they would have repented long ago in sackcloth and ashes. Nevertheless I say to you, it will be more tolerable for Tyre and Sidon in the day of judgment than for you. And you, Capernaum, will not be exalted to heaven, will you? You will descend to Hades; for if the miracles had occurred in Sodom which occurred in you, it would have remained to this day. Nevertheless I say to you that it will be more tolerable for the land of Sodom in the day of judgment, than for you." (Matt. 11:20–24)

3. On Solomon's porch in Jerusalem

If I do not do the works of My Father, do not believe Me; but if I do them, though you do not believe Me, believe the works, so that you may know and understand that the Father is in Me, and I in the Father. (John 10:37–38)

4. During his Farewell Discourse after the Last Supper

If I had not done among them the works which no one else did, they would not have sin; but now they have both seen and hated Me and My Father as well. (John 15:24)

Yet despite the mighty works which Jesus performed, most of the political and religious leaders of the Jewish nation still did not believe that he was the promised Messiah. They rejected both his message and his miracles. The people of the great city of Nineveh had repented of their sins in sackcloth when Jonah, who had been in the belly of a whale for three days, came and preached to them (Jonah 3:4–10). The people of the city of Jerusalem, however, refused to repent of their sins, even though the one sent to preach to them would soon be in the belly of the earth for three days (Matt. 12:40). Jonah was just one of God's prophets; Jesus was God's own son. Jesus told a parable of a man who planted a vineyard, let it out to husbandmen, and then went off into a far country:

> "Listen to another parable. There was a landowner who PLANTED A VINEYARD AND PUT A WALL AROUND IT AND DUG A WINE PRESS IN IT, AND BUILT A TOWER, and rented it out to vine-growers and went on a journey. When the harvest time approached, he sent his slaves to the vine-growers to receive his produce. The vine-growers took his slaves and beat one, and killed another, and stoned a third. Again he sent another group of slaves larger than the first; and they did the same thing to them. But afterward he sent his son to them, saying, 'They will respect my son.' But when the vine-growers saw the son, they said among themselves, 'This is the heir; come, let us kill him and seize his inheritance.' They took him, and threw him out of the vineyard and killed him. Therefore when the owner of the vineyard comes, what will he do to those vine-growers?" (Matt. 21:33–40)

Jesus therefore warned the cities of Galilee where he had performed many of his miracles—Chorazin, Bethsaida, Capernaum—that they would fare far worse at the final judgment than Tyre and Sidon, or even Sodom, because the people in these Galilean cities had failed to repent of their sins, even though he, the Son of God, had performed many great miracles within their walls. Indeed, Jesus went on to say that, had he not performed these miracles, they would have been guiltless, but their rejection of both his words and works had, in effect, made manifest their disdain for both the Son of God and his Father. The Pharisees had also rejected the divinity of Christ, despite the testimony of his Heavenly Father, John the Baptist, and Jesus himself. Finally, like the Galilean cities that Jesus mentioned, the Pharisees has also rejected the miraculous works which Jesus performed, and had therefore sealed their own doom. There was no longer any way for God to reach them. They would believe what they wanted to believe, even if someone came back from the dead. The rejection of Christ's works by nonbelievers inevitably led to their final condemnation. One day, after Jesus had cast out a demon that had made a man both blind and dumb, the Pharisees dismissed this miracle by saying that he did it through the power of Beelzebub the prince of the devils. Jesus then warned them that: "any sin and blasphemy shall be forgiven people, but blasphemy against the Spirit shall not be forgiven" (Matt. 12:31).

In both the Old and New Testament we learn that God's power is manifested through the actions of the Holy Spirit: (1) at the beginning of creation, the Spirit of God was moving upon the waters of the earth (Gen. 1:2); (2) the Spirit of the Lord came mightily upon Samson when he fought the Philistines (Judg. 14:19); (3) David prophesied of the Messiah through the Holy Spirit (Mark 12:36); (4) Mary is found to be with child by the Holy Spirit (Matt. 1:18, 20); (5) John the Baptist would be filled with the Holy Spirit (Luke 1:15); (6) Elizabeth, John the Baptist's mother, was filled with the Holy Spirit and told Mary she was blessed among women (v. 41); (7) Zacharias, John the Baptist's father, was filled with the Holy Spirit and prophesied concerning John (vv. 67–79); (8) the Holy Spirit was upon Simon and he was shown the baby Jesus (Luke 2:25); (9) the Holy Spirit descended upon Jesus in the form of a dove at his baptism (Luke 3:22); (10) Jesus was full of the Holy Spirit (Luke 4:1); (11) John baptized with water but Jesus baptized with the Holy Spirit (Matt. 3:11); (12) during the Last Supper, Jesus promised the apostles that the Spirit would guide them into all truth (John 16:13); (13) the Father gives the Holy Spirit to them that ask (Luke 11:13); and (14) when persecuted and brought before judges, the Holy Spirit will speak for us (Mark 13:11). To see that which is of the Holy Spirit, as that which is profane, is the final step in a man or woman's degradation; it is the point of no return where God ceases to be our Father and Satan fully takes over that role. Satan's eyes become our eyes, his heart becomes our heart. Jesus's birth was the work of the Holy Spirit. The Holy Spirit descended upon Jesus when he was baptized by John. The miraculous works which Jesus performed were through the Holy Spirit which filled him. This is why it was so disastrous for the Pharisees and the cities of Galilee to reject the works which Jesus did. They were saying these works of God were the works of the devil; they were committing blasphemy against the Holy Spirit.

III. MISUNDERSTANDING OF PROPHECIES CONCERNING THE MESSIAH'S DIVINITY

We are now confronted with a dilemma: How could the Pharisees, the acknowledged experts on the law of Moses and its interpretation, the religious leaders of a religious nation, the ones whose very name signified their desire to separate themselves from the world and ungodly influences, have created a theology that was so flawed? After their nation had awaited the coming of the Messiah for more than 1,000 years, how could they persecute and ultimately reject their Messiah when he finally appeared? Why were they so willfully ignorant of the circumstances surrounding the actual place of Jesus's birth? Why did they ignore all the Scriptures that told of the authority God would give to his Holy One? Why did they totally reject the prophecies concerning the divinity of the coming Messiah? In a broad sense, it appears that the answer to all these questions is that the scribes and Pharisees, the chief priests and doctors of the law, had created their own religion. Although this religion was based on the Scriptures and the long interaction of God with their nation, in the end it was a religion that they had fashioned for themselves by picking which Scriptures and prophecies they would accept, ignore, or reject. Over this mosaic of truths, half-truths, and falsehoods, they had spread a thick layer of oral traditions which they themselves had created, and to which they assigned greatest value. This man-made religion was one which most benefited the Pharisees, which gave them honor and positions of authority in their culture. To the common people, the Pharisees had become the final interpreters of the law, the ones who ultimately had the say as to what was right and wrong, behavior. In a sense, they had become their own gods. Small wonder, then, that they so furiously attacked the

Messiah's claims of divinity. They weren't about to give up their position and power to another.

In a narrower sense, however, one might explain the Pharisees' failure to recognize the Messiah as the result of their having believed a lie. Since Satan is the father of lies, it is not surprising that he would attempt to negate God's plan of redemption with a well-placed lie in the hearts of men. In the Gospels, this lie repeatedly appears when the Pharisees and other religious leaders attempt to justify their rejection of Jesus as the Christ. This lie simply states: Jesus was just a man, like us (or perhaps, *a man less than us*, since Jesus was from Nazareth). This lie is repeatedly advanced to negate Jesus's divinity:

A. *The First Rejection of Jesus at Nazareth*

> And He came to Nazareth, where He had been brought up; and as was His custom, He entered the synagogue on the Sabbath, and stood up to read. And the book of the prophet Isaiah was handed to Him. And He opened the book and found the place where it was written, "THE SPIRIT OF THE LORD IS UPON ME, BECAUSE HE ANOINTED ME TO PREACH THE GOSPEL TO THE POOR. HE HAS SENT ME TO PROCLAIM RELEASE TO THE CAPTIVES, AND RECOVERY OF SIGHT TO THE BLIND, TO SET FREE THOSE WHO ARE OPPRESSED, TO PROCLAIM THE FAVORABLE YEAR OF THE LORD." And He closed the book, gave it back to the attendant and sat down; and the eyes of all in the synagogue were fixed on Him. And He began to say to them, "Today this Scripture has been fulfilled in your hearing." And all were speaking well of Him, and wondering at the gracious words which were falling from His lips; and they were saying, "Is this not Joseph's son?" (Luke 4:16–22)

B. *The Second Rejection of Jesus at Nazareth*

> When Jesus had finished these parables, He departed from there. He came to His hometown and began teaching them in their synagogue,

> so that they were astonished, and said, "Where did this man get this
> wisdom and these miraculous powers? Is not this the carpenter's son?
> Is not His mother called Mary, and His brothers, James and Joseph
> and Simon and Judas? And His sisters, are they not all with us? Where
> then did this man get all these things?" And they took offense at Him.
> But Jesus said to them, "A prophet is not without honor except in
> his hometown and in his own household." And He did not do many
> miracles there because of their unbelief. (Matt. 13:53–58)

C. Jesus in Jerusalem

> Therefore the Jews were grumbling about Him, because He said,
> "I am the bread that came down out of heaven." They were saying,
> "Is not this Jesus, the son of Joseph, whose father and mother we
> know? How does He now say, 'I have come down out of heaven'?"
> (John 6:41–42)

D. Jesus in Jerusalem at the Feast of Tabernacles

> So some of the people of Jerusalem were saying, "Is this not the
> man whom they are seeking to kill? Look, He is speaking publicly,
> and they are saying nothing to Him. The rulers do not really know
> that this is the Christ, do they? However, we know where this man
> is from; but whenever the Christ may come, no one knows where
> He is from." (John 7:25–27)

Just as one rotten apple or potato can ruin the lot, one lie can
corrupt our understanding; our thinking can become tainted by
its presence. And what could be a greater lie than that the Son of
God, God's Holy One, was just a man. This lie became a stumbling block, not only for the Pharisees, but for many others down
through the ages. It provided a concise, convenient excuse for non-
belief. Satan's lie that Jesus was just a man was based on the fact
that Christ had parents, as well as brothers and sisters, still living
in Nazareth; therefore, he could not possibly be the Son of God.
Some even argued that the coming Messiah was such a mystery

that no one could know his origin: "but whenever the Christ may come, no one knows where He is from" (John 7:27). This latter argument, of course, was utter non-sense without any scriptural foundation. The Scriptures both foretold how the Messiah would be born—of a virgin, as well as where he would be born—in Bethlehem. However, if the Messiah was to be born of a virgin, as Isaiah (7:14) had prophesied, he had to have a mother living somewhere, and perhaps brothers and sisters as well. One of the titles used throughout the Old Testament prophecies concerning the Messiah was the *Son of David*. Repeatedly in the Scriptures, the Messiah's lineage was traced to the line of King David. Indeed, the prophets sometimes describe the Messiah as *the Branch* (see Table 13):

Table 13: Scriptures concerning The Branch

Then a shoot will spring from the stem of Jesse, And a branch from his roots will bear fruit. The Spirit of the LORD will rest on Him, The spirit of wisdom and understanding, The spirit of counsel and strength, The spirit of knowledge and the fear of the LORD. And He will delight in the fear of the LORD, And He will not judge by what His eyes see, Nor make a decision by what His ears hear; But with righteousness He will judge the poor, And decide with fairness for the afflicted of the earth; And He will strike the earth with the rod of His mouth, And with the breath of His lips He will slay the wicked. Also righteousness will be the belt about His loins, And faithfulness the belt about His waist. (Isa. 11:1–5)

"Behold, the days are coming," declares the LORD, "When I will raise up for David a righteous Branch; And He will reign as king and act wisely And do justice and righteousness in the land." (Jer. 23:5)

Then say to him, "Thus says the LORD of hosts, 'Behold, a man whose name is Branch, for He will branch out from where He is; and He will build the temple of the LORD. Yes, it is He who will build the temple of the LORD, and He who will bear the honor and sit and rule on His throne. Thus, He will be a priest on His throne, and the counsel of peace will be between the two offices.'" (Zech. 6:12–13)

A branch is part of a tree, and the Messiah was a part of the family tree of Jessie and his son David. People that are part of a family tree have ancestors; they also have mothers and fathers, brothers and sisters. Wasn't Joseph, the husband of Mary, of the house and lineage of David (Luke 2:4)? Didn't Matthew (1:1–17) trace the genealogy of Jesus, not only back to King David, but all the way back to Abraham? Didn't Luke (3:23–38) trace the genealogy of Jesus all the way back to Adam? Indeed from Matthew's genealogy, we know that Jesus's ancestors were not only patriarchs and kings, but also included Rahab the Canaanite from Jericho, Ruth the Moabitess, and Bathsheba who was formerly Uriah the Hittite's wife. (What would the Pharisees have said if they had known that these women were also a part of Jesus's ancestry?) Therefore, the real question was not, How could the Son of God have living relatives? but, given the prophecies concerning the Messiah, How could the Messiah *not* have a family and relatives (who were descendants of King David)? Lies have power and longevity, not because they are true, but because they are convenient. They save us from having to do any deep thinking about a problem. Lies often confirm our biases; they allow us to believe what we want to believe, and this was certainly the case with the Pharisees—Jesus of Nazareth was the son of Joseph and Mary, therefore he could not be the Son of God.

CONCLUSION

In conclusion, the mistakes the Pharisees made concerning the Messiah's place of birth, the authority given to him by his Father, and his divinity, all provide classical examples of the limitations of theological truth. Even the most knowledgeable biblical scholars can be led astray in their theological constructions by: (1) their limited knowledge of God and his Word, (2) the unintentional mistakes they may make in interpreting God's Word, and (3) intentional distortions of God's Word they may have fabricated because of their own personal biases. Based on the criticisms and condemnations that Jesus leveled at the Pharisees, it is evident that the bulk of their theological mistakes were the direct result of their own biases and sinful desires, not their ignorance of the Scriptures or their unintentional mistakes in interpreting the Scriptures. Many of the theological mistakes we make today no doubt also arise from our own biases and sinful desires; we also, all too often, only see what we want to see and hear what we want to hear. Therefore, throughout our lives we must constantly reexamine our understanding of the Scriptures and pray to God that he will remove the beams from our eyes so that we might see clearly. Otherwise, we may end up sharing some of the Pharisees' theological mistakes, as well as some of their punishments.

Part 4

Theological Mistakes Concerning the Natural World

Chapter 10

Modern Theological Mistakes concerning the Heavens

Introduction

The limitations of theological truth are very clearly on display in the never-ending debate between science and religion. As was discussed in Chapter 4, we are, in part, a product of the culture into which we are born, educated, and work. Our knowledge and understanding of the natural world, in particular, is a product of that cultural background. Even the words we use to describe nature are derived from our culture. Thus, when we read passages of Scripture that deal with the natural world, our understanding and interpretation of those Scriptures will, inevitably, be strongly influenced by the theories and traditions about nature that we have learned from our culture. Our cultural background provides a lens through which we can view the world around us. Every culture on earth has developed its own theories and traditions as to how nature works and how the heavens and the earth came into existence. These models are based on each culture's own unique experiences, as well as the theories and traditions they have borrowed from other cultures.

The theories and traditions that cultures have concerning nature are not only a product of the cultures in which they arise but also the time period in which they occur. From a historical perspective, it is easy to see how our understanding of the natural world changes through time. Cultures in Europe could not have known that the Americas existed until they were discovered by first the Vikings, and later, Christopher Columbus. They could not have known that the human body was composed of cells until the microscope was invented, they could not have known that Jupiter had moons until the telescope was invented, they could not have explained how heredity worked until genes and DNA were discovered, they could not have explained what powered the sun until nuclear fusion was discovered, and they could not have known what was on the backside of the moon until rockets were invented. As a consequence, the knowledge of the natural world that any culture can even potentially have access to is dependent on the time period during which that culture exists. Here in America, our understanding of the natural world in the time of George Washington in the 1700s was very different from that in the time of Abraham Lincoln in the 1800s, or the time of John Kennedy in the 1900s. From an even broader chronological perspective, Abraham lived in the third millennium B.C., Moses in the second millennium B.C., Isaiah in the first millennium B.C., Paul in the first millennium A.D., Martin Luther in the second millennium A.D., and we, today, in the third millennium A.D. How much greater were the differences between the theories and traditions about nature that must have existed among the various cultures and time periods into which these individuals were born? Through the lens of their own culture and time period, these individuals no doubt had very different understandings and interpretations of scriptural passages that dealt with the natural world. Yet these individuals all shared a common belief in, and love for, God. Moreover, they were called out of their respective cultures to serve Him. Clearly, our salvation is not dependent upon our degree of understanding of the natural world or the accuracy of our theological interpretations of scriptural passages that deal with the natural world. These cultural theories and traditions about nature keep changing from culture to culture and from time to time, as new discoveries are made, new inventions are created, and new models of the physical universe are formulated. As a consequence, our understanding of the natural world continues to change and grow.

Now as we have repeatedly noted in earlier chapters, one of the three primary causes for the limitations of both scientific truth and theological truth is human ignorance. Our individual knowledge and understanding of both nature and the Scriptures is fragmentary and incomplete; it continues to grow and develop, throughout our lives. The same is true of humanity's collective cultural knowledge and understanding of nature down through the centuries and millennia. Unfortunately, many Christians act as though they are ignorant of the fact that humanity's knowledge and understanding of God's creation has grown richer and deeper over time. They are threatened by new scientific discoveries and inventions, and often demand that we confine our understanding of scriptural passages dealing with the natural world to earlier theories and traditions. What they fail to understand is that all theories and traditions, all cultural lenses through which we view nature and interpret scriptural passages about nature, are man-made, imperfect, and subject to change. They demand that we understand and interpret scriptural passages dealing with nature in terms of the science of the seventeenth century when Bishop Ussher lived, or the eighteenth century when Jonathan Edwards lived, or the nineteenth century when D. L. Moody lived, or the twentieth century when Billy Graham lived. But, the scientific tools and models of the cultures that existed during those earlier centuries are no more divinely inspired than those of today in the twenty-first century.

Each culture and time period has a different perspective on the natural world, based on the information that is available to it. If we are born into a culture and time period that believes that the world is flat, we will understand and interpret passages in the Scriptures that deal with the earth, in those terms. If we are born into a culture and time period that believes that the earth is the center of the universe, we will incorporate that idea into our understanding of God's creation. None of these cultural perspectives have the divine stamp of approval; they are just humanity's imperfect attempt to understand God's creation to the best of its knowledge at that time. It is, therefore, the duty of each succeeding generation to try to understand God's creation and the scriptural passages dealing with it in terms of what their culture presently knows about the physical universe. This is the best we can do; we can only work with the information that is available to us. When Christians fail to do this through ignorance or laziness, a schism develops between Christians and the culture(s) in which they live. When Christians linger too long in the past, they begin to advance scriptural interpretations of God's creation that are increasingly out of sync with their culture's current understanding of nature. For example, in America, some Christians now ask us to believe that the heavens and the earth were created in 4,000 B.C. and are, therefore, only slightly older than Stonehenge (3,100 B.C.), or that dinosaurs and humans coexisted. Such models are wildly out of step with our culture's current understanding of the natural world, which is largely based on the empirical evidence presently available to it. By creating this disjunction between faith and empirical evidence, these Christians bring discredit to, and encourage disbelief of, the very Scriptures they hold so dear. What they fail to recognize is that when they reject their culture's current model of the physical universe, they are merely arguing for an earlier cultural model of nature. Since all cultural models of nature are humanly derived and therefore subject to human ignorance, misunderstanding, and bias, these cultural models of nature are inevitably composed of a mixture of truths, half-truths, and falsehoods. Yet, this has been the tendency of Christians over the past two millennia—to found a scriptural interpretation on the science of the time, and then spend the next few centuries, or even millennium, trying to defend that position as the sandy soil beneath its foundation is gradually eroded away by new scientific discoveries. (What was it that Jesus said about choosing one's building sites carefully?) This is why the debate between science and religion has been an unending one. It is my contention that much of the science–religion debate is not really between science and religion. Instead, the debate is between earlier cultural/scientific models of nature which the church previously utilized in its theological interpretations of Scripture, and more recent cultural/scientific models of nature which the church has not (yet) attempted to utilize in its understanding of God's creation.

In this and the following two chapters, I will provide examples of the roles that human ignorance, misinterpretation, and bias have played in the science-religion debate concerning the heavens, the earth, and life. All of these examples illustrate the limitations of theological truth and its transitory nature. Moreover, it should become obvious that the limitations of scientific truth play a significant role in the limitations of theological truth, at least in those areas dealing with God's creation of the natural world. As our cultures learn more and more about the physical universe in terms of: (1) its material structure (what God made), (2) history (when God made it), and (3) the natural laws by which it operates (how God governs it), our understanding and interpretation of those scriptural passages dealing with the natural world may change as well. In other words, as humanity's limited knowledge of God's creation continues to develop and grow, we may gain new insights or perspectives on the majesty and complexity of his Creation that will help us better understand and interpret his Word.

I. THE HEAVENS ARE PERFECT AND UNCHANGING

The idea that the heavens are perfect and unchanging is a classic example of a cultural/scientific model of the physical universe that was subsequently incorporated into a theological interpretation of the Scriptures. This model of the heavens did not even originate during the Christian Period, but can be traced back to the ancient Greeks. Anaximander of Miletus (611–546

B.C.) is sometimes recognized as the father of astronomy since he developed the first mechanistic model to explain the apparent motion of the sun across the vault of the heavens by day and the moon and stars by night. Unlike his predecessors, who explained the movement of these heavenly bodies in terms of gods (Helios) and goddesses (Selena) driving their golden or silvery chariots across the sky, Anaximander created a model composed of a series of rings or tubes of fire that rotated around the earth like cart wheels. These tubes of fire had condensed out of a sphere of fire that originally surrounded the earth. Circular holes in these tubes allowed the light from these fires to shine through. The tube nearest the earth has the smallest and most numerous openings—the stars; the most distant tube had the largest opening—the sun (Freely 2012:9).

By the time of Aristotle (384–322 B.C.), the tubes of Anaximander had grown into a series of rotating spheres in which the spherical bodies of the stars were embedded (Aristotle 1986:179–191). This model had been developed by two of Aristotle's contemporaries: Eudoxus of Cnidus (408–355 B.C.) and Callippus of Cyzicus (c. 370 B.C.–c. 300 B.C.). In an attempt to explain the sometimes retrograde motion of the planets, Eudoxus believed there were twenty-seven of these spheres, while Callippus argued there were thirty-four. While trying to further refine the predictive accuracy of these models, Aristotle expanded the number of rotating spheres to fifty-five (Freely 2012:50, 63). Moreover, since the sphere is the perfect geometrical shape, he argued that these heavenly spheres must be composed of a different substance than that of earth, air, fire, and water out of which the world was fashioned. These latter four substances in the terrestrial realm all moved in a linear fashion, either up (air and fire) or down (earth and water), were subject to change, and were perishable, whereas, this fifth substance (later called aether), only occurred in the celestial realm, always moved in circles, was not subject to change, was imperishable, and was therefore divine (ibid.:59–62). Although Aristotle's model was later refined still further by Claudius Ptolemy (c. A.D. 100–c. 170) of Alexandria in the second century A.D., it dominated Western Civilization's cultural/scientific under-standing of the heavens for the next eighteen centuries. Aristotle's model also dominated Western Civilization's theological inter-pretations of Scriptures about the heavens: they were perfect and unchanging and earth was at the center of the universe.

It was natural that this powerful cultural/scientific model of the heavens, which was developed and refined by Greeks, such as Eudoxus, Callippus, Aristotle, and Claudius Ptolemy, would have a significant impact on the Jews and early Christians living in Pales-tine in the first century A.D. As noted in Chapter 7, after Alexander the Great conquered the Persian Empire in 333 B.C., Judea became a part of Alexander's empire that stretched all the way from Greece to India. After Alexander's death, Judea passed into the hands of Alex-ander's Greek generals, first the Ptolemaic Kingdom of Egypt and later the Seleucid Empire that was centered in Syria. So strong was the Greek influence in Judea that the New Testament was written in Greek, not Hebrew or Aramaic. The Greek culture's knowledge and understanding of the natural world, therefore, also became a part of the Jews' and early Christians' cultural heritage and was utilized by them to help understand those passages of Scripture dealing with the natural world and, in particular, the heavens. Aristotle's belief that the heavens were perfect and unchanging fit easily with the Jews' understanding that God, who was perfect and unchanging, dwelt in heaven, as clearly stated in the Bible (see Table 14):

Table 14: Scriptures concerning the Heavens as God's Dwelling Place
The kings of the earth take their stand And the rulers take counsel together Against the Lord and against His Anointed, saying, "Let us tear their fetters apart And cast away their cords from us!" He who sits in the heavens laughs, The Lord scoffs at them. (Ps. 2:2–4)
God has looked down from heaven upon the sons of men To see if there is anyone who understands, Who seeks after God. (Ps. 53:2)
Thus says the LORD, "Heaven is My throne and the earth is My footstool. Where then is a house you could build for Me? And where is a place that I may rest?" (Isa. 66:1)

Table 14: Scriptures concerning the Heavens as God's Dwelling Place

And He led them out as far as Bethany, and He lifted up His hands and blessed them. While He was blessing them, He parted from them and was carried up into heaven. And they, after worshiping Him, returned to Jerusalem with great joy, and were continually in the temple praising God. (Luke 24:50–53)

But being full of the Holy Spirit, he [Stephen] gazed intently into heaven and saw the glory of God, and Jesus standing at the right hand of God. (Acts 7:55)

But after the three and a half days, the breath of life from God came into them, and they stood on their feet; and great fear fell upon those who were watching them. And they heard a loud voice from heaven saying to them, "Come up here." Then they went up into heaven in the cloud, and their enemies watched them. (Rev. 11:11–12)

After the fall of Jerusalem in A.D. 70 and the later collapse of the Roman Empire in A.D. 476, Western Civilization largely lost touch with the cultures of the eastern Mediterranean. During the Dark Ages (fifth to tenth century) which followed, scholarship declined across Europe and knowledge of the Greek language and the works of Greek scholars, such as Aristotle and Ptolemy, were largely lost. The Crusades to the Holy Land (A.D. 1096–1299), however, stimulated new interest in the cultures, languages, and literature of the peoples living in the Eastern Roman Empire. Many of the crusaders returning to Europe brought back copies of ancient manuscripts from Constantinople, Jerusalem, and Egypt which were subsequently translated into Latin and helped fuel the European Renaissance, which began in the 1300s. Among the scholars who now had access to these ancient works were Albertus Magnus (A.D. 1206–1280), and his student Thomas Aquinas (A.D. 1225–1274). Aquinas would subsequently create a synthesis between the Christian Faith and Aristotelian philosophy that would become an important pillar of both Western thought and theology throughout the remainder of the second millennium, and into the present third millennium.

Given the long history of interaction between Greek culture/science and Christianity, it is not surprising that Aristotle's model of a perfect, unblemished, unchanging heaven was incorporated into theological interpretations, both ancient and modern, of scriptural passages dealing with the heavens. Given Thomas Aquinas's synthesis of Aristotelian philosophy with the Christian faith, it's also not surprising that many church leaders believed that heresy was afoot when later scientific discoveries challenged the validity of Aristotle's model of the heavens. It is at this exact point that the modern debate between science and religion is often said to have begun. In 1608, Galileo Galilei (1564–1642) pointed his improved version of the newly invented telescope at the moon and clearly saw that the moon was not a perfect, unblemished sphere. As Galileo would later write: "It is most beautiful and pleasing to look upon the lunar body...from so near...[T]he moon is by no means endowed with a smooth and polished surface, but is rough and uneven and, just as the face of the Earth itself, crowded everywhere with vast prominences, deep chasms, and convolutions" (Whitehouse 2009:86). Thus, upon closer inspection (with a telescope), the moon, which Aristotle believed was composed of that divine fifth substance aether, showed that it had mountains and valleys, just like the earth—which was composed of the imperfect substances of earth, air, fire, and water.

While visiting Rome during 1611, Galileo undertook a study of the sun. By using his telescope to project an image of the sun onto a screen, he was able to show that the sun (at that time period) was covered by spots or blemishes which were located on or near the surface of the sun and which changed in size over time before eventually disappearing (Shea and Artigas 2003:40–41; Whitehouse 2009:107). Therefore, the sun, like the moon, was not a perfect, unchanging sphere. Galileo believed that this discovery would mark the end of the long reign in astronomy of Aristotle's model of a heavenly realm composed of perfect, unchanging, spherical bodies: "I suspect that this new discovery will be the signal for the funeral, or rather for the last judgment, for pseudo-philosophy. The dirge has already been heard in the moon, the Medicean stars, Saturn, and Venus. And I expect now to see the Peripatetics [members of a school of philosophy in ancient Greece that had a revival in late medieval Europe and promoted Aristotle's doctrines] put forth some grand effort to maintain the immutability of the heavens" (Whitehouse 2009:106). Unfortunately, to the Medieval mind steeped in the cosmology of Aristotle, saying that God's heaven was composed of imperfect spheres was almost akin to saying that God himself was imperfect.

The theological argument that the heavens were perfect and unchanging was a theological mistake that resulted from linking certain biblical passages about God's dwelling place in heaven, with certain Greek cultural/scientific beliefs that the physical heavens were perfect and unchanging. That this was indeed a theological mistake is attested to by the fact that it is no longer an issue—it is a *non-issue*. We have walked on the moon and visited all the other planets in the solar system with our space probes and now know that none of them is perfect and unchanging. In fact, they are very *imperfect*, at least in terms of lifeforms such as ourselves dwelling on these particular heavenly bodies (too hot, too cold, too much pressure, too much radiation, etc.). Moreover, we have witnessed Jupiter being struck by the 21 fragments of Comet Shoemaker-Levy 9 in 1994, recorded the eruption of volcanoes on Io (one of the moons of Jupiter), and documented the highly irregular shape of Miranda (a moon of Uranus, that was apparently shattered by an asteroid or comet impact and gravity has not yet had time to restore it to a spherical state). Consequently, when our astronauts and space probes go out into space, we do not expect to see angels or God just beyond earth's atmosphere, or just beyond the moon, or just beyond Pluto, etc. We now understand that the heaven where God dwells is not a place in this physical universe that can be reached with rockets or radio waves. In fact, the scriptural interpretation that the physical heavens are perfect, which dominated Christian theology for nearly two millennia, was actually illogical from a broader scriptural perspective. Jesus himself told us that: "Heaven and earth will pass away, but My words will not pass away" (Matt. 21:33). Peter told us: "But the day of the Lord will come like a thief, in which the heavens will pass away with a roar and the elements will be destroyed with intense heat, and the earth and its works will be burned up" (2 Peter 3:10). How can the heavens be perfect and unchanging if they are going to pass away and be destroyed? Faulty theological interpretations of Scripture can often be weeded out by simply examining other relevant scriptural passages. Certainly, ignorance or misinterpretation of God's Word seems to have been the primary cause of this particular theological error.

II. The Heavens Are Centered on the Earth

Although Galileo may have first come to the attention of the church authorities because of his discovery of sun spots or mountains and valleys on the moon, he was brought before the inquisition and later put under house arrest for contesting another aspect of Aristotle's model of the heavens—the location of the earth at its center (the geocentric model) (Aristotle 1986:241–245). The better-known Greek astronomical models of the heavens, from the time of Anaximander of Miletus in the sixth century B.C. to the time of Claudius Ptolemy in the second century A.D., placed the earth squarely at the center of the heavens. Whether as tubes filled with fire (Anaximander), celestial spheres of aether (Aristotle), or deferents and epicycles (Ptolemy), they all rotated around a central point, the earth. Earth alone was stationary; the sun, moon, and all the planets and stars orbited around the earth (Freely 2012:9–10, 59–60, 135). Of course, we now know that this centrality of the earth is only the way it *appears* from the surface of the earth; the apparent orbit of the sun, planets, and stars around the earth is, in fact, an optical illusion. Nevertheless, a number of scriptural passages *seemed* to suggest that the earth was fixed in space, while the sun, moon, and stars moved around it (see Table 15):

Table 15: Scriptures concerning the Centrality of the Earth in God's Creation

Then Joshua spoke to the Lord in the day when the Lord delivered up the Amorites before the sons of Israel, and he said in the sight of Israel, "O sun, stand still at Gibeon, And O moon in the valley of Aijalon." So the sun stood still, and the moon stopped, Until the nation avenged themselves of their enemies. Is it not written in the book of Jashar? And the sun stopped in the middle of the sky and did not hasten to go down for about a whole day. There was no day like that before it or after it, when the Lord listened to the voice of a man; for the Lord fought for Israel. (Josh. 10:12–14)

The Lord reigns. He is clothed with majesty; The Lord has clothed and girded Himself with strength; Indeed, the world is firmly established, it will not be moved. Your throne is established from of old; You are from everlasting. (Ps. 93:1–2)

Say among the nations, "The Lord reigns; Indeed, the world is firmly established, it will not be moved; He will judge the peoples with equity." (Ps. 96:10)

He established the earth upon its foundations, So that it will not totter forever and ever. (Ps. 104:5)

Tremble before Him, all the earth; Indeed, the world is firmly established, it will not be moved. Let the heavens be glad, and let the earth rejoice; And let them say among the nations, "The Lord reigns." (1 Chron. 16:30–31)

A generation goes and a generation comes, But the earth remains forever. Also, the sun rises and the sun sets; And hastening to its place it rises there again. (Eccl. 1:4–5)

Moreover, in the book of Genesis (1:26–28) we are told that humans are the final stage of God's creation, made in his image, and given authority over all the other life forms upon earth. Since humans take center stage in the Bible's account of creation, should not the earth on which humans dwell also be at the center of the heavens? Since Aristotle's geocentric model of the heavens placed a fixed, unmoving earth as the focal point of the heavens, it is easy to see why early Christian theologians so readily incorporated this Greek cultural/scientific belief into their understanding and interpretation of scriptural passages about the heavens and the earth.

Unfortunately Aristotle's model of the centrality of earth in the heavens was a scientific model based on human inquiry and insight. Like all scientific truths, it was limited by human ignorance (we don't have all the facts), human mistakes (we sometimes unintentionally misinterpret the facts), and human bias (we sometimes intentionally distort the facts). Therefore, as pointed out in my previous book (Brush 2005), all scientific truths are subject to change or eventual abandonment. It took some eighteen centuries for human knowledge to finally advance to the point where the falsity of Aristotle's model of the heavens could be proven, first through the work of Nicolaus Copernicus (1473–1543), and later by Galileo and other medieval scholars/scientists. Since theologians over the centuries had tightly bound some of their scriptural interpretations with Aristotle's model of the heavens, they naturally resisted Copernicus's discovery that the earth and other planets orbited the sun. Shortly before his death in 1543, Copernicus set forth the evidence for his heliocentric (sun-centered) model of the heavens in a book entitled *On the Revolutions of the Celestial Spheres*. Although some theologians were aware of Copernicus's work on a heliocentric model well before the actual publication of his book, there was relatively little initial condemnation of his book by the Catholic Church when it was published. Indeed, Copernicus, being a loyal Catholic, had received permission from the church authorities to publish the book and had even dedicated it to Pope Paul III. Instead, it was a prominent Protestant, Martin Luther, who, in 1539, became one of the earliest critics of Copernicus:

> Mention was made of a new astronomer who wished to prove that the earth moved and went around, not the sky or the firmament or the sun or the moon. It was just as when one was sitting on a wagon or boat which was moving, it seemed to him that he was standing still and resting, and that the earth and trees moved by. "So it goes," [said Luther], "whoever wants to be clever must not be content with what any one else has done, but must do something of his own and then pretend it was the best ever accomplished. The

> fool wants to change the whole science of astronomy. But the Holy Scripture clearly shows us that Joshua commanded the sun, not the earth, to stand still." (Smith and Gallinger 1915:104)

In fact, it was some seventy-three years later (1616) that the Catholic Church actually placed Copernicus's book on its *Index of Prohibited Books* (where it would remain until 1835). It would be later generations of scientists (such as Galileo) who would bear the wrath of theologians for what they, eventually, came to perceive as the heresy of Copernicus's heliocentric model of the heaven.

As Galileo continued to improve his telescopes and increase their power of magnification, he was able to see deeper into space and discover new stars that were invisible to the human eye. In January 1610, he turned his telescope toward Jupiter and found four new *stars* (the Medicean stars) that were in orbit around Jupiter. These stars were really moons and later came to be known as the Galilean moons: Io, Europa, Ganymede, and Callisto. Realizing that this discovery provided visual proof that not everything revolved around the earth, thereby supporting Copernicus's heliocentric model, Galileo sought to document his discovery as soon as possible. In March 1610 he published a short fifty-six page book entitled *Starry Messenger*, which summarized the astronomical discoveries he had made since he first turned his telescope toward the sky in 1608, culminating in his discovery of these four, never-before seen, stars:

> I should disclose and publish to the world the occasion of discovering and observing four planets, never seen from the beginning of the world up to our own times, their positions, and the observations made during the last two months about their movements and their changes of magnitude; and I summon all astronomers to apply themselves to examine and determine their periodic times, which it has not been permitted me to achieve up to this day.... I therefore concluded, and decided unhesitatingly, that there are three stars in the heavens moving around Jupiter, as Venus and Mercury around the Sun; which was at length established as clear

as daylight by numerous other subsequent observations. These observations also established that there are not only three, but four, erratic sidereal bodies performing their revolutions around Jupiter. (Whitehouse 2009:90)

By December of 1610, Galileo was able to verify Benedetto Castelli's suggestion that, if Copernicus's heliocentric model was correct and the planet Venus was in orbit around the sun, it should display phases just like the earth's moon (full, last quarter, new, first quarter). Through his telescope, Galileo had indeed been able to observe these phases.

Based on his 1608 discovery of mountains and valleys on the moon, his 1610 discovery of the four Medicean stars orbiting Jupiter and the phases of Venus as it orbited around the sun, and his 1611 discovery of sun spots, Galileo publicly came out in support of the Copernican system at the end of 1612 (ibid.:122). The opposition to the heliocentric model of Copernicus that had been building among some of the church's leaders also broke into public view at this time. In November 1612, a Dominican friar and professor of ecclesiastical history in Florence, Niccolò Lorini (1544–1617?) became one of the more vocal opponents of Copernicus: "Preaching on All Soul's Day, [Lorini] said that Copernican doctrine violated Scripture, which clearly places Earth, and not the sun at the center of the universe. If Copernicus were right, he asked, what would be the sense of Joshua 10:13 stating, 'So the sun stood still in the midst of heaven,' or Isaiah 40:22 speaking of 'the heavens stretched out as a curtain' above 'the circle of the earth?'" (ibid.). Two years later, on December 21, 1614, Lorini's friend, Tommaso Caccini (1574–1648), would attack Galileo himself from the pulpit of one of the main churches in Florence:

> Caccini seems to have chosen as his text the passage in the first chapter of the Acts of the Apostles, in which two men clad in white said to the disciples after Jesus's ascension into heaven: "Men of Galilee, why do you stand here looking at the sky?" In the Latin version, which Caccini quoted, "Men of Galilee" is *Viri Galilei*,*

which can be rendered as "Men of [Galileo] Galilei." The pun
startled the congregation, but there was more to come. Caccini
launched into a denunciation of Galileo, the Copernican system,
and all mathematicians, whom he branded as enemies of Church
and State. He was dead serious. He was also bigoted and given to
slander, and he let the Dominicans in Rome know that he had
ferreted out a new heresy. (Shea and Artigas 2003:59)

Shortly after Tommaso Caccini's sermon, Niccolò Lorini
lodged a complaint with the Inquisition concerning the work of
Galileo. Galileo was first summoned before Cardinal Bellarmine
in Rome in 1616 and told to abandon the Copernican model and
stop teaching or defending it. Although Galileo initially agreed to
follow this injunction, he subsequently published *Dialogue on the
Great World Systems* in 1632. In this book he attempted to present
the evidence for and against the Copernican model as a dialogue
between two individuals who held opposing views. This book
was not well received by Pope Urban VIII (1568–1644), a former
friend of Galileo. Galileo was summoned once more to come to
Rome and stand trial for heresy. In 1633 he was found suspect
of heresy, his book was placed on the *Index of Prohibited Books*,
he was forced to recant his support of Copernicus's heliocentric
model of the heavens, and was sentenced to perpetual imprison-
ment—but this latter punishment was subsequently reduced to
house arrest, under which terms he lived until his death in 1642.

It was natural for humans to *assume* that the heavens were
also made for us and that the earth was the focal point for all of
God's creation. On the other hand, according to Genesis, God
only gave us dominion over the earth, nothing was said about
our dominion over the heavens. Perhaps a universe, with all of
its planets, stars, and galaxies, is a necessary prerequisite for life
to exist upon the earth. As Carl Sagan once suggested, "If you
wish to make an apple pie from scratch, you must first invent
the universe" (1980:218). The various ingredients that go into an
apple pie are ultimately made out of elements that were formed
in stars somewhere in the Milky Way Galaxy, which is but one of

billions of galaxies that make up the universe that was formed by the Big Bang some 13.8 billion years ago. On the other hand, God may have created such a vast universe for additional purposes other than just for humans and their apple pies. God may be doing others things in his creation on other planets, in other solar systems, or in other galaxies in this vast universe that are not relevant to the human story. When Peter questioned Jesus as to the future destiny of John, Jesus answered: "If I want him to remain until I come, what is that to you? You follow Me!" (John 21:22). If it is not our business what God is doing in the lives of other individuals here on earth, it is certainly not our business what God is doing throughout the rest of his creation. God's revelation in the Bible is given to men concerning their origin, duty, and destiny; it is very much focused on the earth. It is not about what is happening on Venus, or the solar system surrounding the red dwarf star Gliese 581, or in the Andromeda Galaxy. Thus, although it may have been natural for us to think that the earth was the center of creation, since the biblical narrative is focused on humans and events happening on earth, when we look up into the heavens we find clear evidence that this is not the case. Earth is not even at the center of our solar system, but only one of eight planets orbiting the sun. Our solar system is not at the center of the Milky Way Galaxy or even near its center. Instead we are located in one of the galaxy's outer arms, some 27,000 light years from the galactic center. Given the probable presence of a large black hole and high levels of radiation at the center of our galaxy, we can thank God for his providence that our solar system is not located there. Looking beyond our galaxy we find that our galaxy is but one of a *local group* composed of some 54 galaxies. Out beyond the local group, there are more groups, clusters, and even chains of galaxies stretching out to the edge of time itself (which we now know also had a beginning). One present estimate suggests that there may be more than 170 billion galaxies in the observable universe; some of the largest galaxies may contain up to 100 trillion stars. Therefore, as our knowledge of God's creation continues to grow and we are repeatedly confronted with the vastness of the universe, we should not throw up our hands in despair at the fearful void of space and time. Instead, we, like David, should fall on our knees and proclaim: "When I consider Your heavens, the work of Your fingers, The moon and the stars, which You have ordained; What is man that You take thought of him, And the son of man that You care for him?" (Ps. 8:3–4).

Like the belief in the perfection of the heavens, the belief that the earth was at the center of God's creation also, eventually, ceased to be a problem for theologians. Humans have stood on the moon and watched the earth rotate on its axis. We regularly put our own satellites into orbit around the moon, sun, and planets. With our, now-massive, telescopes on both earth and in orbit around the earth, we can peer ever deeper into space and see other stars and the planets that orbit them; beyond the edge of our own Milky Way Galaxy, we can see countless other galaxies. The belief that the earth was at the center of God's creation was just one more theological mistake that resulted from the incorporation of an earlier human model of nature into our theological interpretations of Scripture. Since the 1600s, the (then) highly controversial scientific insights of Copernicus and Galileo have themselves been altered and enriched by the later work of individuals such as Isaac Newton and Albert Einstein. Our understanding of God's creation and our interpretation of those scriptural passages dealing with the heavens have repeatedly had to be modified as each new discovery was made and finally accepted by the church. Nevertheless, a Pew Research Center report released in 2010 stated that Christianity was still the largest religion in the world with some 2.2 billion adherents. The majority of these Christians still affirm that God created the heavens and the earth and that Christ is the Son of God and our Savior. This bedrock foundation has remained unmoved despite the shifting sands of human scientific understanding and theological interpretations. Perhaps Galileo's insights into theology were even more profound than his insights into science: "In his opinion, Scripture dealt with natural matters cursorily and elusively, reminding us that its proper concern was not natural phenomena, but the soul of man. According to Galileo, Scripture adjusted its notions regarding nature to the simple minds of ordinary people. He argued that Christian sacred writings were not intended to validate science, and defended this point by quoting Cardinal Baronius (1538–1607), a well-known ecclesiastical historian, who had remarked that, 'The Holy Ghost intended to teach us how to go to heaven, not how the heavens go'" (Whitehouse 2009:111).

Four hundred years later Christian apologists are still trying to convince their fellow Christians as to the validity of Galileo's theological insight. For example, John Walton, in his 2009 book entitled *The Lost World of Genesis One*, makes a similar argument to that of Galileo and Cardinal Baronius:

> The view offered of Genesis 1 recognizes that it was never intended to be an account of material origins. Rather it was intended as an account of functional origins in relation to people in the image of God viewing the cosmos as a temple. Though the Bible upholds the idea that God is *responsible* for all origins (functional, material or otherwise), if the Bible does not offer an *account* of material origins we are free to consider contemporary explanations of origins on their own merits, as long as God is seen as ultimately responsible. Therefore whatever explanation scientists may offer in their attempts to explain origins, we could theoretically adopt it as a description of God's handiwork. (Walton 2009:131)

However, whatever cultural or scientific model of the physical universe we may choose to adopt, we should always do so with the knowledge and understanding that all such models are flawed by human ignorance, mistakes, and bias and are therefore subject to change. Current scientific understanding of God's creation should never be so tightly bound with our scriptural interpretations that they become a part of the church's doctrines and confessions of faith. To do so is to invite disaster and perpetuate that long fruitless debate between science and religion—or to be more precise, the debate between older scientific models that were utilized to help interpret scriptural passages dealing with nature, and newer scientific models that have not yet been utilized in our theological interpretations.

III. The Heavens Were Not Created by a "Big Bang"

The current paradigm (master theory) upon which the majority of astronomers base their work is the Big Bang model which was developed in the first half of the twentieth century. Like the Copernican model of the sixteenth and seventeenth centuries, many Christians today oppose the Big Bang Model. The Big Bang Model postulates that the entire universe came into existence some 13.8 billion years ago. This theory was developed by George Gamow (1904–1968), a Ukrainian-born theoretical physicist and cosmologist. His work as a graduate student in Russia was in quantum mechanics. Later, as a post-graduate, he also studied the atomic nucleus, radioactivity, and stellar synthesis in Germany, Sweden, and the United Kingdom. Gamow and his wife immigrated to the United States in the 1934 where he initially taught physics at George Washington University in Washington D.C. (1934–54), then the University of California at Berkeley (1954–56), and finally, the University of Colorado at Boulder (1956–68). His interest in cosmology and the creation of the universe arose out of his earlier work on the formation and transformation of elements within stars, and the formation of the solar system. His knowledge of nuclear fusion eventually led to his development of the hot Big Bang Model that explained how all the matter and energy that make up the universe could have arisen out of an infinitely dense and extremely hot singularity (i.e. single point in space) at the beginning of time.

In 1948, Gamow and his graduate student, Ralph Alpher, published the classic paper on the Big Bang Model. This paper was entitled "The Origin of Chemical Elements," and attempted to explain how the elements themselves were created as the universe expanded out of a singularity. As a joke, Gamow asked another famous nuclear physicist, Hans A. Bethe, if they could include his name on the paper (in absentia) so the paper could be published under the names Alpher, Bethe, and Gamow; Bethe agreed. "To this day, it is known as the 'alpha, beta, gamma' paper, a suitable reflection of the fact that it deals with the beginning of things, and also of the importance of particle physics to cosmology" (Gribbin 1986:154). Alpha, beta, and gamma are the first three letters in the Greek alphabet; they are also the names of three forms of radiation: Alpha Particles, Beta Particles, and Gamma Rays.

It is estimated that 98 percent of the mass of the universe is composed of only two elements: hydrogen (74 percent) and helium (24 percent). These two elements provide the primary fuel for nuclear fusion in stars; they are also the major components of huge clouds of dust and gas (nebula) that are scattered across the galaxies and serve as the nurseries for the birth of new stars. The weakness of Alpher, Bethe, and Gamow's Big Bang Theory was that, although it adequately accounted for the formation of hydrogen and helium during the origin of the universe, the nuclear pathways suggested for the formation of the other, heavier elements, lithium through uranium, were not on nearly as solid theoretical footing (Silk 1989:83, 86–87). Indeed, it would later be discovered that most of the heavier elements had been created well after the Big Bang by fusion processes inside stars. Most stars are largely composed of hydrogen which they burn to form helium. In larger stars, the temperature increases over time and heavier and heavier elements are created by fusion—up to Iron (atomic number 26). Most of the even heavier elements, up to Uranium (atomic 92) or beyond, are created by extremely high pressures and temperatures that occur during the death throes of very massive stars that explode as nova or supernova. Once the problem of the synthesis of heavier elements was resolved by a better understanding of nuclear fusion processes inside stars, the Big Bang Model became much more widely accepted by physicists.

In the same year (1948) that Alpher, Bethe, and Gamow's seminal paper on the Big Bang Model was published, an alternate hypothesis for the universe was advanced by Hermann Bondi, Thomas Gold, and Fred Hoyle. This paper was entitled "The Steady-State Theory of the Expanding Universe." In this model, the authors argued that the universe did not have a beginning—it had always existed and its basic structure had remained unchanged. They attempted to explain the expansion of the universe that Edwin Hubble had observed in the 1920s as the result of the constant creation of new matter. Bondi, Gold, and Hoyle postulated that hydrogen is constantly being created throughout intergalactic space, one atom at a time. The universe is so vast, the creation of only one hydrogen atom per 10 billion cubic meters of space per year would account for its present expansion rate (Gribbin 1996:383). This new hydrogen would provide the raw material for the eventual construction of new stars and galaxies. Therefore the universe expands as it steadily grows larger. Of course, the Steady State Theory flies in the face of the First Law of Thermodynamics, which states that matter cannot be created or destroyed. The same can also be said of the Big Bang Theory, however, although it only requires a single breach of this law at the beginning of the universe. Nevertheless, as Joseph Silk has noted: "If the big bang theory could assert that the universe was created at an instant of time in the remote but finite past, why was it not as reasonable to assert that creation occurs everywhere, in all space and at all times?" (1989:5–6).

During the 1950s and the 1960s Gamow's Big Bang Theory and Hoyle's Steady State Theory were in competition with each other. As astronomers with more powerful telescopes looked ever deeper into space and ever further back in time, however, they began to find evidence that the structure of the universe was not unchanging—as Hoyle's Steady State Theory had proposed. The universe is so vast that light and other forms of electromagnetic radiation emitted by stars, even though traveling at the speed of light (186,200 miles per second), still takes time to travel across the fearful void of space. Therefore, as we are observing stars and galaxies, we are also looking back in time. What astronomers found was that older galaxies were very different from more recent galaxies in terms of activity, size, and density. In the late 1950s, astronomers found a new class of galaxies with very active central cores, which they named quasars. Most of these quasars also displayed large red shifts which showed that they were far more abundant in the early universe than in later time periods (i.e. the Hubbard constant—the greater the distance of a galaxy, the more its light is shifted toward the red end of the spectrum). They also found that galaxies in the early universe were smaller and less dense than those in the later universe, but much more active. For example the most distant galaxy yet discovered, GN-z11, is 25 times smaller and just one percent as massive as our Milky Way Galaxy (which itself is not a very big galaxy). The GN-z11 Galaxy, however, is forming stars twenty times faster than our Milky Way Galaxy (Oesch et al. 2016). The growing body of information on distant (early) galaxies slowly began to reveal that Hoyle's Steady State Theory of the universe was wrong: the universe was neither eternal nor unchanging. Instead, the universe had evolved as it had aged; its stars and galaxies showed a clear progression of growth and development over time.

The final death knell for the Steady State Theory was a discovery made in 1965 by two radio astronomers working for Bell Telephone Laboratories in New Jersey who were searching the skies for the source of electromagnetic noise that was interfering with radio and television transmissions on earth. These two astronomers, Arno Penzias and Robert Wilson, found that the source of this interference was microwaves that were not confined to any particular point in the sky but were pervasive throughout the heavens. This radiation became known as cosmic microwave background radiation and corresponded to a temperature in outer space of around $2.7° K$. This radiation turned out to be the afterglow of the Big Bang when the universe emerged out of a singularity. Such remnant heat from the Big Bang had been predicted (at around $5° K$) by Ralph Alpher and Robert Herman in 1948: "Alpher and Herman calculated that when the universe was young it was very hot, and filled with an intense glow of radiation that should still be visible today in a weakened form. If this cosmic fireball radiation could be detected, it would prove that the universe began in an explosion" (Jastrow 1978:18).

The reason that most astronomers around the world today base their theories and research on the Big Bang Model is the strong empirical evidence that supports this model. Not only does Albert Einstein's Theory of Relativity predict that the universe should either be expanding or contracting, but Edwin Hubble's observation of galaxies and their red shifts with the Hooker 100-inch Telescope on Mount Wilson in California has proved that the universe is indeed expanding as the galaxies speed away from each other. The observed abundance of hydrogen and helium in the universe matches those levels predicted by Alpher, Bethe, and Gamow in their original 1948 paper on the Big Bang. The afterglow of heat from the Big Bang that Alpher and Herman predicted in 1948 was verified by the work of Penzias and Wilson in 1965 with their discovery of the cosmic background radiation. Finally, the discovery of distant quasars in the late 1950s and our continued discovery of distant galaxies, such as GN-z11 in 2016, prove that galaxies in the early universe are quite different from those in the later universe. In other words, the evidence for the Big Bang Model continues to accumulate.

So why do many Christians, almost 70 years after the introduction of the Big Bang Theory, still find it so distasteful and often refer to it in a jeering manner and use quote marks: the "big bang" theory? Nearly 40 years ago, the astrophysicist Robert Jastrow pointed out that, "Now we see how the astronomical evidence leads to a biblical view of the origin of the world. The details differ, but the essential elements in the astronomical and biblical accounts of Genesis are the same: the chain of events leading to man commenced suddenly and sharply at a definite moment in time, in a flash of light and energy" (1978:14). Jastrow went on to note that it was not the theologians who were upset over this theory, but the scientists: "Theologians generally are delighted with the proof that the universe had a beginning, but astronomers are curiously upset. Their reactions provide an interesting demonstration of the response of the scientific mind—supposedly a very objective mind—when evidence uncovered by science itself leads to a conflict with the articles of faith in our profession. It turns out that the scientist behaves the way the rest of us do when our beliefs are in conflict with the evidence. We become irritated, we pretend the conflict does not exist, or we paper it over with meaningless phrases" (ibid.:16). Indeed, Jastrow went so far as to suggest that, to many scientists, the Big Bang Theory was like a nightmare: "For the scientist who has lived by his faith in the power of reason, the story ends like a bad dream. He has scaled the mountains of ignorance; he is about to conquer the highest peak; as he pulls himself over the final rock, he is greeted by a band of theologians who have been sitting there for centuries" (ibid.:116).

Yet, today, we see the tables have turned once again and it is some of the theologians, as well as many Christian laymen, who object to the Big Bang Theory. But why should Christians object to a scientific theory that actually agrees with the Bible: the universe had a beginning? At the very beginning of the Old Testament we are told that: "In the beginning God created the heavens and the earth" (Gen. 1:1). In the New Testament it is stated: "By faith we understand that the worlds were prepared by the word of God, so that what is seen was not made out of things which are visible" (Heb. 11:3). The Big Bang Theory tells much the same story, the universe had a beginning (at 13.8 billion years ago); it arose out of that which is not visible (a singularity). It was the other theory, the Steady State Theory, which was in direct opposition to the Bible. It was the theory that said the heavens were eternal and unchanging, the theory that left no room for creation. Not surprisingly, we can trace the steady state back to the Greeks, back to Aristotle (among others), who, with his belief in the perfection of the heavenly spheres, also could find no room or justification for creation. Perfect spheres and circles have no beginning or end. This was the theory which, if true, would have presented a grave challenge to the Christian faith and the biblical account. But the empirical evidence has shown us otherwise; the Steady State Theory has been disproven and rejected by scientists.

Perhaps some Christians reject the Big Bang Theory because they find it offensive to refer to the majesty of God's creation as a *big bang*. The name, however, has little to do with the power and significance of the theory. In fact, the name applied to this theory is actually an accident of history and not the result of its creators' irreverence. The theory was actually given this name by its arch-enemy, Fred Hoyle, the leading advocate of the Steady State Theory. He certainly meant to use the term in a derogatory manner: George Gamow's *Big Bang* Theory, "a theory he regarded as about as elegant as 'a party girl jumping out of a cake'" (Gribbin 1996:52). Unfortunately, the name stuck, possibly because—unlike Bondi, Gold, and Hoyle—Alpher, Bethe, and Gamow did not include a catchy name in the title of their 1948 article that introduced the Big Bang Theory. On the other hand, perhaps many Christians reject the Big Bang Theory because of the devil in the details. It is so much simpler to imagine God speaking the universe into existence (or singing it into existence as Aslan did with Narnia) (Lewis 1955b:98–102), rather than getting involved with subatomic particles, the laws of physics, and galactic evolution. And then there is also that nasty bit about how long ago scientists say this event happened: 13.8 *billion* years ago, but we will discuss the question of geologic time in the next chapter. On the other hand, perhaps the present reticence of some Christians to consider the merits of the Big Bang Model is just one more example of people tying their theological interpretations too tightly to older cultural/scientific models that have ceased to be viable in light of the current empirical evidence that is available to us.

CONCLUSION

In this chapter we have seen that two of the most commonly cited examples of the debate between science and Christianity were not really about actual conflicts between Scripture and science. Instead, these debates were really about the merits of earlier versus later cultural/scientific models of the universe: Aristotle's perfect heavenly spheres model verses Galileo's imperfect heavenly bodies model; Anaximander's geocentric model versus Copernicus's heliocentric model. Because theologians had previously incorporated Aristotle's and Anaximander's models into their theological interpretations, they mistakenly believed that Galileo's and Copernicus's models contradicted Scripture and were therefore heretical. They were badly mistaken on both counts. Christianity's eventual acceptance of Galileo's and Copernicus's discoveries, and theologians' use of these new models to help them understand and interpret Scripture, has had no impact whatsoever on "the faith which was once for all handed down to the saints" (Jude 1:3). The eventual acceptance of George Gamow's Big Bang Model for the creation of the universe will have a similar null impact on Christians' faith. As our knowledge and understanding of God's creation continues to expand and deepen, our current cultural/scientific models of the natural world will, no doubt, repeatedly be replaced by newer and (hopefully) more accurate models. However, with regard to the natural world, we must never assume that any particular scientific model or theological interpretation will be the final, definitive word on the subject. To do so would be to repeat the same mistakes of our ancestors and engage in the same futile debates over which humanly derived scientific model or theological interpretation is the correct one.

As finite human beings, we can only work with the knowledge and information that is available to us during our limited lifetimes. We must always be aware of our limitations—our ignorance, mistakes, and biases—that can easily undermine the validity of our scientific models or our theological interpretations about the natural world that God has created. We desire an end to this long quest for understanding the natural world. We long for the rest and security that would come with absolute truth. God, however, has not seen fit to grant us this desire of our heart. Thus, each generation must wrestle with the cultural/scientific knowledge available to it, and try to understand how each new scientific discovery *might* be understood in terms of the scriptural account. In this manner we live as faithful servants, always dependent upon the Holy Spirit to guide our understanding and lead us into new and ever-deeper truths.

Chapter 11

Modern Theological Mistakes Concerning the Earth

Introduction

Theologians have not only made significant mistakes about the heavens, but also about the earth. Once again, these mistakes have often arisen from theologians linking their theological interpretations to older cultural/scientific models of nature and then attempting to defend these interpretations long after those cultural/scientific models of nature have been disproven and abandoned by scientists and the rest of society. Many Christians today know very little about church history and even less about earth history. As a result of their lack of knowledge about church history, they easily fall prey to new fads and movements within the church, often embracing and repeating the same errors that were popular centuries earlier. In this manner they validate George Santayana's observation that: "Those who cannot remember the past are condemned to repeat it" (Evans 1968:511). Moreover, because of their limited understanding of earth history, many Christians are easily led astray by those who themselves, have either a distorted or very rudimentary knowledge of science.

The end results of these two deficiencies are half-baked ideas and theories that have neither a solid scriptural nor solid scientific foundation. Instead of creating a bridge between religion and science where Christians and scientists can find common ground, this situation has created an intellectual bog where neither party can find solid footing.

I. THE EARTH IS ONLY A FEW THOUSAND YEARS OLD

Down through the ages, debate has continued as to whether the heavens and earth are eternal or temporal. Aristotle (384–322 B.C.) believed that the heavens were eternal and unchanging; Anaxagoras (510–c. 428 B.C.) believed that the universe had a beginning. This same issue was still being debated in the twentieth century between Fred Hoyle with his Steady State Theory and George Gamow with his Big Bang Theory. Over the past two millennia, theologians who believed in a young heaven and earth often used the genealogies in the Bible to arrive at a date for the beginning of God's creation (see Table 16):

Table 16: Estimates for the Age of the Earth based on Biblical Genealogies	
3761 B.C.	Jewish Rabbi, Jose ben Halafta (second century A.D.)
3952 B.C.	English monk, Saint Bede (c. 673–735)
3949 B.C.	French religious leader and scholar, Joseph Justus Scaliger (1540–1609)
3992 B.C.	German mathematician and astronomer, Johannes Kepler (1571–1630)
4004 B.C.	Irish Archbishop, James Ussher (1581–1656)
3929 B.C.	English scholar, John Lightfoot (1602–1675)
3998 B.C.	English physicist and mathematician, Sir Isaac Newton (1643–1727)

Remarkably, all the individuals listed above, whether they were theologians or scientists, arrived at dates for the beginning of the heavens and earth that were within 243 years of each other. Six of the seven dates fell within 75 years of each other; the date with the greatest deviation (that of Jose ben Halafta), was also the oldest (second century A.D.). Therefore, if the date of creation can be established from biblical genealogies, the end results are pretty uniform—the heavens and earth are only around 6,000 years old.

A number of prominent theologians over the past two millennia, however, have argued that it is incorrect hermeneutics to use biblical genealogies for chronology. One of the problems is that when we compare the various genealogies in the Bible, we often find that some of the generations have been left out. For example, 1 Chronicles 6:3–15 and Ezra 7:1–5 both trace the line of Aaron's descendants to the Babylonian captivity. In Ezra's genealogy, however, the four generations between Meraioth and Azariah are left out, as well as two generations between Azariah and Amariah. A second example of skipped generations can be found when comparing 1 Chronicles 6:3–15 with 1 Chronicles 26:24, the latter of which briefly traces the descent of Shebuel, ruler of the treasures for King David, to Moses. 1 Chronicles 6:3–15 lists eight generations between Aaron/Moses/Miriam and Zadok, who was the priest for King David; 1 Chronicles 26:24 lists only one generation between Aaron and Shebuel, ruler of King David's treasures (a period of some 400 years). A third example of skipped generations occurs when comparing 1 Chronicles 3:1–16, which traces the descent of the kings of Judea from King David to the Babylonian captivity, with Matthew 1:6–11, which traces the descent of Christ from King David. Matthew's genealogy skips three generations between Joram and Azariah that are recorded in 1 Chronicles 3:1–16. Therefore, it appears that God was more concerned with having his writers show the connections and relationships between individuals, rather than providing readers with an exact record of every generation in these lines of descent. It has sometimes been suggested that even the most detailed genealogies may be abbreviated, only listing some of the better-known individuals in these ancestral lines. As

Francis Schaeffer, a well-known conservative theologian from the latter part of the twentieth century noted in his book, *Genesis in Space and Time:*, "A second reason why we must not take genealogy for chronology is that several passages make it obvious that the writers knew the chronology but that they still deliberately omitted several steps in the genealogy. . . . Thus we are reminded that the purpose of all this is to indicate the flow of official, historical lines. It is important to say, 'This man comes from such and such an origin'" (1972:123–124). In addition, from the perspective of an ancient Israelite or Jew, the term father can be applied not only to one's biological father, but also to direct ancestors in previous generations. If your grandfather, great grandfather, etc. hadn't existed, you wouldn't exist either, so they are also your fathers. For example, many Jews still refer to *Father Abraham* and Christians sing a hymn about *Faith of our fathers.* Therefore, in the biblical genealogies, the links between individuals may not necessarily represent a literal-father-to-literal-son pathway; several generations may be skipped.

Another problem with using biblical genealogy to date the heavens and earth is that all the individuals listed in Table 16 either left out the seven days of creation or assumed that they only represented seven twenty-four-hour days. The Hebrew word for *day*, as well as the English word for day, can have three *literal* meanings: (1) the period of light from sunrise to sunset (which of course varies from season to season), (2) the twenty-four-hour period between sunrise on one day and sunrise on the next day, and (3) an indefinite period of time. The very same Hebrew word for day that is used with regard to the days of creation in Genesis 1:1–32 and 2:1–4 is also used for the *day of the Lord* (see Table 17):

Table 17: Scriptures concerning the Day of the Lord
The sun will be turned into darkness And the moon into blood Before the great and awesome day of the LORD comes. (Joel 2:31)
Alas, you who are longing for the day of the LORD, For what purpose will the day of the LORD be to you? It will be darkness and not light. (Amos 5:18)
Near is the great day of the LORD, Near and coming very quickly; Listen, the day of the LORD! In it the warrior cries out bitterly. (Zeph. 1:14)

Since the day of the Lord will be at the end of the world when Christ returns, this day is probably not a twenty-four-hour day, so what assurance do we have that the days of creation were twenty-four-hour days? Strong arguments have certainly been made for creation days being twenty-four-hour days, but equally strong arguments have been made for creation days being indefinite periods of time.

Many Christians today are fearful that any suggestion that the creation days are not normal twenty-four-hour days is a rejection of the authority of the Scriptures in favor of the teachings of modern science. The debate over the interpretation of the word day in the Genesis account, however, has deep roots in both Jewish and church history, long before the development of modern science. Philo (20 B.C.-A.D. 45) was a Jewish philosopher, born of a noble family in Alexandria, Egypt. He devoted his life to knowing God through the study of the Scriptures. With regard to the creation account in Genesis, Philo pointed out that time is measured in terms of the movement of the sun across the heavens. Since the heavens were part of God's creation, creation itself must have occurred outside of time as we understand it, so the days of creation could not have been literal days:

> It is quite foolish to think that the world was created in six days or in a space of time at all. Why? Because every period of time is a series of days and nights, and these can only be made such by the movement of the sun as it goes over and under the earth: but the sun is a part of heaven, so that time is confessedly more recent than the world. It would therefore be correct to say that the world was not made in time, but that time was formed by means of the world, for it was heaven's movement that was the index of the nature of time. When, then, Moses says, "He finished His work on the sixth day," we must understand him to be adducing not a quantity of days, but a perfect number, namely six. (Philo 1929:147–149)

Writing some three centuries after the time of Philo, Saint Augustine (A.D. 354–430) also believed that the days of creation were symbolic days, not literal ones. Augustine was a Christian theologian and philosopher who lived in a Roman Province in North Africa (now Algeria). He eventually became Bishop of Hippo and wrote two well-known Christian classics, *The Confessions of Saint Augustine* (1961) and *City of God*. In *City of God*, Book 11, Chapter 6, Augustine argues that:

> Moreover, when the sacred and wholly truth-laden Scriptures say that "In the beginning God created the heavens and the earth", this is so that we may know that nothing was made before the heavens and the earth; for if something was made before them, it is this something that would then be said to have been made "in the beginning". Beyond doubt, then, the world was made not in time, but simultaneously with time. For that which is made in time is made both after and before some time: after that which is past, and before that which is to come. But there could have been no "past" before the creation, because there was then no creature by whose changing movements time could be enacted. If change and movement were created when the world was created, then, time and the world were created simultaneously; and this seems to be borne out by the order of the first six or seven days. For the morning and the evening of these days are all counted, until, on the sixth day, all the things which God has made are finished; and, on the seventh, there is established the great mystery of God's rest. But what kind of days these were it is extremely difficult, or even impossible, for us to conceive, still less to express. (1998:456–457)

On the other hand, although Saint Augustine did not interpret the days of creation as literal days, he still came to the conclusion, in *City of God*, Book 12, Chapter 13, that the earth was less than 6,000 years old (ibid:514), presumably because that was the common cultural/scientific belief at the time. Nevertheless, Augustine was open to other interpretations of Scripture if new information was found. As McGrath has noted, "Augustine was deeply concerned that biblical interpreters might get locked into reading the Bible according to the scientific assumptions of the age" (2009:40). In *The Literal Interpretation of Genesis*, Book 1, Chapter 18, Verse 37, Augustine cautions his readers:

> In matters that are obscure and far beyond our vision, even in such as we may find treated in Holy Scripture, different interpretations are sometimes possible without prejudice to the faith we have received. In such a case, we should not rush in headlong and so firmly take our stand on one side that, if further progress in the search of truth justly undermines this position, we too fall with it. That would be to battle not for the teaching of Holy Scripture but for our own, wishing its teaching to conform to ours, whereas we ought to wish ours to conform to that of Sacred Scripture. (1983:41)

Nearly one thousand years later, Saint Thomas Aquinas (1225–1274) offered the same advice to his fellow Christians in his book *Summa Theologica* (1,68,1): "Since Holy Scripture can be explained in a multiplicity of senses, one should adhere to a particular explanation, only in such measure as to be ready to abandon it, if it be proved with certainty to be false; lest Holy Scripture be exposed to the ridicule of unbelievers, and obstacles be placed to their believing" (Westerholm and Westerholm 2016:182).

As noted previously, scriptural passages dealing with the natural world are particularly prone to error and vulnerable to subsequent reinterpretation as our cultural/scientific knowledge of the physical universe continues to expand and deepen. For reasons such as those noted previously, the use of biblical genealogies to assign an absolute date for the creation of the heavens and earth is particularly suspect. As Francis Schaeffer has argued in his book, *A Christian View of the Bible as Truth*, "we can say very clearly that the Bible does not invite us to use genealogies in Scripture as a chronology" (1982:88). The popular 6,000-year date for the heavens and earth began to come under sustained attack during the Renaissance as the foundations of modern science were being laid.

Leonardo da Vinci (1452–1519) was an Italian polymath whose interests and skills knew no bounds. He made significant contributions as a painter, sculpture, architect, hydrologist, cartographer, engineer, inventor, mathematician, anatomist, botanist, astronomer, and geologist. Being both an artist and a scientist, da Vinci was a particularly keen observer of nature. While living in Milan, he would often take walks along the Po River Valley and its tributaries. Every year, however, these walks would be interrupted by a seasonal flood. Da Vinci noticed that after each flood a thin layer of sediment would be left behind in the fields and on the pathways near the river. On his walks in these valleys he also observed wells being dug down to the water table. On closer inspection he found that the wells had been excavated through a series of sedimentary layers which he concluded had also been laid down by the repeated flooding of the valley. Comparing the depths of the sediments in these wells with the thin layer of sediment deposited on the ground's surface each year by the seasonal flood, he calculated that it had probably taken around 200,000 years for the sediments in the Po Valley to form (DiPietro 2013:321; Müntz 2006:94). Therefore, the man, perhaps most famous for his painting of the *Mona Lisa* and the *Last Supper*, also discovered some of the earliest evidence that the earth might be much older than the 6,000 years commonly assigned to creation by theologians and other scientists in his day.

Nearly three centuries after da Vinci's observations of sedimentation rates in the Po Valley and its tributaries, a Scottish farmer/physician, James Hutton (1726–1797), would make even more startling discoveries about the age of the earth. At the heart of Edinburgh, where Hutton lived, is a huge rocky outcrop called Arthur's Seat that provides a panoramic view of the city that surrounds it and is the site of Edinburgh Castle. What attracted Hutton's attention was the composition of the rocks in this outcrop; they were volcanic, just like those found around active volcanoes in Italy such as Mount Etna or Mount Vesuvius. Yet, there were no historical records of active volcanoes in Scotland or Britain, nor was there even a hint of volcanism in ancient Celtic mythology.

Therefore, this volcano at the center of Edinburgh must have been active long before even the oral folktales about Celtic heroes and gods were created.

Although Hutton could not assign a date to the volcanic rocks in Arthur's Seat, there were other rocks in Scotland that could be dated, such as the rocks in Hadrian's Wall. This wall had been built across northern England from sea to sea by the Roman Emperor Hadrian (76–138 CE). It had been garrisoned with Roman soldiers to keep out Scottish invaders from the north. This wall marked the northern-most boundary of the Roman Empire at that time. Although work on this wall had begun in A.D. 122, parts of the wall were still standing in Hutton's time (although many of the stone blocks had been removed and incorporated into later houses and churches). What got Hutton's attention, however, was the fact that the edges of the cut stone blocks in this wall were still relatively sharp after some sixteen centuries of exposure to the winds, rains, and snows of Scotland. On the other hand, the sandy beach at St. Andrews on the North Sea was composed of quartz, the hardest and most weather-resistant mineral in granite. Mountains are composed of granite. The streams that had deposited this sand at the edge of the North Sea near St. Andrews could be followed upstream to their sources in the mountains of the Scottish Highlands, mountains composed of granite. Hutton realized that the contrast between the relatively unweathered blocks in Hadrian's Wall and the highly weathered remains of an ancient mountain range on the beach at St. Andrews proved that the earth must be much older than a few thousand years. How long would it take to weather away part of a mountain range and reduce it to sand, if Hadrian's Wall was still standing and relatively unweathered after nearly 1600 years?

Hutton found an even more telling example of the depth of geologic time at Siccar Point, also on the North Sea. At this site, quartz sand, the weathered remains of an ancient mountain range, had been lithified into sandstone, turned on its side so that the originally horizontal beds of sand were nearly vertical, and then partially weathered away, leaving an irregular erosion surface. Deposited on top of this erosion surface was more sand from the weathered remains of another ancient mountain range. This sand had also been lithified into sandstone and then turned on its side at an oblique angle. How much time was represented by the sandstones at Siccar Point? Hutton had no way of knowing. All he could say was that when we study the history of the earth we find "no vestige of a beginning, nor prospect of an end" (Marshak 2012:402). Through these four sites in Scotland, Hutton proved that the earth must be much older than we had ever imagined. This idea of the passage of vast amounts of time (i.e. geologic time) was to become one of the pillars of modern geology. Hutton himself would subsequently be honored as the *father* of modern geology.

Today, geologists can do what Hutton could not do, assign absolute dates to earth history. In the process, geologists have found that earth does have a beginning, although it is some 4.6 billion years in the past. Geologists and other scientists have devised a variety of techniques for dating things in the physical universe (see Table 18):

Table 18: Chronological Range of Modern Dating Techniques		
Tree Rings	12,460 Years Ago	thick/thin rings formed seasonally
Varves	13,200 Years Ago	thick/thin sediments deposited seasonally
Carbon-14	50,000 Years Ago	half-life of 5,730 yrs/50,000 maximum
Ice Cores	800,000 Years Ago	dense/less dense ice deposited seasonally
Potassium/Argon	1.3 Billion Years Ago	half-life of 1.3 Ga
Uranium/Lead	4.5 Billion Years Ago	half-life of 4.5 Ga
Radius of Universe	13.8 Billion Years Ago	travel time of light from distant galaxies

Some of these techniques are as simple as counting layers that were deposited on a seasonal basis: tree rings, varves (layers of sediment in lakes), and ice cores. For even older dates, however, scientists have had to resort to radioactive clocks with various half-lives, or even the time it takes for electromagnetic radiation to travel across space at the speed of light.

Perhaps the simplest of all dating techniques is dendrochronology, counting the growth rings in trees (something many of us have done as children). A thick growth ring composed of large cells is produced each spring and early summer when the leaves come out; a thin growth ring composed of small cells is created in the late summer and early fall before the leaves drop. Since the width of these growth rings varies from year to year, based on temperature, moisture, and the length of the growing season, a unique pattern of growth is recorded in the wood from year to year, decade to decade, and century to century. Dendrochronologists can compare these unique patterns in two or more samples of wood in order to determine if they are from trees that were growing at roughly the same time. By collecting thousands of samples from living trees, recently dead trees, older trees that were incorporated into buildings, and ancient trees that have been preserved in bogs or beneath glacial till, dendrochronologists have been able to construct an unbroken record of tree growth that now stretches back some 12,460 years (twice the age of the earth as derived from biblical genealogies).

Northern lakes produce similar thick and thin sediment layers (called varves) on a seasonal basis. During the spring and summer, water flow is stronger and streams are able to carry coarser sediment into lakes, thereby producing a thicker, light-colored layer; during the fall and winter, water flow is weaker and streams are only able to carry in finer sediments that produce a thinner, dark-colored layer. By removing sediment cores from the bottom of a number of lakes across Europe, sedimentologists have been able to create an unbroken record of varves that stretches back some 13,200 years. Unfortunately, since tree rings and varves are typically found in northern forests and lakes, these two chronologies come to an abrupt end at 12–13,000 years ago because of the Ice Age, which buried these northern forests and lakes under a thick sheet of ice.

Glaciers themselves, however, can also create a seasonal record in the form of a layer of dense and less dense ice. In the winter, winds blowing across the snowpack are stronger and the ice that is formed is denser; in the summer winds are weaker and the ice that is formed is less dense. By shining a strong light or laser through thin slices of glacial ice these dense and less dense layers can be clearly seen and counted (just like tree rings or varves). Although many of the glaciers that formed during the Ice Age have melted away, glaciers in Greenland and Antarctica, as well as those in high mountains, are still intact. Scientists have recovered a series of ice cores from Dome C in Antarctica that extends over a vertical distance of some two miles and which record some 800,000 years of ice deposition. Scientists working in Antarctica hope to eventually find a thicker deposit of ice that will take them back to about 1 million years ago. Beyond that date, however, the ice record will also come to an abrupt end. Although Antarctica has probably been covered with ice for the past 20–30 million years, most of that ice has melted away and been returned to the atmosphere and oceans. Ice will melt under pressure and the pressure beneath a couple of miles of ice is great enough to melt the ice at the bottom of an ice sheet. Consequently, as new ice is deposited at the top of the Antarctica ice sheet, old ice at the bottom of the ice sheets melts away. Nevertheless, by the simple technique of counting layers, the ice sheets that still exist have allowed scientists to create an unbroken chronology back to at least 800,000 years ago.

In addition to wood, sediment, and ice cores, there are also rock layers that geologists can use to date the earth. Most of these rock layers, however, were not deposited on a seasonal basis but instead were laid down over centuries, millennia, or even millions of years. Fortunately, minerals in these rock layers often contain radioactive isotopes that can be used to date these layers. Scientists have identified various radioactive isotopes with different half-lives that can be used in this process. These isotopes transform themselves from unstable to stable isotopes at a known rate (their half-life). By comparing the ratio between the parent (original) isotopes and the daughter (decay product) isotopes, scientists can determine how much time has elapsed since a rock or mineral was formed. For example, uranium-238 has a half-life of 4.5 billion years. After 4.5 billion years, half the unstable uranium-238 atoms will have decayed into stable lead-206 atoms; after another 4.5 billion years, half of those remaining unstable uranium-238 atoms will have decayed into stable lead-206 atoms, etc. Based on the fact that meteorites from the asteroid belt (which contain rocks and minerals that date to the formation of the solar system) have slightly higher amounts of lead-206 than uranium-238, we can date the origin of the earth and other planets to approximately 4.6 billion years ago (just over one half-life for uranium-238). Very old rocks are difficult to find on earth because it is a dynamic planet where older rocks are constantly being weathered away and newer rocks formed. After much diligent searching, however, geologists, have found an outcrop of rocks along Hudson Bay in Canada (Faux Amphibolite) that dates to 4.3 billion years ago, as well as zircons in rocks from Australia (Jack Hills Conglomerate) that date to 4.4 billion years ago. Therefore, although most really old rocks on the earth have been weathered away, geologist have found a few minerals and rocks that are nearly as old as the 4.6 billion year old meteorites that were formed at the beginning of the solar system.

We do not have any rock or mineral samples from other stars, solar systems, or galaxies, so we cannot use radioactive isotopes to date these heavenly bodies, or the universe itself. We do, however, have access to light from the stars and galaxies in outer space and scientists have been very creative in extracting information from this light to learn such things as: (1) the temperature of stars (based on their color), (2) the elemental composition of stars and nebula (based on black absorption bands within the light), and (3) the speed at which stars and galaxies are moving toward or away from us (based on the doppler effect, light is either shifted toward the blue or red end of the spectrum). We have also become accustomed to using other forms of electromagnetic radiation that travel at the speed of light (186,200 miles per second), such as radio waves, to communicate with our satellites and probes on distant planets. In 2012, based on the location of Mars relative to earth, it took 13 minutes and 48 seconds to send a message to or receive a message from the Curiosity Rover on the surface of Mars. When the New Horizon space probe flew by Pluto in 2016, it took 4 hours and 20 minutes for the first pictures to reach earth. Currently, it takes over nineteen hours for communication to travel between earth and the Voyager I space probe, a spacecraft which was launched in 1977 and is now over 13 billion miles from earth. Thus, even within our solar system, we have become accustomed to vast distances and the time it takes light or other forms of electromagnetic radiation to travel across these dark voids.

Beyond our solar system, however, distances become truly staggering. Light can travel approximately 6 trillion miles in a year (a light year). It takes light from the nearest star, Proxima Centauri, 4.25 light years to reach the earth, the Gliese Solar System is 20.3 light years away, the center of our galaxy is 27,000 light years away, and the neighboring Andromeda Galaxy is 2.2 million light years away. However, the most distant galaxy yet recorded (GN-z11) has a red shift of 11.1 and is located some 13.4 billion light years from earth. This means that this galaxy was formed just 400 million years after the Big Bang (Makishima 2017:22–23). Cosmic microwave background radiation from the Big Bang has taken about 13.8 billion light years to reach the earth. Therefore, based on distance which light travels in a year (6 trillion miles), we assume the universe is about 13.8 billion years old. Although 13.8 billion years may seem almost unimaginable from the perspective of our short lifetimes, and wildly out of step with our previous estimates of around 6,000 years for the age of the heavens and earth, it is not really that big a number or that vast a time period, especially from the perspective of our eternal God.

Given the work of da Vinci in the 1400s on sediment rates in the Po Valley and the work of Hutton on various ancient structures and landforms in Scotland in the 1700s, as well as the many dating techniques available to scientists today (from tree rings to light waves), the current cultural and scientific evidences for an old earth are rather overwhelming. When we work a math problem in two or three different ways and always get the same result, we are pretty confident that our answer is correct. When one dating technique after another gives us results that are thousands, millions, or billions of years older than earlier estimates based on biblical genealogies, we become pretty confident that the heavens and earth are indeed a great deal older than 6,000 years. Therefore, it is not surprising that those Christians today, whose theological interpretations are still firmly linked to the science of the Middle Ages, find themselves in a rather precarious position. Like their counterparts in the days of Copernicus and Galileo, they have fabricated various models and theories and even created colleges and museums to defend their position and explain away the empirical evidence for an old earth. In reality, they are just defending an older cultural/scientific understanding of nature that they are more comfortable with, against a newer cultural/scientific model of nature that they still distrust. In the end, the age of the earth and the heavens will probably also become a non-issue, just like the perfection of the heavens or the centrality of the earth. Christians will continue to follow Christ and nonbelievers will continue to reject him, and new battles will arise over humanly flawed theological and cultural/scientific interpretations of nature. Presently, however, this debate over the age of the earth in churches across America is a great distraction. It threatens the peace of mind of Christians within the church, as well as hinders their ability to share the gospel with non-Christians (especially those who know much about science).

II. THE GEOLOGICAL COLUMN IS THE RESULT OF A SINGLE GREAT FLOOD

A much more recent debate between geologists and some theologians has arisen over the nature of fossils found in the rocks of the earth. The preserved remnants of ancient life forms have repeatedly been found and wondered at down through the ages. Indeed, a polished brachiopod has even been found at a Neanderthal site in Europe, suggesting it had been collected and carried about in a skin pouch, either because of its interesting shape and beauty, or as some type of magic token. The Greeks, of course, were among the ancient peoples who speculated about the origin of fossils. It has been suggested that some of the monsters in Greek mythology were based on actual fossils (Mayor 2011). A 2007 display at the American Museum of Natural History in New York entitled "Mythic Creatures: Dragons, Unicorns & Mermaids" suggested that the fossilized remains of animals such as narwhal tusks and mammoth skulls may have given rise to the belief in mythical animals, such as unicorns (horses with horns) and cyclopes (a race of one-eyed giants). Fossils sharing a closer resemblance to modern forms, however, were explained in less imaginative terms. Xenophanes of Colophon (c. 570–c. 475 B.C.) argued that the presence of fossilized sea creatures and sea shells on land was the result of a wetter period in earth history when the earth was covered with water and the land had turned to mud. Herodotus (484–425 B.C.) observed fossil shells in Egypt that he believed were evidence that this land had once been beneath the sea. A thousand years later, Leonardo da Vinci (1452–1519) would also explain the presence of fossilized shark's teeth and sea shells in the Alps as evidence that these mountains had once been beneath the sea (Moore and Moore 2006:51). It would not be until the late eighteenth century, however, that the British engineer, William Smith (1769–1839), would be able to make sense of all the various fossilized remains that were sprinkled among the rocks of the earth.

William Smith was an English canal engineer. Although irrigation canals had first been constructed in Iraq and Syria around 4000 B.C., and a canal for transport had been cut around the cataract on the Nile around 2000 B.C., the Industrial Revolution, which began in Britain in the mid-1700s, ushered in a period of intensive canal building to facilitate the movement of raw materials and finished products. One of the problems that an engineer like Smith encountered was determining the amount of time, money, and manpower necessary to excavate a canal channel across a given area of the countryside. These expenditures were determined, in large part, by the type and depth of the soil, as well as the type and depth of the underlying bedrock. Soft rocks, such as mudstone and siltstone were much easier to remove than the harder and more massive sandstones and limestones. While the former might be removed with picks and shovels, the latter often required drilling and dynamite. Moreover, some shales were quite soft and pliable while others were hard and brittle; some sandstones were composed of sand grains that were only loosely compacted together while others had grains that were tightly cemented to each other. Once Smith determined the ease or difficulty of cutting through any particular rock strata, how could he determine when this same rock stratum was encountered elsewhere? He needed some method for recognizing the various rock strata wherever he ran into them as he excavated canals across the English countryside. Smith's solution to this problem was the fossils that the rocks contained. Each rock strata not only had unique physical properties such as hardness and mineral composition, but also unique fossil assemblages. Rocks formed in shallow waters would contain the fossils of animals and plants that thrived in such high energy, high light environments; rocks formed in deeper waters would contain fossils of animals that were adapted to those settings. Each rock strata had its only unique set of fossils based on the environment in which the rock had formed.

In addition to recognizing that each rock strata had a unique assemblage of fossils, Smith also recognized that the fossils in these assemblages changed over time. Although Smith did not have knowledge of the radioactive isotopes that we now use to date rocks, he could assign relative dates to the rock strata, from oldest to youngest, based on the vertical position of these strata relative to each other. In the 1600s, the Danish priest and scientist, Nicolas Steno, formulated the Law of Superposition. In any sequence of rocks, the ones at the bottom of the sequence were deposited first and are therefore the oldest; the ones at the top were deposited last and are therefore the youngest. The same principle applies to making a bed or a layered cake—one doesn't put the bedspread or frosting on first and then try to slide the sheets or cake layers underneath. The bottom-most layer is always laid down first. Using Steno's Law of Superposition, Smith found that, although marine fossils such as brachiopods (a type of sea shell) occurred in many different limestone strata, those in one strata were often morphologically somewhat different from those in the strata above or below (i.e. although of the same genus, there were a different species). Even more importantly, the lower-most fossils were always the more primitive, the upper-most fossils, the more advanced. While the type of ecosystem (terrestrial, shallow water, mid-depth, deep water) might repeatedly occur over and over again from one rock strata to the next, the type of organisms occupying those ecosystems changed their forms through time. This became known as the Principle of Faunal Succession. This discovery allowed Smith to precisely identify individual rock strata, not only based on the type of ecosystem in which the rock strata and its fossils had formed, but also on the morphology of the fossils occupying those ecosystems. With Steno's Law of Superposition and Smith's own Principle of Faunal Succession, Smith would subsequently map all the surface rocks of Great Britain and thereby produce the world's very first geological map (Winchester 2009). His work would become the foundation for the geologic column which would incorporate all the geologic rock strata of the earth and the unique fossil assemblages that each strata contained. The geologic column in turn would give us a better understanding of the progression of life upon the earth: The Age of Invertebrates, The Age of Fishes, The Age of Amphibians, The Age of Reptiles (Dinosaurs), and The Age of Mammals.

Young Earth Creationists often argued that geologists created the geologic column in order to validate the evolutionary theory of Charles Darwin. This is not true since Smith developed his Principle of Faunal Succession in the first decade of the nineteenth century, some 50 years before Darwin published his *On the Origin of Species* in 1859. How, then, did scientists in the first half of the nineteenth century explain Smith's discovery of the succession of life from primitive to more advanced forms? Many scientists used the Bible. The book of Genesis tell us that God created swarms of living creatures in the water and birds in the air on the fifth day of creation. The cattle, creeping things, and beasts of the earth were created on the sixth day, which concluded with Adam and Eve. A similar progression of life, from simple to complex, could be seen in the rock record.

After Darwin developed his theory of evolution, this progression of life could also be explained in terms of evolution, with simple forms of life giving rise to more complex forms through processes such as natural selection and the survival of the fittest. Many scientists, who were agnostics or atheists, often used the theory of evolution to buttress their belief that there was no God and the appearance of life on the earth was just the result of random processes. Some scientists who were Christians, however, accepted evolution as a possible method by which God chose to create life and populate the earth with a diversity of creatures. Other Christians saw evolution as a direct challenge to their faith and totally rejected Darwin's theory. Once again, we see scientists and theologians interpreting empirical evidence in terms of their particular biases, even as they also did concerning the evidence for an ancient earth in geology or the evidence for the Big Bang in astronomy.

Many Christians in American today have been strongly influenced by the Young Earth Creationists movement, which often rejects, not only evolution, but also geologic time, as well as the Big Bang theory. Thus, they have set themselves and the churches which they attend at odds with the three major natural science disciplines humans use to study the physical universe: biology, geology, and astronomy. This is a very precariously position that both Saint Augustine and Saint Aquinas warned their fellow Christians against taking, many centuries ago.

According to Ronald Numbers in his book *The Creationists: The Evolution of Scientific Creationism* (1992), the origin of the modern Young Earth Creationist movement can be traced to the writings of Ellen G. White (1827–1915), who was one of the founders of the Seventh-day Adventist Church. White claimed to have received messages from God in the form of visions that gave

her a deeper understanding of events recorded in the Bible, such
as creation and Noah's flood. Her writings were incorporated into
the doctrines of the Seventh-day Adventist's Church and were
given equal authority with the Scriptures (Numbers 1992:73–74).
White's visions concerning Noah's flood provided an explanation
for the presence of fossils in the rocks of the earth:

> In a published gloss on the Mosaic cosmogony, White endorsed
> the largely discarded view of Noah's flood as a worldwide catas-
> trophe that had buried the fossils and reshaped the earth's surface.
> After the flood waters had subsided, exposing the rotting carcasses
> of antediluvian life, God had buried the organic debris, she
> explained, by causing "a powerful wind to pass over the earth…in
> some instances carrying away the tops of mountains like mighty
> avalanches, forming huge hills and high mountains where there
> were none to be seen before, and burying the dead bodies with
> trees, stones, and earth." The buried forests subsequently turned
> into coal and oil, which God occasionally ignited to produce
> "earthquakes, volcanoes and fiery issues." (ibid.:74)

White's visions were popularized, both inside and outside
the Adventist Church, by George McCready Price (1870–1963),
a largely self-taught geologist who incorporated her ideas on
fossils and the flood into his 726-page book entitled, *The New
Geology* (1923). As Numbers has noted, "*The New Geology*, like
so many of Price's previous works, featured the Genesis flood as
the central geological event in the history of earth" (1992:82). In
this context it is worth noting that the rejection of the paradigm
of catastrophism and the rise of the paradigm of uniformitari-
anism in the eighteenth century was precipitated, in part, by the
earlier emphasis on the flood as a mainstay of geology. For centuries, the flood had been used to explain anything and everything
about earth history; it was the primary agent responsible for
shaping the face of the earth and a host of other things. Sometimes it seemed as though the ultimate answer to any geologic
question was—Noah's flood. However, when every question

can be explained by the same answer, the answer has become so generalized that it contains little informative content. Therefore, it was like a breath of fresh air when other earth-shaping processes were identified by James Hutton (1726–1797), Charles Lyell (1797–1875), and Louis Agassiz (1807–1873). Instead of focusing on a single event (the flood) for explaining earth history, Hutton argued that "the present is the key to the past." In other words, the processes that are shaping the earth today (i.e. running water, wind, wave action, ice, etc.) had shaped the earth in the past. Hutton's disciple, Charles Lyell, in his book *Principles of Geology* (1811–1813), attempted to identify all the processes that had shaped the earth. Louis Agassiz explained many landforms that were previously thought to have been created by the flood, as instead having been formed by huge glaciers during an Ice Age. Therefore, Price's return to the flood as the centerpiece of earth history seemed like déjà vu to most professional geologists in the twentieth century.

Price's ideas concerning flood geology had a particularly strong impact on some biblical scholars in other denominations, specifically John C. Whitcomb, Jr. (1924–present), a member of the Grace Brethren Church, and Henry M. Morris (1918–2006), who was a Baptist (Numbers 1992:187–189, 192–194). Together, Whitcomb and Morris published a book entitled *The Genesis Flood: The Biblical Record and Its Scientific Implications* (1961) that would capture the imagination and support of members in thousands of fundamentalist and evangelical churches across America. Tens of thousands of copies were sold during its first decade in print (Numbers 1992:204); after 5 decades and 48 printings, it had sold more than 300,000 copies (Scharf 2010). Karl Giberson describes this publication as the book that "launched the modern creationist movement and helped convince half of America that the earth was just a few thousand years old" (2008:124). This book also helped Henry Morris to later become recognized in many churches as the *father of modern creation science*. The book itself, however, was largely a restatement of Price's and White's ideas:

Although Morris had deleted all but a few direct references to Price [in Whitcomb's original manuscript], his section read like an updated version of *The New Geology*. In arguing for a worldwide flood that deposited most of the fossil-bearing rocks, he followed Price in discarding the principle of uniformity, in questioning the notion of multiple ice ages, and in rejecting the so-called geological column. The apparent order of the column he attributed to such factors as the early death of marine creatures, buried by sediments deposited during the first stages of the flood; the hydrodynamic selectivity of moving water, which sorted out particles of similar sizes and shapes; and the superior mobility of vertebrates, which allowed them to escape early destruction. (Numbers 1992:202)

According to Whitcomb and Morris, and now many theologians and laymen in various churches across the country, William Smith's Principle of Faunal Succession and the geologic column are simply fallacious interpretations of the rock record. They argued that the great majority of fossils found in the rocks of the earth are from animals that all lived at roughly the same time, including humans and dinosaurs. Most of the organisms represented by these fossils also died at roughly the same time, during Noah's flood. Smith's Principle of Faunal Succession is explained in terms of Noah's flood. Invertebrates are found at the bottom of the geologic column because they already lived on the sea floor and were rapidly killed and buried as sediment from the land began to pour into the sea as the rains began. Fish which live in the water column were subsequently overwhelmed by the flood waters and buried on top of the invertebrates. Amphibians, which live near water, were next as the oceans began to rise and submerge the lowlands surrounding the seas, rivers, and lakes. The reptiles which creep or slither on the ground were the first fully terrestrial creatures to be drowned, and were later followed by the other, more mobile, mammals. Finally, even the humans, who had fled to the highest elevations, were drowned as the flood waters reached the tops of the mountains (Whitcomb and Morris 1961:265–266).

Although Whitcomb and Morris's explanation of Smith's Principle of Faunal Succession is very ingenious, it betrays a fundamental ignorance of the richness and complexity of the record of past life forms that God has left for us in the rocks of the earth. Although geologists have designated the Cambrian and Ordovician periods as *The Age of Invertebrates*, fish were also present in these rocks, but not nearly as abundant as the invertebrates during this time period. The Silurian and Devonian periods are designated as *The Age of Fish* because fish were going through a process of proliferation and diversification at this time. Nevertheless, invertebrates were still present. *The Age of Amphibians* encompasses the Mississippian, Pennsylvanian, and Permian Periods, but both invertebrates and fish were also present in the rocks of these periods. The same is true of *The Age of Reptiles* in the Triassic, Jurassic, and Cretaceous periods. Dinosaurs may have come to rule the earth by the middle of the Jurassic Period, but invertebrates, fish, amphibians, and even birds and mammals were also a part of the rock record from that time period. Although dinosaurs disappeared from the face of the earth at the end of the Cretaceous Period, many reptiles, such as turtles, crocodiles, and snakes, did not go extinct. During the Tertiary and Quaternary periods, mammals, which had remained in the background during the reign of the dinosaurs, now moved to center stage and began to fill many of the ecological niches left empty by the demise of the dinosaurs; thus, geologists call this time period the *Age of Mammals*. Representatives of all the other life forms (invertebrates, fish, amphibians, reptiles, and birds), however, were still present, they had not disappeared beneath the sediments deposited by the rising waters of Noah's flood.

Therefore, the fossils which occur in rock strata do not represent just one type of organism (such as invertebrates or amphibians), but a whole host of organisms that lived together as a community in various ecosystems. Just like today, the ecosystems preserved in the rock record represented a variety of different environments, including: low or high elevations, deserts or rainforests, swamps or grassy steppes, marine or fresh water, and deep or shallow water. Many of the organisms living in these various ecosystems were periodically wiped out at the same time by great world-wide mass extinction events that resulted from such natural processes as flood basalts, ice ages, or asteroid impacts. The survivors of these catastrophic upheavals then repopulated the earth and a whole new series of ecosystems developed. Moreover, the various types of plants and animals that had been members of the ecosystems that had perished often reappeared again in the rock record, although in slightly different forms (i.e. as new species). For example, trilobites, which first appeared at the beginning of the Age of Invertebrates in the Cambrian Period, are also found in the Age of Fishes and the Age of Amphibians, before finally disappearing from the fossil record at the end of the Permian Period. During this vast period of time, older species of trilobites that went extinct were repeatedly replaced by newer species of trilobites. Fish, which also first appeared in the Cambrian Period, but are still with us today, display a similar pattern of death and rebirth as older species of fish were replaced with newer species of fish. Amphibians, reptiles, and mammals that lived and died with the dinosaurs are still with us today, although in new and different forms. Indeed our natural history museums are filled with the fossils of many different species of invertebrates, fish, amphibians, reptiles, birds, and mammals representing a host of different ecosystems that appeared and disappeared down through the ages, yet their descendants are still living amongst us. As God commanded, the waters still teem with swarms of living creatures (Gen. 1:20), and the earth still brings forth living creatures (v. 24), despite repeated catastrophes and extinction events.

These different ecosystems and the various organisms of which they are composed, as well as the environments in which they lived (i.e. deserts, swamps, grasslands, forests lakes, rivers, oceans), occur over and over again in the geologic column, not in a smooth progression from the sea floor to the mountain tops as Young Earth Creationists would have us believe. Over the past 500–600 million years sea levels have experienced six major rises and falls (Sauk, Tippecanoe, Absaroka, Kakaskian, Zuni, and

Tejas), resulting in the oceans transgressing onto the continents, and then regressing. Each of these marine transgressions leaves a mantle of sedimentary rock composed of sandstones, shales, and limestones. Embedded within these sedimentary rocks are the fossils of marine creatures such as trilobites and brachiopods that are unique to the time period during which each of these transgressions occurred. During this same time period, there were three major ice ages (Ordovician, Permo-Carboniferous, and Pleistocene) that covered parts of continents in the Northern and Southern Hemispheres with glacial ice. Each time the ice retreated, it left behind glacial landforms that can only be created by ice. Within these glacial sediments are the fossils of terrestrial creatures (such a mammoth and sabertooth cats) that were specially adapted to the cold and are unique to the time period during which each of these ice ages occurred. During the past 500–600 million years, there were five major mass extinctions (Ordovician, Devonian, Permian, Triassic, and Cretaceous) in which 50 percent or more of all species on the earth went extinct (Ward and Kirschvink 2015:146). Within the rocks that date to these extinction events are the fossils of both marine and terrestrial organisms that are unique to the time period during which each of these major extinctions occurred.

The belief that a single flood (even Noah's flood) can account for the rich diversity of organisms, ecosystems, and environments, as well as the many marine transgressions, ice ages, and mass extinction events that are recorded in the rock record, is simply not tenable. Only to those with little or no knowledge of earth history will Whitcomb and Morris's model seem logical and believable. As the astronomer, Hugh Ross, has noted, "Many Young-Earth Creationist leaders declare that their view is reality and that virtually all of what has been discovered in the hard sciences is *not* what scientists think it is. This apparent anti-science position obscures physical reality in a dense fog. Galaxies, stars, fossils, dinosaurs, Neanderthals and many other subjects of scientific inquiry remain cloaked in mystery, supposedly lacking satisfactory explanation. The refusal of Young Earth Creationists to acknowledge established facts causes many people to dismiss belief in creationism as either complete idiocy or downright deception" (2004:207). We as humans, however, have been given the gift of free will, so we can believe what we want to believe. When inconvenient facts get in the way we can simply shove them aside and ignore them or reinterpret them to fit our biases. Many theologians and laymen in evangelical and fundamentalist churches have gone to great pains to create models that can preserve their badly flawed understanding of the earth and its history. One has to wonder how much further along we might all be in our spiritual development if these same individuals had devoted their time and effort to trying to build models that would allow us to maintain our faith, while still being able to accept (at least tentatively) our culture's current scientific understanding of the world which God has created. Although our present understanding of nature may someday also be shown to be flawed, all we can do is work with the knowledge and information that is presently available to us. Yet, many theologians and Christian laymen have chosen to reject or remain ignorant of our present scientific knowledge and information concerning the world and universe in which we live. Unfortunately, to be willfully ignorant is a sin that has consequences.

III. THE EARTH'S CLIMATE CANNOT BE ALTERED BY HUMAN ACTIVITY

A sin of willful ignorance for which we may already be suffering the consequences is global warming. Many Christians, because of their opposition to current scientific understanding of such things as evolution, geologic time, the Principal of Faunal Succession, and the geologic column, have come to hate science in general; it is an enemy not to be trusted. As one of my former Bible college roommates, who is now a Bible college professor, once informed me: My students hate science; no, let me rephrase that, they really, really HATE science. As a result of this growing antipathy with regards to all things scientific, many Christians are now rejecting other scientific discoveries that seem to have no bearing on their faith. Indeed, in some cases, they are actually rejecting scientific knowledge that could support their faith, and global warming is one of those areas.

The foundation for the science behind global warming was laid nearly 200 years ago. In the 1820s, the French mathematician and physicist, Joseph Fourier (1768–1830), noted that the earth should actually be cooler than it is, given its size and distance from the sun. He went on to speculate that the atmosphere might somehow be acting as an insulator to keep the earth warmer than one would expect it to be. In 1861, John Tyndall (1820–1893), an Irish physicist and chemist, found that certain gases in the earth's atmosphere (including carbon dioxide) had the power to absorb infrared radiation (radiant heat), thereby producing a greenhouse effect. In 1896, the Swedish physicist and chemist, Svante Arrhenius (1859–1927), was the first scientist to attempt to calculate how changing carbon dioxide levels in the atmosphere could cause earth's climate to heat up or cool down. Moreover, he suggested that the release of carbon dioxide from the burning of fossil fuels (coal, oil, gas) could cause future global warming. However, it was not until the late 1950s that scientists were able to begin collecting accurate data as to how rapidly the level of carbon dioxide in the atmosphere was increasing. In 1958, the American chemist and oceanographer, Charles David Keeling (1928–2005), set up an observatory on top of Mauna Loa in Hawaii in order to measure the amount of carbon dioxide in the atmosphere. He chose this remote location in the middle of the Pacific Ocean, on a mountaintop some two miles above sea level, in order to ensure that his samples of gases in the atmosphere were thoroughly mixed, being located far from major industrial areas on the continents. By 1961 he was able to show that carbon dioxide levels in earth's atmosphere were rising, and doing so on a yearly basis. This steady rise in carbon dioxide became known as the Keeling Curve. In 1958 there were 315 ppm (parts per million) of carbon dioxide in the atmosphere, by August 20, 2016 the Scripps Institute of Oceanography in San Diego, California, reported that that figure had risen to 400.42 ppm. Scientists have also devised a technique for determining the amount of carbon dioxide in earth's atmosphere that extends back in time thousands of years before Keeling began his measurements on Mauna Loa. Air bubbles trapped in glacial ice in Antarctica provide scientists with samples of atmospheric gases at the time when any particular layer of ice formed. By counting the yearly layers of dense and less dense ice, this record goes back some 800,000 years. At no time in this vast time period did carbon dioxide levels ever exceed 280 ppm, until after the Industrial Revolution began in 1700.

By the end of the 1970s, most environmental scientist had concluded that the continued rise in carbon dioxide would inevitably lead to global warming, probably starting around the year 2000. However, near the end of the 1980s (the hottest decade on record at that time), James Hansen (1941-present), director of the NASA Goddard Institute for Space Studies in New York City, testified before Congress (1988) that global warming was already beginning to cause climate change. As Hanson later described his testimony: "I declared, with 99 percent confidence, that it was time to stop waffling: Earth was being affected by human-made greenhouse gases, and the planet had entered a period of long-term warming" (Hansen 2009:xv). In the three decades since Hanson's testimony, the climate has continued to grow warmer and the impacts of climate change more devastating. The string of hottest years on record in the 1980s was broken in the 1990s. The string of hottest years on record in the 1990s was broken again in the 2000s. Global warming in the present decade seems to be rapidly accelerating. A new record for the hottest year was set in 2014, but this was eclipsed by an even hotter year in 2015, which was subsequently replaced by even hotter year in 2016. Yet, the naysayers of global warming have only increased the volume and intensity of their protests. Hansen, on the other hand, in 2009 published a book entitled *Storms of My Grandchildren: The Truth About the Coming Climate Catastrophe and Our Last Chance to Save Humanity*. In 2013 he retired from NASA, "giving himself more freedom to pursue political and legal efforts to limit greenhouse gases" (Gillis 2013).

Many Christians today continue to reject the science of global warming for a variety of reasons. One of the weakest arguments is that the scientists promoting the idea of global warming and the need to protect our environment are tree-huggers who worship nature more than God. It seems odd that some Christians should ascribe religious motives to the same scientists whom they usually castigate as agnostics and atheists. Moreover, from a biblical standpoint, it seems evident that God intended that we should care for that which he has created. Was not the first profession of man, that of a gardener?: "Then the Lord God took the man and put him into the garden of Eden to cultivate it and keep it" (Gen. 2:15).

Another argument that some Christians make against global warming is that scientists believe that humans are responsible for climate change, whereas they, being Christians, believe that only God can control the climate. It is obvious, however, that God has allowed mankind to wantonly slaughter the animals he has created, cut down the forests, and pollute the air and water, and then suffer the consequences. Why, then, should many Christians believe that the climate is off-limits for man's misuse? According to the Bible, the fact that God is not pleased with our misuse of the world he had created for us will become frighteningly evident at the last judgment: "And the nations were enraged, and Your wrath came, and the time came for the dead to be judged, and the time to reward Your bond-servants the prophets and the saints and those who fear Your name, the small and the great, and to destroy those who destroy the earth" (Rev. 11:18).

A third reason many Christians in America have rejected the scientific evidence for global warming is that they have aligned themselves with a particular political party that, for the past few decades, has made a point of rejecting the scientific evidence for global warming, even when that evidence was collected by the government's own scientists and agencies. This political party's feud with environmentalists goes back to World War II when America was developing the atomic bomb. A number of envi-ronmental scientists opposed open-air testing of nuclear weapons because clouds of radioactive isotopes from these tests were drifting across America and contaminating the land and water (Commoner 2003:29–30). The nuclear scientists running these tests, however, saw this work as essential to national security, especially after the nuclear arms race began with the Soviet Union. Therefore, many nuclear scientists came to view environmental scientists as little better than traitors whose attempts to stop open-air testing and the subsequent nuclear arms race were aiding and abetting the enemy. They convinced themselves that environmentalists were friends of the Communists. Out of this conflict arose the caricature of environmentalists as being like watermelons, green on the outside, but red on the inside. Therefore, any attempt to get the government to regulate nuclear testing was a drift toward socialism and communism (Oreskes and Conway 2010:248–249). This mantra against regulation was also adopted by businessmen within the party who saw other forms of government regulation, such as those governing air pollution, water pollution, or product safety, as being detrimental to their business practices and profit margins. Interestingly, many of the same individuals who opposed government regulation of nuclear testing also opposed government regulation of toxic pesticides (such as DDT), the tobacco industry, acid rain, chlorofluorocarbons, *and* greenhouse gases (ibid.:216–242). This rejection of any type of government regulation has grown to an irrational obsession within that party and includes many of the most divisive issues in America today: the regulation of guns, banks, and healthcare, as well as greenhouse gases. As a result, many Christians who flocked to this party because of its promise (ironically) to pass laws to *regulate* abortion and marriage now find they are supporting other ideas and practices that the rest of society sees as being immoral and very un-Christian. As Oreskes and Conway note, self-proclaimed warriors in America's so called *cultural wars* have ended up in a similar situation to that of the *Cold War Warriors*: "…who had dedicated their lives to fighting Soviet Communism, joined forces with the self-appointed defenders of the free market to blame the messenger, to undermine science, to deny the truth, and to market doubt. People who began their careers as fact find-ers ended them as fact fighters. Evidently accepting that their ends justified their means, they embraced the tactics of their enemy, the very things they had hated Soviet Communism for: its lies, its deceit, its denial of the very realities it had created" (2010:238).

The fact that many Christians today reject the scientific evidence for the greenhouse effect and global warming seems highly illogical from a biblical standpoint. Many of these same Christians are very interested in biblical prophecy and look forward to the eminent fulfillment of prophecies about the end-times as constituting a strong affirmation of their faith. For decades, the works of dispensationalists and other end times preachers and writers such as Jack Van Impe, Herbert W. Armstrong, Hal Lind-sey, and Tim LaHaye/Jerry B. Jenkins have been highly popu-lar among evangelical and fundamentalist churches. Yet, global warming and its effects can very easily be seen as a literal fulfill-ment of some of these prophecies. In the fifteenth chapter of the book of Revelation, the apostle John records: "Then I saw another sign in heaven, great and marvelous, seven angels who had seven plagues, which are the last, because in them the wrath of God is finished" (15:1). These follow the seven messages to the churches in Asia Minor (Rev. 1:11–3:22); the seven seals (Rev. 5:1–8:1); and the seven trumpets (Rev. 8:2–11:19). These seven last plagues are in bowls which the angels pour out upon the earth. The fourth bowl *could* be fulfilled by the greenhouse effect and global warm-ing since carbon dioxide certainly does trap heat from the sun and thereby increases the sun's power upon the earth: "The fourth angel poured out his bowl upon the sun, and it was given to it to scorch men with fire. Men were scorched with fierce heat; and they blasphemed the name of God who has the power over these plagues, and they did not repent so as to give Him glory" (Rev. 16:8–9).

The geologist, Peter D. Ward, has written a book entitled: *Under a Green Sky: Global Warming, the Mass Extinctions of the Past and What They Can Tell Us About Our Future* (2007). In this book, Ward suggests that global warming, which was caused by a period of intense volcanism and carbon dioxide release in Siberia, may have brought about the Great Permian Mass Extinction during which 90–95 percent of all species on earth went extinct. As Ward notes in this book, global warming can have a number of negative consequences that lead to greater and greater ecological devastation. At least four of the other plagues that are released when the angels pour out their bowls upon the earth could also be caused by intense global warming. The first bowl that is poured out upon the earth causes a loathsome and malignant sore (Rev. 16:2). An increased level of ultraviolet radiation from the sun causes skin cancer, as we have witnessed in recent years. This recent increase in ultraviolet radiation has resulted from damage to the ozone layer and was caused by the manufacture and release of chlorofluorocarbons into the atmosphere. Hydrogen sulfide, a bi-product of intense global warming, can also destroy the ozone layer (Ward 2007:118). The second bowl poured out upon the earth by one of the angels causes everything in the oceans to die (Rev. 16:3). Global warming eventually heats the ocean waters and warm water holds less oxygen than cold water so the oceans become more anoxic as they warm. Less oxygen in the water also allows various types of anoxic bacteria to proliferate, one of which produces hydrogen sulfide (a deadly poison) as a byproduct of its metabolic activity (Ward 2007:112–113). The fifth bowl causes darkness upon the earth (Rev. 16:10–11). Such darkness might be caused by increased fires across the surface of a warming and drying earth (as we are seeing in the Western United States today and as Russia experienced in 2010). The sixth bowl causes the waters of the Euphrates River to dry up (v. 12), a likely result of increased droughts in a warming earth (this happened to portions of the River Rhine during the heat wave in 2003 which killed 35,000 people in northern Europe) (Maslin 2009:225).

God can bring about the fulfillment of the prophecies in the book of Revelation and the other prophetic books by any means he chooses. Global Warming resulting from the burning of fossil fuels and the subsequent release of greenhouse gases is just one possible scenario. However, based on our current scientific understanding, earlier worlds, as recorded in the geologic record, also perished by similar means. In a recent book entitled: *The Worst of Times: How Life on Earth Survived Eighty Million Years of Extinctions* (2015), Paul B. Wignall presents detailed evidence of at least six extinction events that occurred between the middle of the Permian Period and the early Jurassic Period. According to Wignall, each of these mass extinction events was caused by global warming that was precipitated by huge volcanic flood basalt events that released massive amounts of carbon dioxide into the atmosphere. The question naturally arises, has God allowed scientists to discover these ancient catastrophes and their causes as a warning of how our world will also end? If so, many Christians are not listening, perhaps because they have rejected geologic time and the geologic column upon which this evidence is based.

God could certainly use another flood basalt event to bring about another catastrophic period of global warming on the earth. Unfortunately, that may not be necessary. One of the primary gases that volcanoes release is carbon dioxide. Today the average yearly amount of carbon dioxide released into the atmosphere by volcanism is about 300 *million* tons. By contrast, human industry is presently releasing about 32 *billion* tons, far in excess of the natural rate of volcanism, but more in line with the amount released during huge flood basalt events. Therefore, our burning of coal, oil, and natural gas is, on a yearly basis, releasing massive amounts of carbon dioxide into the atmosphere that are in the same range as those released by large flood basalt eruptions in the past, which caused major mass extinctions of life upon the earth. Throughout the Scriptures we see numerous examples where God has allowed people's sins to become the agents of their punishment, such as when Samson's eyes were put out after his affair with Delilah (Judg. 16:15–21), the death of David's first son with Bathsheba, Uriah the Hittite's wife (2 Sam. 12:15–19), or the eventual Babylonian capture of Jerusalem after King Hezekiah showed all that was in his treasure house to the Babylonian envoys from King Baladan (2 Kings 20:12–18). Consequently, would it be a surprise if a God of justice should choose to punish us with the fruits (i.e. global warming) of our greed for material things, our misuse and pollution of the natural world to obtain those items, our willful ignorance of the evidence of past climatic disasters resulting from excess carbon dioxide, and the distorted theological interpretations by which we attempt to justify our actions and beliefs? Will we become those very people described in Revelation 16:8–9 who blaspheme God because of these plagues and refuse to repent, perhaps never recognizing that the instrument of our punishment (global warming) was forged by our own hands? Watching the evening news about the increasing number of natural disasters that are occurring as global temperatures and sea levels continue to rise, the prognosis is not hopeful. The ice caps continue to melt, sea waters continue to acidify, periods of drought lengthen, fires spread, flood waters rise, and the power of hurricanes increases, but many continue to say: "all continues just as it was from the beginning of creation" (2 Peter 3:4).

Conclusion

In geology, as well as astronomy, we see conflicts arising between science and religion because earlier theologians both utilized and incorporated *then* current cultural/scientific knowledge and understanding of nature into their interpretations of scriptural passages that deal with the creation and functioning of the natural world. At various times in the past, the scientific ideas of Aristotle, Ptolemy, Newton, and others were called upon to lend insight and clarity to certainly theological interpretations of Scripture. Unfortunately, like the Pharisees we often value tradition over truth. When more recent scientific discoveries sweep away many of these older scientific theories and ideas, theologians and Christian laymen often reject these discoveries and castigate them as being attacks upon the validity of the Scriptures. In reality, these new scientific insights and discoveries are primarily attacks, not upon Scripture, but upon earlier scientific theories and beliefs. Theologians and laymen are inevitably pulled into these battles when they too closely tie their interpretations of Scripture to these older, now obviously flawed, cultural/ scientific theories and models about the natural world. They have hitched their wagons to a dying horse and later, when the horse dies, choose to argue that the horse is not dead; it is in fine health. It is the new scientific theories and ideas that are flawed, not the old ones. The heavens and earth are only a few thousand years old, just as Jose ben Halafta, Saint Bede, James Ussher, and Isaac Newton had believed. The thousands of feet of sedimentary rock, the millions upon millions of fossils they contain, and the great diversity of ecosystems these strata record, are the result of a single great flood, just as Ellen G. White, George McCready Price, John C. Whitcomb, and Henry M. Morris had said. There is no evidence of global warming, just ignore all the natural disasters that are occurring around you today.

Just as there is a price to be paid for willful ignorance, there is also a price to be paid for trying to link the eternal truths of the Scripture too closely with the very temporal and transitory truths of human disciplines, such as science. The price to be paid is a never-ending disjunction between science and religion because science continues to change as new discoveries are made and deeper insights into the workings of nature are acquired. Since theology, like science, is also a human discipline, theologians cannot avoid using humanly derived cultural/scientific knowledge upon which to base some of their scriptural interpretations, especially with regard to the natural world. They must constantly keep in mind, however, the transitory nature of this source of information and the resulting transitory nature of their interpretations of Scripture that are based on this source of information. Consequently, they should be, as Saint Aquinas suggested, "ready to abandon it, if it be proved with certainty to be false; lest Holy Scripture be exposed to the ridicule of unbelievers, and obstacles be placed to their believing" (Westerholm and Westerholm 2016:182).

Chapter 12

MODERN THEOLOGICAL
MISTAKES CONCERNING LIFE

INTRODUCTION: THE PERFECTION OF LIFE

Down through the ages, theologians have made three fundamental mistakes concerning life upon the earth: (1) the various types of life that God made are perfect, there was no death before sin; (2) the various types of life that God made are perfect, they do not go extinct; (3) the various types of life that God made are perfect, they do not evolve. All of these mistakes are based on God's pronouncements at the end of days 3, 4, and 6 in the Genesis account (see Table 19):

Table 19: Scriptures concerning the Goodness of God's Creation
Then God said, "Let the earth sprout vegetation: plants yielding seed, and fruit trees on the earth bearing fruit after their kind with seed in them"; and it was so. The earth brought forth vegetation, plants yielding seed after their kind, and trees bearing fruit with seed in them, after their kind; and God saw that it was good. There was evening and there was morning, a third day. (Gen. 1:11–13)

Table 19: Scriptures concerning the Goodness of God's Creation

Then God said, "Let the waters teem with swarms of living creatures, and let birds fly above the earth in the open expanse of the heavens." God created the great sea monsters and every living creature that moves, with which the waters swarmed after their kind, and every winged bird after its kind; and God saw that it was good. God blessed them, saying, "Be fruitful and multiply, and fill the waters in the seas, and let birds multiply on the earth." There was evening and there was morning, a fifth day. (vv. 20–23)

Then God said, "Let the earth bring forth living creatures after their kind: cattle and creeping things and beasts of the earth after their kind"; and it was so. God made the beasts of the earth after their kind, and the cattle after their kind, and everything that creeps on the ground after its kind; and God saw that it was good. Then God said, "Let Us make man in Our image, according to Our likeness; and let them rule over the fish of the sea and over the birds of the sky and over the cattle and over all the earth, and over every creeping thing that creeps on the earth." God created man in His own image, in the image of God He created him; male and female He created them. God blessed them; and God said to them, "Be fruitful and multiply, and fill the earth, and subdue it; and rule over the fish of the sea and over the birds of the sky and over every living thing that moves on the earth." Then God said, "Behold, I have given you every plant yielding seed that is on the surface of all the earth, and every tree which has fruit yielding seed; it shall be food for you; and to every beast of the earth and to every bird of the sky and to every thing that moves on the earth which has life, I have given every green plant for food"; and it was so. God saw all that He had made, and behold, it was very good. And there was evening and there was morning, the sixth day. (vv. 24–31)

Many theologians have long assumed that, if God said his creation was *good* or *very good*, it must be perfect or as near perfect as humans could imagine. Here, however, we see human bias and interpretation entering into the creation account. In an attempt to elevate God and his ways above man, theologians reasoned that, if God says his creation is good or very good, then from the human perspective, it must be perfect. In doing this, however, theologians have made the Bible say what it does not say. If God had wanted to pronounce his creation as being perfect, he could have certainly done so. For example, Jesus said, "Therefore you are to be perfect, as your heavenly Father is perfect" (Matt. 5:48). Instead God pronounces his creation as being *good* and *very good*. But good or very good in what sense? Can God's creation *do good* in a moral sense, such as not sinning (like the Good Shepherd) or doing good deeds (like the Good Samaritan)? This cannot be the case since Adam and Eve were not only capable of sinning, but chose to do so. Can animals really do good when they don't know right from wrong? It seems much more likely that God's creation is good or very good in the sense that it can (and does) fulfill that for which it was created, like a good design, story, tool, or weapon. Therefore, for theologians to attribute perfection to that which God has only designated as being good or very good, is an example of bad theology; theologians are displaying their fallen nature by unintentionally misunderstanding the facts because of their limited knowledge or intentionally misinterpreting the facts in the Genesis account because of their biases.

I. Species Are Perfect—They Do Not Die (until Adam and Eve Sinned)

Some conservative Christians today argue that, although organisms now die, this was not the case before Adam and Eve sinned in the garden of Eden. In fact, these groups believe that there was no death at all in the garden of Eden—either for man and woman or for the animals—until Adam and Eve disobeyed God and ate from the Tree of Knowledge of Good and Evil. In his article, "Did Death of Any Kind Exist Before the Fall?," Simon Turpin advances this argument: "The gospel according to those who believe that God created a world which had animals and humans dying, destruction, and catastrophe before Adam's disobedience is faith in the Creator, Christ, who 'creates' by using evolutionary processes, which is faith in a 'god' who said He created all things 'very good' when he really used aeons of death and struggle. How then can He be trusted to make a new and good creation as His definition of 'good' may well mean an eternity of death and struggle?" (2013:114). Biblical *proof texts* for this position include (see Table 20):

Table 20: Scriptures Used as Proof-Texts That There Was No Physical Death before Sin
For since by a man came death, by a man also came the resurrection of the dead. For as in Adam all die, so also in Christ all will be made alive. (1 Cor. 15:21–22)
For the anxious longing of the creation waits eagerly for the revealing of the sons of God. For the creation was subjected to futility, not willingly, but because of Him who subjected it, in hope that the creation itself also will be set free from its slavery to corruption into the freedom of the glory of the children of God. For we know that the whole creation groans and suffers the pains of childbirth together until now. And not only this, but also we ourselves, having the first fruits of the Spirit, even we ourselves groan within ourselves, waiting eagerly for our adoption as sons, the redemption of our body. (Rom. 8:19–23)
Therefore, just as through one man sin entered into the world, and death through sin, and so death spread to all men, because all sinned—for until the Law sin was in the world, but sin is not imputed when there is no law. Nevertheless death reigned from Adam until Moses, even over those who had not sinned in the likeness of the offense of Adam, who is a type of Him who was to come. (Rom. 5:12–14)

Proponents of this view believe that the garden of Eden was a heaven on earth with no sin, suffering, or death. In Romans 5, however, Paul also notes that "for until the Law sin was in the world, but sin is not imputed when there is no law" (v. 13). Is there a possible parallel here between the giving of the law and the command not to eat the fruit of the Tree of Knowledge of Good and Evil in the garden of Eden? Were Adam and Eve innocent of sin, not due to their inherent purity or goodness, but instead, because they were like very young children who do not know right from wrong and, therefore, are not accountable for their actions—until God gave them this prohibition? As God explained to Jonah: "Should I not have compassion on Nineveh, the great city in which there are more than 120,000 persons who do not know the difference between their right and left hand, as well as many animals?" (Jonah 4:9). As Jesus noted when speaking of those towns and villages he had visited, "If I had not come and spoken to them, they would not have sin, but now they have no excuse for their sin" (John 15:22). We do know that sin was present in the garden of Eden before Adam and Eve disobeyed God because Satan, the father of lies, was already there in the form of a Serpent. If sin was already present before Adam and Eve sinned, perhaps death was as well?

The argument that there was no death before the Fall has very deep roots in Christian History. For example, in A.D. 418 at the African Council held in Carthage, it was stated that: "Whosoever says, that Adam was created mortal, and would, even without sin, have died by natural necessity, let him be anathema" (Schaff 1891:799). Now there is no doubt that the accounts in Genesis 3:14–19, Romans 5:12, and 1 Corinthians 15:21 clearly teach that Adam and Eve's disobedience in the garden of Eden brought the penalty of death upon all humanity. It does not necessarily follow, however, that there was no death before the Fall. In Genesis chapter 2, God gives Adam and Eve permission to eat of any of the trees in the garden of Eden, *except* for one tree:

> Then the LORD God took the man and put him into the garden of Eden to cultivate it and keep it. The LORD God commanded the man, saying, "From any tree of the garden you may eat freely; but from the tree of the knowledge of good and evil you shall not eat, for in the day that you eat from it you will surely die." (Gen. 2:15–17)

> The woman said to the serpent, "From the fruit of the trees of the garden we may eat; but from the fruit of the tree which is in the middle of the garden, God has said, 'You shall not eat from it or touch it, or you will die.'" (Gen. 3:2–3)

Now among the trees in the garden of Eden was also the Tree of Life (v. 22). Why would such a tree be present in the garden of Eden if there was no death upon the earth before Adam and Eve sinned? Rather than death being absent, it seems that the opportunity was present to escape from death, but Adam and Eve failed to eat from this tree, preferring to eat from the one tree in the garden which was denied to them. After their disobedience, God then denied Adam and Eve, and their descendants, the opportunity to eat from the Tree of Life. In fact, the Bible states that this is the very reason that God drove them out of the garden of Eden: "Then the LORD God said, 'Behold, the man has become like one of Us, knowing good and evil; and now, he might stretch out his hand, and take also from the tree of life, and eat, and live forever'—therefore the LORD God sent him out from the garden of Eden, to cultivate the ground from which he was taken. So He drove the man out; and at the east of the garden of Eden He stationed the cherubim and the flaming sword which turned every direction to guard the way to the tree of life" (vv. 22–24). Therefore, the Genesis account does not teach that Adam and Eve were immortal before the fall (let alone the animals). Instead, Adam and Eve were given the opportunity to become immortal by eating of the Tree of Life, but, through their disobedience, they lost that opportunity and were driven from the garden. Now, through Christ who has paid the debt for our sins, we will have the opportunity, once again, to eat from the Tree of Life and live forever with our God in the place he is preparing for us, as John foresaw in the final chapter of the book of Revelation:

> Then the angel showed me the river of the water of life, as clear as crystal, flowing from the throne of God and of the Lamb down the middle of the great street of the city. On each side of the river stood the Tree of Life, bearing twelve crops of fruit, yielding its fruit every month. And the leaves of the tree are for the healing of the nations. No longer will there be any curse. The throne of God and of the Lamb will be in the city, and his servants will serve him. They will see his face, and his name will be on their foreheads. There will be no more night. They will not need the light of a lamp or the light of the sun, for the Lord God will give them light. And they will reign for ever and ever. (Rev. 22:1–5)

The idea that there was no death in the world before Adam and Eve's sin is another flight of fancy that is based more on our human desires and theological misinterpretations than scriptural teachings. It is certainly more appealing to imagine ourselves as noble, immortal beings who formerly lived in a heaven on earth, but who lost our position through the wiles of the devil, rather than foolish mortal beings who were created from the dust of the earth and chose disobedience over eternal life and are still suffering the consequences. However, the garden of Eden we have created in our minds does not correspond with the one found in the scriptural record, nor with the one found in the fossil record, which records the death of untold multitudes of organisms long before the appearance of humans upon the earth.

II. Species Are Perfect—They Do Not Go Extinct

Another debate between science and religion arose over whether or not any species of animal that God had created could ever totally disappear from the face of the earth (i.e. go extinct). If, as many theologians and Christians believed, God's creation was perfect, then of course this was impossible, since it would imply that at least some of God's creation was imperfect or flawed, thus contradicting the Bible—or at least what we assumed the Bible was saying. This theological interpretation of the Scriptures, like those discussed in the previous two chapters, was based, in part, on humanities' earlier cultural/scientific knowledge and understanding of living organisms. As usual in Western Civilization, the roots of this idea can be traced back to the ancient Greeks—particularly Aristotle (384–322 B.C.). Aristotle attempted to make sense out of the diversity of living organisms upon the earth by organizing them into groups according to certain traits which they possessed, such as whether or not they had blood, their ability to sense or move, how they gave birth to their offspring, the power of their *souls* etc. Moreover, based on these characteristics, he believed that nature could be arranged in a hierarchy from inanimate objects, through plants and animals, to humans (Archibald 2014:2; Freely 2012:64; Lovejoy 1961:58–59). As Aristotle noted in Book VIII of his *The History of Animals*:

Nature proceeds little by little from things lifeless to animal life in such a way that it is impossible to determine the exact line of demarcation, nor on which side thereof an intermediate form should lie. Thus, next after lifeless things in the upward scale comes the plant, and of plants one will differ from another as to its amount of apparent vitality; and, in a word, the whole genus of plants, whilst it is devoid of life as compared with an animal, is endowed with life as compared with other corporeal entities. Indeed, as we just remarked, there is observed in plants a continuous scale of ascent towards the animal. So, in the sea, there are certain objects concerning which one would be at a loss to determine whether they be animal or vegetable. (McKeon 1941:635)

Aristotle's ranking of nature and living organisms came to be described as a ladder, a staircase, a scale (*scala naturae*), or a chain (the Great Chain of Being), with the simplest organism on the bottom and the most complex organism on the top. Once again, a Greek cultural/scientific model of nature easily made its way into Jewish and Christian theological interpretations via the Greek domination of Judea after Alexander the Great's conquest of the Persian Empire. Like Aristotle's model of the heavens, his model of living organisms seemed to complement rather than contest the biblical account. After all, the Bible presented a similar order for creation—from simple to more complex: birds, great sea monsters, cattle, creeping things, beasts of the earth, man and woman (Gen. 1:20–21, 24, 26).

In the Middle Ages, with the rediscovery of Greek language and literature and Thomas Aquinas's incorporation of Aristotelian philosophy into Christian theology, Aristotle's hierarchical model of life would be adopted into church teachings and scriptural interpretations. Theologians would also modify and expand Aristotle's ladder in two significant ways, creating what would become known as the Great Chain of Being. First, the model would now include heavenly beings, with angels above humans and God at the very apex of life. Second, theologians would expand upon Aristotle's belief that there were no gaps between the organisms in his hierarchy: "Certainly species across groups share characters; thus Aristotle sees the scale or ladder as forming a continuum, a succession without gaps from inanimate objects through plants and then to animals, thus *natura non facit saltus* (nature makes no leaps). Boundaries between groups do occur; we simply cannot discern them because of the continuous nature of characters shared by the various groups" (Archibald 2014:2). Medieval church fathers took this idea one step further. Not only were there no gaps between the groups in Aristotle's hierarchy of life, there could *never* be gaps between these groups because God had pronounced his creation good or very good (i.e. read perfect). Therefore, if any group ever disappeared (went extinct) the Great Chain of Being linking all living organisms to God would be broken and the perfection of God's creation shown to be imperfect. As the saying goes, a chain is only as strong as its weakest link or, as the poet Alexander Pope once put to verse:

> Vast chain of being! which from God began,
> Natures aethereal, human, angel, man,
> Beast, bird, fish, insect, what no eye can see,
> No glass can reach; from Infinite to thee,
> From thee to nothing,—On superior pow'rs
> Were we to press, inferior might on ours;
> Or in the full creation leave a void,
> Where, one step broken, the great scale's destroy'd;
> From Nature's chain whatever link you strike,
> Tenth, or ten thousandth, breaks the chain alike.
>
> (Lovejoy 1961:60)

During the Renaissance (fourteenth to seventeenth centuries), European cultures turned their attention not only to the classical world of Greece and Rome, but also to the natural world. The foundations for many of the modern sciences were laid at this time, including biology, geology, archaeology, and astronomy. As these early scientists studied the earth's surface more carefully or probed beneath its surface, they often found what appeared to be the remains of plants and animals—some the likes of which had never been seen before. Fortunately, the European voyages of discovery (fifteenth to eighteenth centuries) overlapped the Renaissance and brought Western Civilization into contact with many new lands, peoples, animals, and plants. Therefore, a convenient explanation was readily at hand for any strange animal or plant fossils that were found by the pioneers of science during this period. It was simply assumed that, no matter how strange or foreign a fossil might be, its living counterpart no doubt existed somewhere on the face of the earth in an, as yet, unexplored region. This assumption preserved the Great Chain of Being from developing any gaps; all animals created by God were present and accounted for, or soon would be (with a little more exploration). Such was the case when Europeans and Americans in the 1700s begin to dig up the bones of large elephant-like creatures which are now called mammoths.

The best-preserved exotic fossils, as well as those nearest the surface where they might most easily be found, were animals that had lived during the Ice Age, since the most recent glacial advance had ended only some 10,000 years ago. These Ice Age animals were often quite large (to preserve body heat) and included: mammoths, mastodons, glyptodonts, giant ground sloths, and giant short-faced bears. Thomas Jefferson was not only one of the founding fathers of America, principal author of the Declaration of Independence, and the third president of the United States; he is often honored as the father of both paleontology and archaeology in America. Through his efforts, the bones of a number of Ice Age animals were recovered from New York, West Virginia, and Big Bone Lick in Kentucky. Some of these bones were brought to Washington D.C. for display. Two of the Ice Age animals recovered through Jefferson's interest and patronage would eventually be named in his honor: the Jefferson's Ground Sloth (Megalonyx jeffersoni) and the Jefferson's Mammoth (Mammuthus jeffersonii).

Jefferson first became interested in fossil vertebrates in 1780–81 while writing *Notes on the State of Virginia* (1982). In this book he noted that the bones of *incognitum* (mammoth) had been found in Virginia and suggests that living examples might still exist somewhere in the United States:

> In his table of American and European mammals found in *Notes on the State of Virginia*, Jefferson listed the mammoth first. In defense of this decision he wrote: "It may be asked, why I insert the Mammoth as if it still existed? It may be asked in return, why I should omit it, as if it did not exist? Such is the economy of nature, that no instance can be produced of her having permitted any one race of her animals to become extinct; of her having formed any link in her great work so weak as to be broken." Beyond this basic philosophical objection to extinction was the "traditionary testimony of the Indians, that this animal still existed in the northern and western parts of America," regions that remained "in their aboriginal state, unexplored and undisturbed." (Barrow 2009:18)

Moreover, the large bones of these Ice Age creatures that had been recovered from various sites, such as Big Bone Lick in Kentucky, still appeared to be fresh and relatively unaltered by time, suggesting that these animals had died only a short time ago. So strong was Jefferson's belief that mammoths might still exist in as yet unexplored areas of America that, when he commissioned the Lewis and Clark Expedition to the Pacific Northwest (1804–1806), he gave them orders not only to record the native plants and animals in the region but also to be on the lookout for mammoths that might still be living in the west.

Lewis and Clark failed to find living mammoths in the Pacific Northwest. Other explorers failed to find them in the jungles of South America and Africa; the frozen wastes of Canada, Alaska, and Antarctica; or the deserts of Mexico or Australia. This was the basis of George Cuvier's (1769–1832) argument as he would pound the lectern and shake his vivid red hair at his audiences: mammoths were very large animals, you could not hide one under a bushel or even behind a tree. No one had ever found a living mammoth because they no longer existed. They were extinct! Cuvier was one of the earliest and greatest naturalists and became known as the father of paleontology and comparative anatomy (Gould 1993:viii). When a circus elephant died in Paris, Cuvier recovered the carcass and butchered it so that he could compare its bones with similar-sized bones of incognitum (mammoth) that had been found in both Europe and Siberia. Through this effort he conclusively proved that, although these bones were similar to modern elephants, they were not the same, they were a different species, a species that no modern man had ever seen alive. With these two pieces of empirical evidence, Cuvier eventually convinced the world that incognitum (the Siberian Mammoth) was really an extinct form of animal that no longer existed upon the earth. In other words, a link in the Great Chain of Being had been broken! Many other breaks were to follow. As Cuvier noted in his *Discourse on the Revolutions of the Surface of the Globe*: "Existence has thus been often troubled on this earth by appalling events. Living creatures without number have fallen victims to these catastrophes: some, the inhabitants of dry land, have been swallowed up by a deluge; others, who peopled the depths of the waters, have been cast on land by the sudden receding of the waters, their very race became extinct, and only a few remains left of them in the world, scarcely recognized by the naturalist" (1829:11). Among the extinct species that Cuvier would subsequently identify as having gone extinct were a number of animals that had previously roamed across Europe, including the Irish Elk, mastodons, rhinoceros, and hippopotamus (Barrow 2009:42).

Today we know of tens-of-thousands of species that have gone extinct—our museums are filled with their fossils and our geology textbooks with their pictures. All of the dinosaurs went extinct 66 million years ago and have never been seen again. Many of the Ice Age megafauna, such as mammoth and mastodon, that were here a mere 10,000 years ago, are also gone. Geologists and paleontologists have now identified five major mass extinctions (The Big 5) which have occurred in the past 500 million years, each of which swept away 75 percent or more of all living organisms on the earth at the time of those extinction events. Indeed, by one estimate, 99.9 percent of all species that have ever lived upon the earth are now extinct (Raup 1991:3–4).

The Great Chain of Being, that was a staple of religious and scientific belief for many centuries, has been proven to be outrageously wrong, yet the faith of millions of Christians still endures.

Theologians and laymen alike were wrong about the perfection of life, just as they were wrong about the perfection of the heavens. After much hand-wringing, soul-searching, and untold thousands of pamphlets, books, and sermons, it turns out that this was just another *non-issue*, a theological firestorm in a teacup that resulted from, once again, basing some of our theological interpretations about God's creation on outdated cultural/scientific models. Indeed, "the faith which was once for all handed down to the saints" (Jude 1:3) has remained unaltered and unaffected.

III. Species Are Perfect—They Do Not Evolve

Bad ideas sometimes take on a life of their own. They are like a fire which, once ignited, starts to spread and is often very difficult to put out. Just when we think we have the flames stamped out, they quietly smolder for a while and then reignite, or hot ashes are blown downwind and start fires in new areas. The idea that God's creation was perfect is just such an idea. Despite our theological interpretations of Genesis, God's creation was good—not perfect. In the real universe that God created, the heavens are not perfect: planets are struck by comets and asteroids, stars explode, and galaxies collide. In the real world that God created, living organisms are not perfect: individual organisms die (even before the Fall) and entire species go extinct. Yet, many Christians today are still desperately trying to cling to that last vestige of our old theological mistake concerning the perfection of God's creation. They may (or may not) accept the fact that plants and animals were dying long before Adam and Eve sinned in the garden of Eden; they may (or may not) accept the fact that many animals, such as dinosaurs and mammoths, are now extinct; but they certainly do not accept the fact that plants and animals can change (evolve) over time. In the face of these other evidences of change, many Christians remain resolute in their belief that at least one of the pillars in our earlier theological interpretations of the creation account remains standing: the types of living organisms that God created were perfect and unchanging—species are fixed, they do not *evolve*. They say, "Doesn't the Genesis account clearly state: 'Then God said, "Let the earth bring forth living creatures after their kind: cattle and creeping things and beasts of the earth after their kind"; and it was so'" (Gen. 1:24)?

Now once we accept the fact that millions upon millions of species have indeed gone extinct, that they are not hiding somewhere in deepest, darkest Africa or in the wilderness of the Pacific Northwest, the question naturally arises, How were they replaced? If they were not replaced, do we live in a world that is biologically impoverished, a world where life presents but a shadow of its former rich biodiversity? This is certainly not the case, as everywhere we look we are astonished at the seemingly endless variety of life forms. In the garden of Eden, God brought the animals to Adam so he could name them (Gen. 2:19–20). Thousands of years later, scientists are still working on that project with no end in sight. In the 250 years since Carl Linnaeus (1707–1778) created a taxonomic system for naming plants and animals, scientists have identified approximately 1.25 million separate animal species on the earth. A report released in 2011, however, estimated that there may be approximately 8.7 million species presently living on the earth, and given the present rates of discovery, it may take us another thousand years or so to identify these species—if they don't go extinct first:

> Our current estimate of ~8.7 million species narrows the range of 3 to 100 million species suggested by taxonomic experts and it suggests that after 250 years of taxonomic classification only a small fraction of species on Earth (~14%) and in the ocean (~9%) have been indexed in a central database.... Closing this knowledge gap may still take a lot longer. Considering current rates of description of eukaryote species in the last 20 years (i.e., 6,200 species per year; ±811 SD; Figure 3F–3J), the average number of new species described per taxonomist's career (i.e., 24.8 species), and the estimated average cost to describe animal species (i.e., US $48,500 per species) and assuming that these values remain constant and are general among taxonomic groups, describing Earth's remaining species may take as long as 1,200 years and would require

303,000 taxonomists at an approximated cost of US $364 billion. With extinction rates now exceeding natural background rates by a factor of 100 to 1,000, our results also suggest that this slow advance in the description of species will lead to species becoming extinct before we know they even existed. (Mora et al. 2011:5)

Now the Bible clearly states that the heavens and the earth were completed after six days; on the seventh day God rested from his creative works: "Thus the heavens and the earth were completed, and all their hosts. By the seventh day God completed His work which He had done, and He rested on the seventh day from all His work which He had done. Then God blessed the seventh day and sanctified it, because in it He rested from all His work which God had created and made" (Gen. 2:1–3). Therefore how do we harmonize the fact of past extinctions with the fact of the rich biological diversity that we see around us today? Did God begin his creative work again on the eighth day, replacing each creature that goes extinct, with a new creature? Speaking of the Sabbath, Jesus said that: My Father works and so do I. But is this work a *creative* work, or instead, a *sustaining* work, as many theologians have suggested? Is this present, temporal heaven and earth sufficient to accomplish all of God's purposes until he brings it to an end and creates a new heaven and earth (Isa. 65:17; Rev. 21:1)? Perhaps the goodness of God's creation is that the life which he has created in all its various forms is so vibrant, pervasive, and enduring. In C. S. Lewis's sixth book in *The Chronicles of Narnia*, Aslan sings Narnia into existence. So powerful was this creative act that even the cross-bar from the lamppost in London, which the witch had ripped loose and later threw at Aslan, took root in the grass and grew into a new lamppost that became the namesake for *Lantern Waste* in later Narnian history (1955b:107–111). Perhaps a part of the great beauty and goodness of God's creation is that the living organisms he has created upon the earth continue to not only survive, but thrive, down through the ages despite repeated changes and even catastrophic events. Life has resilience, it keeps coming back, it rolls with the punches, it adapts, it even changes/evolves when necessary, but it is still here. It may have taken many forms and guises but it is still the life that God created. The waters still teem with fish and the air with birds, the earth still brings forth living creatures as God commanded them to do on the sixth day of creation. As Charles Kingsley once wrote in a letter to Charles Darwin in 1859: "I have gradually learnt to see that it is just as noble a conception of Deity, to believe that he created primal forms capable of self-development into all forms needful *pro tempore* and *pro loco*, as to believe that he required a fresh act of intervention to supply the *lacunas* which He himself had made. I question whether the former be not the loftier thought" (Young 1985:106).

If the earth and heavens were perfect, they would not change; but they are not perfect and they do change. The record that God has etched into the rocks of the earth tells a story of continents colliding together and pulling apart, of mountains growing and weathering away, of sea levels rising and falling, of ice sheets waxing and waning, of whole ecosystems coming into existence and then ceasing to exist. Both the heavens and the earth change and grow old (see Table 21):

Table 21: Scriptures concerning the Temporal Nature of the Heavens and Earth
And all the host of heaven will wear away, And the sky will be rolled up like a scroll; All their hosts will also wither away As a leaf withers from the vine Or as one withers from the fig tree. (Isa. 34:4)
Lift up your eyes to the sky, Then look to the earth beneath; For the sky will vanish like smoke, And the earth will wear out like a garment And its inhabitants will die in like manner; But My salvation will be forever, And My righteousness will not wane. (Isa. 51:6)
Of old You founded the earth, And the heavens are the work of Your hands. Even they will perish, but You endure; And all of them will wear out like a garment; Like clothing You will change them and they will be changed. (Ps. 102:25–26)

In such a temporal, ever-changing heaven and earth, unchanging life forms (fixed species) would obviously be at a great disadvantage. Instead, God has given life the ability to adapt to these changes both on a behavioral and a physiological level. As the world changes, life changes as well, thereby fulfilling Gods command after the flood: "Bring out with you every living thing of all flesh that is with you, birds and animals and every creeping thing that creeps on the earth, that they may breed abundantly on the earth, and be fruitful and multiply on the earth" (Gen. 8:17). This ability of life to repopulate the earth after the flood is also evident in other great mass extinction events that occurred long before the flood in Noah's time. The fossil record reveals that survivors of such disasters go through a period of relatively rapid evolutionary change and adaptive radiation, by which means the world is once more filled with life. As the world changes, living organisms must also change in order to survive and thrive under these new conditions. Such is the nature of God's providential care, he not only gives good gifts to his children, but also to the other life forms he has created: "Are not two sparrows sold for a cent? And yet not one of them will fall to the ground apart from your Father. But the very hairs of your head are all numbered. So do not fear; you are more valuable than many sparrows" (Matt. 10:29–31).

Because evolution is such a slow, gradual process, living organisms do not disobey God's command that the "earth bring fourth creatures after their kind." Cats do not give birth to dogs nor cattle to birds. Genetic traits, as well as genetic mutations, are faithfully passed from parents to offspring, just as God commanded. The slight genetic changes from generation to generation, which arise from mutations, however, do gradually build up and provide the variability that allows organisms to become better adapted to the changing world about them. Eventually these alterations in the genetic code become numerous enough that we can begin to distinguish significant morphological differences between offspring and their ancestral forbearers, thereby allowing us to recognize the appearance of new species. This evolutionary process, however, is achieved by each species producing offspring after its own kind, over and over again, for many generations.

CONCLUSION

In conclusion, the debates between science and Christianity over life are very similar to those over the heavens and the earth. As theologians, laymen, and laywomen, our point of reference for understanding and interpreting Scriptures concerning the physical universe is always based on what we presently know, or our forebears knew, about the heavens, earth, and life. However, since our cultural/scientific knowledge of the physical universe keeps changing, both throughout our lives, as well as the lives of many generations throughout the past and into the future, we must constantly reevaluate our interpretations of those particular passages in the Bible that deal with the natural world. We are only responsible for what we presently know, not for what future generations may learn. Since our interpretations of those Scriptures dealing with nature are so strongly colored by our cultural/scientific understanding of nature, it does no good, and often much harm, to elevate these interpretations to a doctrinal level. Like children, we still have much to learn about God's creation. Because of our limited knowledge, we, like T. S. Eliot's J. Alfred Prufrock, live in a twilight zone between fact and fiction where our beliefs about the minutia of God's creation will always be subject to revision:

> And time yet for a hundred indecisions,
> And for a hundred visions and revisions,
> Before the taking of a toast and tea.
>
> (Eliot 1998:6–7)

Instead of focusing on the temporal natural realm, our focus should be on those aspects of the eternal supernatural realm that have been clearly revealed to us, and upon which our salvation depends. As Paul proclaimed: "And when I came to you, brethren, I did not come with superiority of speech or of wisdom, proclaiming to you the testimony of God. For I determined to know nothing among you except Jesus Christ, and Him crucified" (1 Cor. 2:1–2).

PART 5

THE DIVINE FACTOR

Chapter 13

CEASING TO DISAGREE

I. SUMMATION

There are three important lessons to be learned from our examination of the limitations of theological truth. First is the fact that theology is a very human discipline: created by humans, practiced by humans, and flawed by human weaknesses, the foremost of which is our sinful nature. Based on our examination of some of the theological errors of the apostles, the Pharisees, and the church, we see the same problems arising over and over again. The problems are the direct result of human ignorance (we don't have all the facts), human mistakes (we sometimes unintentionally misinterpret the facts that we do have), and human bias (we sometimes intentionally distort the facts to fit our own personal beliefs or desires). Whether individuals loved Jesus, such as the disciples and apostles, or hated him, like many of the scribes and Pharisees, all humans make similar mistakes as they try to understand and interpret the Word of God. These errors occur whether we were sitting at the feet of Jesus as he preaches to a crowd on the shores of the Sea of Galilee, or quietly reading the Scriptures in our homes many centuries later. Although God is our Creator and Father, his holiness, omniscience, and omnipotence—as compared to our sinfulness, ignorance, and weakness—present nearly insurmountable barriers to our fully comprehending the truths that he desires to share with us. Only by his mercy and through the intercession of the Holy Spirit can we approach his throne and hear his words of grace.

The second lesson that we need to learn from past theological mistakes is that our understanding and interpretation of the Scriptures is, in part, based on what we have already learned through our own culture. This is particularly true of scriptural passages dealing with nature and the physical universe. We acquire knowledge and understanding of the world around us, both through our own experiences, as well as from what we have learned from our parents, friends, and teachers. The content of this cultural/scientific knowledge, unfortunately, is highly dependent on both the place and time in which we live, and is subject to change as new discoveries are made and new models and theories are developed. It is quite logical that we would start with what we already know as we try to understand those things that we do not yet know. It is a mistake, however, to allow this cultural/scientific knowledge (and our scriptural interpretations based on this information) to become too closely bound with the eternal, unchanging Word of God. To do so makes it appear that the Word of God is faulty or outdated whenever new discoveries about the physical world are made. Older, less precise cultural/scientific models of the world are inevitably replaced with newer, more accurate ones as time goes by. Much of the so-called conflict between science and religion over the past 500 years has been the result of theologians and church fathers putting too much faith in older cultural/scientific beliefs about the physical universe, such as Aristotle' model of a perfect heaven or Ptolemy's geocentric model. Since theologians had built some of their interpretations of Scripture around these scientific models, they came to believe that these were also divinely inspired—which they were not. As time would later show, Aristotle's and Ptolemy's models of the heavens and earth were wrong, as were the theologians' interpretations of the Scripture that were based on these models. Therefore, the conflicts between the church and scientists, such as Copernicus or Galileo, were really debates about the merits of older scientific theories versus newer scientific theories, and really had nothing to do with the truthfulness of the Scriptures. Trying to mix the eternal truths of Scripture with the temporal, ever-changing truths of science and theology is like trying to mix oil and water: the two will eventually separate from each other.

The third lesson to be learned from our study of past theological mistakes is the fact that Christian apologetics is never a finished project; it is always a work in progress. Since scientific models are constantly changing, so must our scriptural interpretations that are based on those models. We are like children playing with a jigsaw puzzle: We keep trying to see how the pieces fit together so we can finally view the overall picture that is hidden among the fragments. What we need to understand, however, is that we do not have all the pieces of the puzzle; our knowledge is finite. Over time, we continue to find new pieces that will enlarge and enrich the picture that we are trying to assemble: maybe a bit of blue sky over here, more pieces of the red barn down in the corner, etc. As new scientific discoveries are made in the sciences, such as biology, geology, and astronomy, it is both natural and good that we should try to see how these new pieces of the puzzle might fit into the picture of the heavens and earth that we are trying to assemble through our study of God's Word and God's world. Indeed, our Lord has invited us to consider the works of his hands (see Table 22):

Table 22: Scriptures inviting Us to Examine God's Handiwork

Consider the ravens, for they neither sow nor reap; they have no storeroom nor barn, and yet God feeds them; how much more valuable you are than the birds! (Luke 12:24)

Consider the lilies, how they grow: they neither toil nor spin; but I tell you, not even Solomon in all his glory clothed himself like one of these. (v. 27)

Have you entered the storehouses of the snow, Or have you seen the storehouses of the hail, Which I have reserved for the time of distress, For the day of war and battle? Where is the way that the light is divided, Or the east wind scattered on the earth? (Job 38:22–24)

It is also natural that we should look upon that which our Father has created with wonder, awe, and praise. As David said, "I will give thanks to You, for I am fearfully and wonderfully made; Wonderful are Your works, And my soul knows it very well" (Ps. 139:14). It is a mistake, however, to assume that the picture we have assembled of God's creation thus far is complete, or even partially complete. After thousands of years of effort, humans have only just begun to probe the depths of God's wisdom and creativity. Therefore, trying to harmonize Scripture with science is an ongoing process. It is not a finished body of knowledge that we can incorporate into a religious creed to which all Christians must adhere or be cast out of the church. Our interpretations of Scripture based on current or past culture/scientific knowledge should never be codified into dogma because such interpretations are ever subject to changes as new information about the natural world becomes available. Therefore, human interpretations of Scripture concerning the natural realm should never be elevated to equal status with the Word of God or added as appendages to the everlasting gospel. As Paul warned: "But even if we, or an angel from heaven, should preach to you a gospel contrary to what we have preached to you, he is to be accursed!" (Gal. 1:8). The Pharisees did this with their interpretations and human traditions, but were soundly condemned by Christ for having done so (Matt. 15:9).

We can only work with the knowledge that is available to us during the course of our lives, but as good stewards and students of the Word, God expects us to use that which he has given us and not to live in willful ignorance. Unfortunately, many Christians in America today have chosen this latter pathway and largely reject most *new* scientific knowledge. Each generation of Christians, however, has the sacred task, not only to remain faithful to the Scriptures, but also to try and understand the Scriptures in terms of what we currently know about the world around us. We cannot rest upon what others have done in previous generations. The attempts that were made to harmonize Scripture with the science of the sixteenth, seventeenth, or eighteenth centuries are not particularly relevant or useful today. But, when we try to understand and interpret passages in the Scripture that deal with creation and the natural world in terms of twenty-first-century science, we must resist the temptation to think that our interpretations are the final ones, as so many individuals in previous generations have done. It is our duty to try and see the Hand of God at work throughout all his creation no matter what century or age we live in. Since we know that our understanding and interpretations of Scripture and the world around us are imperfect, we also understand that the models and theories we build will not be perfect. Nevertheless, it is our duty to do the best we can with the materials that we have at hand: "Be diligent to present yourself approved to God as a workman who does not need to be ashamed, accurately handling the word of truth" (2 Tim. 2:15). In each generation, we live with the hope that God will take our imperfect work, and perfect it for the accomplishment of his will. Many people's faith is threatened by new scientific discoveries so Christian theologians and laymen need to have thought deeply about these matters so that they will have a ready answer to allay such fears and doubts. Since Christ made all things (John 1:3), there is nothing that science can ever discover that was not made by him and ordained by God. As Peter encouraged us: "DO NOT FEAR THEIR INTIMIDATION, AND DO NOT BE TROUBLED, but sanctify Christ as Lord in your hearts, always being ready to make a defense to everyone who asks you to give an account for the hope that is in you, yet with gentleness and reverence" (1 Peter 3:14–15).

II. Application

If Christians are ever going to stop disagreeing and fighting over theological interpretations of Scripture that are probably all flawed to one degree or another, they will have to become more like Christ, and less like their former, unsaved selves.

A. Keeping Things Simple—A Child's Faith

> Truly I say to you, unless you are converted and become like children, you will not enter the kingdom of heaven. (Matt. 18:3)

When we tie our religious beliefs too tightly to the scientific beliefs of the past or the present, we doom ourselves to perpetual warfare with our culture as the pace of scientific discovery accelerates. Meanwhile, God's creation swirls around us in a kaleidoscope of ever-changing colors and forms, as it always has, but we are too caught up with our thoughts and theories to truly understand and enjoy what God has made for us. We must cease being intellectual adults, forever locked into a rigid perception of the world. Instead, we must become as little children once more, surprised and enchanted by the discoveries that each new day brings, always willing to see the hand of our Father at work in whatever we find. This is the true task of the Christian who is also a scientist, to help his brothers and sisters cast aside the shackles that seek to cloud our vision of God's Creation. We have allowed our understanding and appreciation of God's creation to harden into yesterday's joys that grow steadily dimmer and less exciting with time. We become like the aged who can no longer see or hear clearly, who can no longer get around very well in the world that God has made. We become cranky and self-centered, demanding that everyone around us see the world in exactly the same way that we do. In the few decades we have been allotted upon the earth, we should make every effort to continue to grow each day into beings more like our Father who is in heaven, to never be satisfied with who we are or what we know, but ever-ready to deepen our understanding of his Word and the present world which he has given us. This will not only be pleasing to our Father, but will better prepare us to understand and appreciate the new heaven and new earth that he is preparing for us.

B. Keeping Things Truthful—A Servant's Humility

> And what does the Lord require of you
> But to do justice, to love kindness,
> And to walk humbly with your God?
>
> (Mic. 6:8)

The things we don't know, God will eventually reveal to us, either in this life or the next. If we acknowledge that our scientific and theological understanding is flawed, that it contains gaping holes, we are admitting nothing more than what is true. Why try to hide it? Why act as though we know more than we really do? What does it profit us to pretend we are someone who we are not? To live a lie is to live a life that is not our own. To claim to have knowledge and understanding that we do not have, is to deceive ourselves, as well as others. The problem is that we keep forgetting who we are in the present and who we were in the past. In the present, we are brothers and sisters of Christ and sons and daughters of God. We are people whose sins have been forgiven and who have the promise of everlasting life. So what more do we want? Why are we not happy? Why do we spend our time arguing with each other over things that are not important? Do we want more respect, or power, or wealth? Have we forgotten that we are already dead and the dead have no need of such things?

> I have been crucified with Christ; and it is no longer I who live, but Christ lives in me; and the life which I now live in the flesh I live by faith in the Son of God, who loved me and gave Himself up for me. (Gal. 2:20)

> Or do you not know that all of us who have been baptized into Christ Jesus have been baptized into his death? Therefore we have been buried with Him through baptism into death, so that as Christ was raised from the dead through the glory of the Father, so we too might walk in newness of life. (Rom. 6:3–4)

Have we forgotten who we were before we came to Christ? It's often not a pretty tale. Self-centered, arrogant, liars, cheats, fornicators—many of us were walking billboards of the seven deadly sins. Do we want to go back to that? Have we gone back to that? Have we ever really changed? Has our own personal man-of-sin followed us into the church, only to re-emerge now dressed in white, but still stained within with sin? To many, the people in many churches today do not seem much different than the people in the world. Indeed, in some cases, they seem worse than the people in the world. And it's our fault. We are the ones who have forgotten who we are, as well as who we were. If anyone in the world has a right to be humble, it is a Christian. We can certainly empathize with Paul: "Wretched man that I am! Who will set me free from the body of this death?" (Rom. 7:24). We of all people have a reason to be humble as we can plainly see the stark contrast between what we should be, what God wants us to be, and who we actually are! If we finally remember who we are and who we were, our proclivity for argument and disagreement, even on theological matters, will no doubt be greatly diminished. The truly humble man or woman has little desire to engage in such disputes since they do not value their opinions over that of others. Humility would also greatly improve the quality of our theological work. As Witherington has noted, "Above all, this enterprise of discovering and doing NT theology requires humility, not hubris. It requires a willingness to say 'I don't know how to hold these things in tension,' a willingness to resist the Evangelical lust for certainty, a willingness to embrace the mystery and be willing to accept some paradoxes" (Witherington 2005:247).

C. Keeping Things Peaceful—A Saint's Patience

> Blessed are the peacemakers, for they shall be called sons of God. (Matt. 5:9)

In serving the Prince of Peace, it makes sense that we should also try to be peacemakers, not troublemakers who are always looking for an argument or a fight. Surely the many fragments into which the church has shattered have not been the result of men and women seeking the will of God. No, instead they are the result of strong-willed individuals in conflict with each other; individuals who are sure of the rightness of their own personal views and the total incompetence, if not the downright sinfulness, of their opponents. What matters to them is not peace, but victory: the vindication of their ideas, the banishment of their foes. Pride is not a

peaceful beast; like its father the Devil, it goes about "seeking someone to devour" (1 Peter 5:8). A peacemaker is one who is willing to
subjugate his own desires for the benefit of others. Indeed, our Lord
has provided us with the preeminent example to follow:

> Then He poured water into the basin, and began to wash the
> disciples' feet and to wipe them with the towel with which He
> was girded.... So when He had washed their feet, and taken His
> garments and reclined at the table again, He said to them, "Do
> you know what I have done to you? You call Me Teacher and Lord;
> and you are right, for so I am. If I then, the Lord and the Teacher,
> washed your feet, you also ought to wash one another's feet. For I
> gave you an example that you also should do as I did to you. Truly,
> truly, I say to you, a slave is not greater than his master, nor is one
> who is sent greater than the one who sent him." (John 13:5, 12–16)

> Have this attitude in yourselves which was also in Christ Jesus, who,
> although He existed in the form of God, did not regard equality with
> God a thing to be grasped, but emptied Himself, taking the form of
> a bond-servant, and being made in the likeness of men. Being found
> in appearance as a man, He humbled Himself by becoming obedient
> to the point of death, even death on a cross. (Phil. 2:5–8)

No wonder that he is the Prince of Peace. He to whom
"EVERY KNEE WILL BOW, of those who are in heaven and on
earth and under the earth" (v. 10), himself bowed down to wash
the feet of man whom he had created. How different from so
many *religious* leaders down through the ages—scribes and Pharisees, patriarchs and popes, preachers and priests—who dressed
themselves in colorful robes and fine linen, lived in palaces and
mansions, surrounded themselves with material wealth, and
ceaselessly argued with each other over the finer points of the law
and the Scriptures. Jesus, on the other hand, summarized all that
was found in the law with two simple commands: "'YOU SHALL
LOVE THE LORD YOUR GOD WITH ALL YOUR HEART,
AND WITH ALL YOUR SOUL, AND WITH ALL YOUR MIND.'

This is the great and foremost commandment. The second is like it, 'YOU SHALL LOVE YOUR NEIGHBOR AS YOURSELF.' On these two commandments depend the whole Law and the Prophets" (Matt. 22:37–39). Christ laid down his life so that our sins could be forgiven and we could be reconciled to God, so that we might be at peace with God. During the Last Supper, before Christ went off to the garden of Gethsemane where he would be betrayed, he said to his disciples: "Peace I leave with you; My peace I give to you; not as the world gives do I give to you. Do not let your heart be troubled, nor let it be fearful" (John 14:27). Those who have the peace of Christ do not seek out controversy and disagreement with their brothers and sisters.

CONCLUSION

As we discussed at the beginning of this book, there are many limitations to theological truth, all of them arising from the imperfect nature of the humans who practice this discipline. As Alister McGrath has noted: "Evangelicals, after all, believe in the infallibility of Scripture, not the infallibility of its interpreters" (2009:40). Given this severe limitation, how then can Christians avoid the controversies and disagreements that have plagued the church down through the ages? Knowing our limitations is a very good place to start.

By becoming like little children as Jesus commanded, we open our hearts and minds to the leading of the Holy Spirit, rather than grounding our faith on the interpretations and traditions of men. We cease to be dependent upon our own knowledge, or that of our fellow man, and turn our focus to our Heavenly Father. By walking humbly before our God, we acknowledge our ignorance and sinfulness and cease to have an inflated opinion as to the value of our own understanding and interpretations of his Word. By seeking peace with our brothers and sisters in Christ, instead of trying to force our understanding and interpretations of Scripture upon them, we emulate our Lord who is the Prince of Peace. By taking these three steps, we will move a long way toward resolving the conflicts and disagreements that have arisen in the church over the centuries because of the limitations of theological truth.

REFERENCES

Aquinas, Thomas. *Summa Theologica*. Westminster, MD: Christian Classics, 1948.

Archibald, J. David. *Aristotle's Ladder, Darwin's Tree: The Evolution of Visual Metaphors for Biological Order*. New York: Columbia University Press, 2014.

Aristotle. *On the Heavens*. Translated by W. K. C. Guthrie. Vol. 6. Loeb Classical Library. Cambridge, MA: Harvard University Press, 1986.

Atkinson, Kenneth. *Queen Salome: Jerusalem's Warrior Monarch of the First Century B.C.E.* Jefferson, NC: McFarland & Company, 2012.

Augustine. *The City of God Against the Pagans*. Edited by R. W. Dyson. Cambridge, UK: Cambridge University Press, 1998.

_____. *The Literal Meaning of Genesis*. Edited by John Hammond Taylor. Vol. 1. Ancient Christian Writers Series. Mahwah, NJ: Paulist Press, 1983.

_____. *Confessions*. New York: Penguin Classics, 1961.

Avi-Yonah, M. "The Hasmonean Revolt and Judah Maccabee's War Against the Syrians." In *The Hellenistic Age: Political History of Jewish Palestine from 332 B.C.E. to 67 B.C.E.* Edited by Abraham Schalit, 147–182. New Brunswick, NJ: Rutgers University Press, 1972.

Barrow, Mark V. Jr. *Nature's Ghosts: Confronting Extinction from the Age of Jefferson to the Age of Ecology.* Chicago: The University of Chicago Press, 2009.

Berkhof, L. *Systematic Theology.* Grand Rapids, MI: Wm. B. Eerdmans, 1941.

Brush, Nigel. *The Limitations of Scientific Truth: Why Science Can't Answer Life's Ultimate Questions.* Grand Rapids, MI: Kregel, 2005.

Chadwick, Owen. *A History of Christianity.* New York: Thomas Dunne/St. Martin's Griffin, 1995.

Commoner, Barry. "A Cautionary Tale." In *Environmental Science and Preventive Public Policy.* Edited by Joel A. Tickner, 29–36. Washington, DC: Island Press, 2003.

Cuvier, Baron G. *A Discourse on the Revolutions of the Surface of the Globe: And the Changes Thereby Produced in the Animal Kingdom.* London, UK: Whittaker, Treacher and Arnot, 1829.

Danby, Herbert, trans. *The Mishnah.* Oxford, UK: Clarendon Press, 1933.

Darwin, Charles. *On the Origin of Species.* New York: Bantam Classics, 1999.

DiPietro, Joseph A. *Landscape Evolution in the United States: An Introduction to the Geography, Geology, and Natural History.* New York: Elsevier, 2013.

Eliot, T. S. "The Love Song of J. Alfred Prufrock." In *The Waste Land and Other Poems.* Edited by Helen Vendler, 5–11. New York: Signet Classic, 1998.

Evans, Bergen. *Dictionary of Quotations.* New York: Delacorte Press, 1968.

Fairclough, H. R., trans. *Horace: Satires, Epistles, and Ars Poetica.* New York: G. P. Putnam's Sons, 1932.

Ferris, Timothy. *Coming of Age in the Milky Way.* New York: William Morrow, 1988.

Freely, John. *The Flame of Miletus: The Birth of Science in Ancient Greece (And How It Changed the World).* New York: I. B. Tauris, 2012.

Giberson, Karl W. *Saving Darwin: How to Be a Christian and Believe in Evolution.* New York: HarperOne, 2008.

Gillis, Justin. "Climate Maverick to Quit NASA." *The New York Times*, April 1, 2013.

Gould, Stephen Jay. "Forward." In *Georges Cuvier: An Annotated Bibliography of His Published Works*. Edited by Jean Chandler Smith, vii–xi. Washington, DC: Smithsonian Institution Press, 1993.

———. *The Mismeasure of Man*. New York: W. W. Norton, 1981.

Grainger, John D. *The Wars of the Maccabees: The Jewish Struggle for Freedom, 167–37* b.c.. Barnsley, UK: Pen & Sword, 2012.

Grenz, Stanley J. *The Millennial Maze: Sorting Out Evangelical Options*. Downers Grove, IL: InterVarsity Press, 1992.

Gribbin, John. *Companion to the Cosmos*. New York: Little, Brown and Company, 1996.

———. *In Search of the Big Bang: Quantum Physics and Cosmology*. New York: Bantam Books, 1986.

Grun, Bernard. *The Timetables of History: A Horizontal Linkage of People and Events*. New York: Simon and Schuster, 1979.

Hansen, James. *Storms of My Grandchildren: The Truth about the Coming Climate Catastrophe and Our Last Chance to Save Humanity*. New York: Bloomsbury, 2009.

Hodge, Charles. *Systematic Theology* Vol. 1. Grand Rapids, MI: Wm. B. Eerdmans, 1995.

Holy Bible. *New American Standard Bible*. Grand Rapids, MI: Zondervan, 1995.

Jastrow, Robert. *God and the Astronomers*. New York: W. W. Norton, 1978.

Jefferson, Thomas. *Notes on the State of Virginia*. Edited by William Peden. Chapel Hill: University of North Carolina Press, 1982.

Josephus, Flavius. "The Wars of the Jews." In *The Works of Flavius Josephus*. Translated by William Whiston, 427–605. Grand Rapids, MI: Associated Publishers and Authors, 1970a.

———. "The Antiquities of the Jews." In *The Works of Flavius Josephus*. Translated by William Whiston, 23–426. Grand Rapids, MI: Associated Publishers and Authors, 1970b.

Keathley, Kenneth D., and Mark F. Rooker. *40 Questions about Creation and Evolution*. Grand Rapids, MI: Kregel, 2014.

Latourette, Kenneth Scott. "The Twentieth Century in Europe: The Roman Catholic, Protestant, and Eastern Churches," Vol. 4. In *Christianity in a Revolutionary Age: A History of Christianity in the Nineteenth and Twentieth Centuries*. Grand Rapids, MI: Zondervan, 1961.

_____. *A History of Christianity*. New York: Harper & Row, 1953.

Lewis, C. Day. *The Aeneid of Virgil*. Garden City, NY: Doubleday, 1952.

Lewis, C. S. *Surprised by Joy: The Shape of My Early Life*. New York: Harcourt Brace Jovanovich, 1955a.

_____. *The Magician's Nephew*. New York: Collier, 1955b.

_____. *Mere Christianity*. New York: HarperSanFrancisco, 1952.

_____. *Perelandra*. New York: Macmillan, 1944.

Linnaeus, Carolus. *Systema Naturae*. Nieuwkoop, Netherlands: B. De Graaf, 1964.

Lovejoy, Arthur O. *The Great Chain of Being: A Study of the History of an Idea*. Cambridge, MA: Harvard University Press, 1961.

Lyell, Charles. *Principles of Geology*. London: Penguin Books, 1997.

Makishima, Akio. *Origins of the Earth, Moon, and Life: An Interdisciplinary Approach*. New York: Elsevier, 2017.

Marshak, Stephen. *Earth: Portrait of a Planet*. New York: W. W. Norton, 2012.

Maslin, Mark. "Hot or Cold Future?" In *The Complete Ice Age: How Climate Change Shaped the World*, edited by Brian Fagan. London: Thames & Hudson, 2009.

Mayor, Adrienne. *The First Fossil Hunters: Dinosaurs, Mammoths, and Myth in Greek and Roman Times*. Princeton, NJ: Princeton University Press, 2011.

McGrath, Alister E. *Christian Theology: An Introduction*. Oxford, UK: Wiley-Blackwell, 2011.

_____. "Augustine's Origin of Species: How the Great Theologian Might Weigh in on the Darwin Debate." *Christianity Today* 53, no. 5 (2009): 38–41.

McKeon, Richard, ed. *The Basic Works of Aristotle*. New York: The Modern Library, 1941.

McKim, Donald K. *Theological Turning Points: Major Issues in Christian Thought*. Atlanta: John Knox Press, 1988.

Moore, Randy, and Janice Moore. *Evolution 101*. Westport, CT: Greenwood Press, 2006.

Mora, C., D. P. Tittensor, S. Adl, A. G. B. Simpson, and B. Worm. "How Many Species Are There on Earth and in the Ocean?" *PLOS Biology* 9, no. 8 (2011): e1001127. https://doi.org/10.1371/journal.pbio.1001127

Müntz, Eugène. *Leonardo da Vinci: Artist, Thinker, and Man of Science*, Vol. 2. New York: Parkstone Press, 2006.

Newton, John. "Amazing Grace." In *Great Songs of the Church*. No. 2. Compiled by E. L. Jorgenson, p. 337. Cincinnati: Standard Publishing, 1937.

Numbers, Ronald L. *The Creationists: The Evolution of Scientific Creationism*. Berkeley: University of California Press, 1992.

Oesch, P. A., G. Brammer, P. G. van Dokkum, G. D. Illingworth, R. J. Bouwens, I. Labbe, M. Franx, I. Momcheva, M. L. N. Ashby, G. G. Fazio, V. Gonzalez, B. Holden, D. Magee, R. E. Skelton, R. Smit, L. R. Spitler, M. Trenti, and S. P. Willner. "A Remarkably Luminous Galaxy at z=11.1 Measured with Hubble Space Telescope Grism Spectroscopy." *The Astrophysical Journal* 819, no. 2 (2016): 129–139.

Oreskes, Naomi, and Erik M. Conway. *Merchants of Doubt: How a Handful of Scientists Obscured the Truth on Issues from Tobacco Smoke to Global Warming*. New York: Bloomsbury Press, 2010.

Oxford. *The Oxford Dictionary of Quotations*. 3rd ed. Oxford, UK: Oxford University Press, 1979.

Philo. "Allegorical Interpretation of Genesis II, III." In *Philo*. Vol 1. Translated by F. H. Colson, and G. H. Whitaker. New York: G. P. Putnam's Sons, 1929.

Price, George McCready. *The New Geology*. Mountain View, CA: Pacific Press Publishing Association, 1923.

Ptolemy, Claudius. *Almagest*. In *The Almagest: On the Revolutions of the Heavenly Spheres / Epitome of Copernican Astronomy / Harmonies of the World*. Translated by R. Catesby Taliaferro and Charles Glenn Wallis. Great Books Edition. London, UK: Encyclopaedia Britannica, 1952.

Randall, Lisa. *Dark Matter and the Dinosaurs: The Astounding Interconnectedness of the Universe*. New York: HarperCollins, 2015.

Raup, David M. *Extinction: Bad Genes or Bad Luck?* New York: W. W. Norton, 1991.

Ross, Hugh. *A Matter of Days: Resolving a Creation Controversy*. Colorado Springs: NavPress, 2004.

_____. *The Creator and the Cosmos: How the Greatest Scientific Discoveries of the Century Reveal God*. Colorado Springs: NavPress, 1993.

Rovelli, Carlo. *Reality Is Not What It Seems: The Journey to Quantum Gravity*. New York: Riverhead Books, 2017.

_____. *Seven Brief Lessons on Physics*. New York: Riverhead Books, 2016.

Sagan, Carl. *Cosmos*. New York: Random House, 1980.

_____. *Pale Blue Dot: A Vision of the Human Future in Space*. New York: Ballantine Books, 1997.

Schaeffer, Francis A. *A Christian View of the Bible as Truth*, Vol. 2. In The Complete Works of Francis A. Schaeffer: A Christian Worldview. Westchester, IL: Crossway Books, 1982.

_____. *Genesis in Space and Time: The Flow of Biblical History*. Downers Grove, IL: InterVarsity Press, 1972.

Schaff, Philip. *Nicene and Post-Nicene Christianity: From Constantine the Great to Gregory the Great*, A.D. *311–600*. Vol. 2. *History of the Christian Church*. Edinburgh: T. & T. Clark, 1891.

Schalit, Abraham. "Domestic Politics and Political Institutions." In *The Hellenistic Age: Political History of Jewish Palestine from 332 B.C.E. to 67 B.C.E.* Edited by Abraham Schalit, 255–297. New Brunswick, NJ: Rutgers University Press, 1972.

Scharf, Paul J. "The Genesis Flood, Tidal Wave of Change." *Baptist Bulletin* (2010): July. https://sharperiron.org/article/genesis-flood-tidal-wave-of-change.

Shea, William R., and Mariano Artigas. *Galileo in Rome: The Rise and Fall of a Troublesome Genius.* Oxford, UK: Oxford University Press, 2003.

Sievers, Joseph. *The Hasmoneans and Their Supporters: From Mattathias to the Death of John Hyrcanus I.* Atlanta, GA: Scholars Press, 1990.

Silk, Joseph. *The Big Bang: Revised and Updated Edition.* New York: W. H. Freeman and Company, 1989.

Smith, Preserved, and Herbert Percival Gallinger, eds. and trans. *Conversations with Luther: Selections from Recently Published Sources of the Table Talk.* New York: The Pilgrim Press, 1915.

Tcherikover, V. "The Hellenistic Movement in Jerusalem and Antiochus' Persecutions." In *The Hellenistic Age: Political History of Jewish Palestine from 332 B.C.E. to 67 B.C.E.* Edited by Abraham Schalit, 115–144. New Brunswick, NJ: Rutgers University Press, 1972.

Tenney, Merrill C., ed. Pharisees. In *The Zondervan Pictorial Encyclopedia of the Bible.* Vol. 4, pp. 745–752. Grand Rapids, MI: Zondervan, 1976.

Turpin, Simon. "Did Death of Any Kind Exist Before the Fall?: What the Bible Says about the Origin of Death and Suffering." *Answers Research Journal* 6 (2013): 99–116.

Walker, Williston. *A History of the Christian Church.* New York: Charles Scribner's Sons, 1959.

Walton, John H. *The Lost World of Genesis One: Ancient Cosmology and the Origins Debate.* Downers Grove, IL: InterVarsity Press, 2009.

Walton, Robert C. *Chronological and Background Charts of Church History.* Grand Rapids, MI: Zondervan, 1986.

Ward, Peter D. *Under a Green Sky: Global Warming, the Mass Extinctions of the Past, and What They Can Tell Us about Our Future.* New York: HarperCollins, 2007.

Ward, Peter, and Joe Kirschvink. *A New History of Life: The Radical New Discoveries about the Origins and Evolution of Life on Earth*. New York: Bloomsbury Press, 2015.

Westerholm, Stephen, and Martin Westerholm. *Reading Sacred Scripture: Voices from the History of Biblical Interpretation*. Grand Rapids, MI: Eerdmans, 2016.

Whitcomb, John C., and Henry M. Morris. *The Genesis Flood: The biblical Record and Its Scientific Implicatio*ns. Philadelphia: Presbyterian and Reformed Publishing Company, 1961.

Whitehouse, David. *Renaissance Genius: Galileo Galilei & His Legacy to Modern Science*. New York: Sterling, 2009.

Wignall, Paul B. *The Worst of Times: How Life on Earth Survived Eighty Million Years of Extinctions*. Princeton, NJ: Princeton University Press, 2015.

Winchester, Simon. *The Map that Changed the World: William Smith and the Birth of Modern Geology*. New York: Harper-Collins, 2009.

Witherington, Ben III. *The Problem with Evangelical Theology; Testing the Exegetical Foundations of Calvinism, Dispensationalism, and Wesleyanism*. Waco, TX: Baylor University Press, 2005.

Woolf, Henry Bosley, ed. *Webster's New Collegiate Dictionary*. Springfield, MA: G. & C. Merriam, 1981.

Young, Robert M. *Darwin's Metaphor: Nature's Place in Victorian Culture*. Cambridge, UK: Cambridge University Press, 1985.

About the Author

Nigel Brush began his academic career at the Cincinnati Bible College and held student ministries in Ohio, Indiana, and Kentucky. He went on to pursue graduate work in archaeology and anthropology at Ohio State University, the University of Southampton in England, and the University of California in Los Angeles. During these years he was blessed with the opportunity to study under several brilliant scholars: Dr. Reuben Bullard, a pioneer in the field of geoarchaeology; Dr. William Sumner, later director of the Oriental Institute at the University of Chicago; Dr. Colin Renfrew, later Disney Chair of Archaeology at Cambridge University; and Rainer Berger, Director of the Radiocarbon Laboratory at UCLA. After graduation, he continued to take postdoctoral classes in geology. Nigel taught classes in anthropology, archaeology, environmental studies, and geology as a visiting professor and adjunct faculty for 15 years at Ohio State University, Kent State University, University of Akron, the College of Wooster, and Wayne College. He is now a professor of geology at Ashland University, where he has taught for the past 18 years. He and his wife Anne live near Wooster, Ohio, at the edge of Amish country. They have two cats and a yard filled with trees, gardens, flowers, and interesting rocks.

INDEX